Steve,

With warmest regards,

Selina

JAMESIAN CENTERS OF CONSCIOUSNESS AS READERS AND TELLERS OF STORIES

S. Selina Jamil

University Press of America,® Inc.
Lanham · New York · Oxford

Copyright © 2001 by
University Press of America,® Inc.
4720 Boston Way
Lanham, Maryland 20706

12 Hid's Copse Rd.
Cumnor Hill, Oxford OX2 9JJ

All rights reserved
Printed in the United States of America
British Library Cataloging in Publication Information Available

Library of Congress Cataloging-in-Publication Data

Jamil, S. Selina.
Jamesian centers of consciousness as readers and tellers of stories /
S. Selina Jamil.
p. cm
Includes bibliographical references and index.
1. James, Henry, 1843-1916—Technique. 2. Books and reading
in literature. 3. Consciousness in literature. 4. Storytelling in literature.
5. Point of view (literature) 6. First person narrative.
7. Narration (Rhetoric) 8. Fiction—Technique. I. Title.
PS2127.T4 J35   2000   813'.4—dc21   00-048908 CIP

ISBN 0-7618-1914-2 (cloth: alk. ppr.)

∞™ The paper used in this publication meets the minimum
requirements of American National Standard for Information
Sciences—Permanence of Paper for Printed Library Materials,
ANSI Z39.48—1984

Contents

Preface   v

Acknowledgements   vii

Narrative Authority in the Jamesian Center of Consciousness: 1
An Introduction

Chapter 1   In the Cage of Commonness   15

Chapter 2   Spencer Brydon's Aesthetic Quest in the   49
"Human Actual Social" World

Chapter 3   The Changing of Old Stories in   81
<u>The Golden Bowl</u>

Chapter 4   The Changing Imaginative Consciousness   123
of Lambert Strether

Conclusion   159

Bibliography   163

Index   173

Preface

Much critical attention has been devoted to the Jamesian centers of consciousness as watchers or readers and "artists," but not to their specific activity of reading and telling stories about their surroundings and about themselves with their wondering, interpretive, and creative imagination. Because the Jamesian reflectors are readers and tellers of stories, they create meaning, experience perceptual growth, and develop representational skills, and thus exert narrative authority. This project is a study of Henry James's portrayal of narrative authority through his technique of the center of consciousness as embodied by the reflector characters of *In the Cage*, "The Jolly Corner," *The Golden Bowl*, and *The Ambassadors*. As readers of stories the reflectors make narrative connections, and consequently engage themselves in a struggle to create epistemological patterns, which continue to grow just as their imagination continues to grow. *In the Cage* reveals how the imaginative reflector, although she does not grow to become a successful storyteller, grows to be an acute reader of stories, for she ultimately frees herself from an involvement with sentimental narratives, and thus creates mental refinement for herself. "The Jolly Corner," *The Golden Bowl*, and *The Ambassadors*, reveal how the reflectors' imaginative growth enables these readers of stories to become figurative storytellers who at some point watch their environment from their house of fiction through their interpretive imagination and create their relation with that environment. As a result of his exertion of narrative authority, Brydon ultimately finds self-fulfillment through his aesthetic quest; Maggie changes an old story into a new one, and helps Amerigo to make use of his own interpretive imagination; and Strether, whose changing and growing imaginative consciousness enables him to understand that there is nothing final or stable within himself, finds the narrative connection between his past, present and future. And although these reflectors' systems of representation are often indistinguishable from those of the third-person narrators of these works of fiction, as successful storytellers they create vivid and well-developed images which ultimately reveal their imaginative sophistication and independence from the narrators.

Acknowledgements

This project would never have been completed without the guidance, patience, understanding, of my advisor, Dr. Sheila Teahan. Her questions and comments, and hence, all her suggestions have been invaluable during the entire process of my writing of this dissertation. She has read every word I have written for this project with such diligence and thoroughness, such insight and acuteness, that I shall forever be grateful to her. And I shall forever treasure her friendship and critical advice.

I would also like to thank Dr. Douglas Peterson, Dr. Barry Gross, Dr. Stephen Arch, and Dr. Kathleen Rout for reading my dissertation and discussing it with me, and also for being helpful and supportive.

I could not have written this book without the patience, love, and support of my son, Angshu, and my husband, Nazre. Therefore it is dedicated to them.

Narrative Authority in the Jamesian Center of Consciousness: An Introduction

This project examines Henry James's portrayal of narrative authority in *In the Cage*, "The Jolly Corner," *The Golden Bowl*, and *The Ambassadors* through his technique of the center of consciousness. In his prefaces, collected together in *The Art of the Novel*, James discusses his method of approaching the subject-matter within his fiction not through an omniscient narrator but through characters who embody centers of consciousness. For the center of consciousness, as James conceives it, is the "centre" from which the "subject" of each of his narratives is "treated," and therefore it is "a principle of composition" that makes the stories "hang together."[1] As he mentions in the preface to *The Golden Bowl*, James presents "an imagined observer's, a projected, charmed painter's or poet's" view or impression because he does not care for the "muffled majesty of irresponsible 'authorship,'" that is, for the authority displayed by an omniscient narrator, the power that stays beyond the realm of the fiction but that makes mere puppets of the characters within the fiction (*AN* 328). As a responsible author he is mindful, as he points out in another preface, of "the art of guiding ... [the subject] with consequent authority - since this sense of 'authority' is for the master-builder the treasure of treasures" (*AN* 328,123). As the storyteller he is the "master-builder"[2] who guides the subjects of his narratives and authorizes the centers of consciousness, his "deput[ies] or delegate[s]," as he describes them in the preface to *The Golden Bowl*, with the task of carrying out the work of constructing the narratives, as it were (*AN* 327). Thus the "consequent" and therefore responsible authority he finds himself exerting as the "master-builder," and that he delegates his centers of consciousness to exert by allowing the action to be seen from their points of view (although it is recorded in third-person narration), is narrative authority. Vivienne Rundle argues that "James contrives to regain mastery" through the prefaces over his novels in which, by claiming "to share narrative authority with his characters" and staging "his own disappearance from the narrative system, [and] allowing the reader to assume substantial authority over the text," he stages "a drama of authorial abdication".[3] But as Mark Seltzer, who argues that "the art of the novel is an art of power," observes, "James's organic principle of composition ... allows for a recession of narrative authority and makes for a dispersal of narrative control that is nonetheless immanent in every movement and gesture of character and plot."[4] As I see the question of James's narrative authority, because his centers of consciousness are cast in the likeness of James,[5] that is, they function in ways that remind us of the James who describes himself as author in the Prefaces, he does not show an abdication but rather an assertion of narrative authority by "dispers[ing]" it through the characters who represent the centers of consciousness. To share narrative authority with his characters is not to "abdicat[e]" it but, as a reading of the preface to *The Golden Bowl* suggests, a manner in which the "impersonal author[]" reveals it through imaginary but "concrete" characters (*AN* 327).

James describes these characters as "mirrors" and "intense *perceivers*," in *The Art of the Novel* (*AN* 70,71). Thus what is significant in *The Ambassadors* for the author, as he writes in the preface to that novel, is that Strether, the protagonist who embodies the center of consciousness in that novel, and who suffers from a sense of not having "live[d]" his life, "now at all events *sees*; so that the business of my tale and the march of my action, not to say the precious moral of everything, is just my demonstration of this process of vision" (*AN* 308). Because they are acute watchers, who are "burnished ... by the intelligence, the curiosity, the passion, the force of the moment," James makes his protagonists "registers or 'reflectors'" (*AN* 300). The intensity of the drama within his fiction, then, even for James himself comes from the changing and growing, thinking and feeling, contemplative and interpretive intelligence of his fictive characters who register and reflect the action: "I confess I never see the *leading* interest of any human hazard but in a consciousness (on the part of the moved and moving creature) subject to fine intensification and wide enlargement. It is as mirrored in that consciousness that the gross fools, the headlong fools, the fatal fools play their part for us - they have much less to show us in themselves" (*AN* 67). And as James writes in the preface to *The Ambassadors*, "Art deals with what we see" (*AN* 312). Consequently, much critical attention has been devoted to James's technique of the center of consciousness and its ability to see or interpret.

As Laurence Holland argues, the central intelligence takes part in "observing the action and constructing its image" with the author.[6] And although Tony Tanner does not mention the center of consciousness, he also discusses the speculative activity performed by the Jamesian spectator. Both Holland and Tanner, then, are concerned with the artistic activity in which the Jamesian observer is involved. Also, like Holland, Tanner is concerned with the price that the Jamesian spectator pays for his or her vision. While Holland discusses the "sacrifice that at once measures and becomes the expense of vision,"[6] Tanner discusses the "exclusion from participation" that the Jamesian spectator pays for his or her vision.[7] Ora Segal, who is also concerned with the center of consciousness embodied by the Jamesian observer, and the "authorial functions" fulfilled by this fictive character, argues that seeing does not lead the Jamesian observer to a vicarious but rather to an "authentic" form of being.[8] And Carolyn Porter, who discusses the artist in the Jamesian watcher as an embodiment of the center of consciousness as well, argues that the seer is a complicit participant in the events he or she observes.[9] My own project, which grows from such readings of the authorial role played by the reflectors, and thus from the questions of losses and gains encountered by the reflectors that these readings raise, however, is concerned with the reflectors' ability to exert narrative authority as a result of their ability to observe and interpret, and thus to make meaning.

Thus my reading of James's fiction has also grown out of Paul Armstrong's discussion of the epistemological implications of "the composing powers of consciousness".[10] Armstrong focuses on James's portrayal of consciousness because "consciousness is the activity of making and interpreting meaning".[10] Further, my reading has also grown out of Sharon Cameron's discussion of what consciousness achieves in the novels, for example, of how it determines meanings, and of the "tension between the empowering of consciousness ... and the disrupting of that power".[11] Picking up the thread of the consciousness's power to compose or determine meanings from these arguments, my own exploration of the meaning-making activities of James's centers of consciousness has taken me to a study of the reflectors' exertion of narrative control by way of their perceptual quest, which originates in their imaginative faculty.

For it is the imaginative faculty that the center of consciousness uses to interpret meanings. As I see James's portrayal of the imagination, meanings cannot be interpreted without the help of the imaginative faculty because it is the imagination which makes the center of consciousness see. For Daniel Mark Fogel, James's concept of "vision" involves "the imagination as much as the eye," and it is "a power of discrimination" as well as "a moral process". Fogel also maintains that Strether is "gifted with a Coleridgean secondary imagination".[12] On the other hand, William Goetz, in his reading of James, associates the imagination not simply with triumphs but also with failures: "the imaginative life triumphs in the production of a world full of artistic meaning and ... [encounters] failures when it confronts another world outside of its imaginative orbit".[13] But as I see James's portrayal of the imaginative faculty, although it may not necessarily lead the centers of consciousness to a synthetic vision, it certainly is not the cause of any of their failures. As James writes in the preface to *The Ambassadors*, it is Strether's "blest imagination" that helps him "to discriminate" (*AN* 316). For James, then, it is not the rational but the imaginative faculty that plays the most significant role in producing analytical activity. And as he writes in the preface to *In the Cage* in regards to the wondering imagination of the telegraphist, the center of consciousness in that novella, it is the "imagination" that "continues to abound in questions and to supply answers to as many of them as possible" (*AN* 155). Consequently, even the imagination of the "little," nameless, "brooding telegraphist" is endowed with epistemological concerns (*AN* 156). Thus the dramatic intensity of this novella, too, comes from the center of consciousness's interpretive imagination: "The action of the drama is simply the girl's 'subjective' adventure - that of her quite definitely winged intelligence" (*AN* 157). Thus not only has James endowed his fictive protagonists with a vivid imagination, but, in the preface to *The Golden Bowl*, he even calls the center of consciousness "a convenient substitute ... for the [author's] creative power otherwise so veiled and disembodied" (*AN* 327).

As I see these centers of consciousness, characters who represent the "veiled and disembodied" "creative" faculty of the storyteller's imagination, a significant manner in which they exert their narrative authority is by reading stories about the people around them and about themselves with the help of their acute imagination. It is with her imagination that the telegraphist "guess[es] all sorts of impossible things" and creates "theories and interpretations" which become evident in her "read[ing] into the immensity of [upper class people's telegraphic] intercourse stories and meanings without end."[14] These may hardly have any accuracy, as James ironically suggests in the novella, but her reading of stories is still significant because it ultimately enables her to broaden her imagination, and consequently to move beyond the desire to read sentimental narratives. The centers of consciousness's ability to watch, and thus read, is inseparably connected with their ability to imagine, for what they use is an interpretive imagination. And their ability to imagine interpretations, and thus create meaning, makes them acute readers of stories. To read stories, then, is to make meaning. This is why James refers to his designated centers of consciousness of the first and second volumes in

The Golden Bowl, Prince Amerigo and Maggie Verver respectively, as "the admirably endowed pair ... [who] point ... for me the moral of the endless interest, endless worth for 'delight,' of the compositional contribution" (*AN* 329). Indeed, the Jamesian spectators who embody the central intelligence make a kind of "compositional contribution" as acute readers of stories because of their intensely active imagination. This is why, in the preface to "The Jolly Corner," James writes of the protagonist who embodies the center of consciousness in the tale, Spencer Brydon, that the "thickness" of the appeal to "mystification" is in the consciousness that "amplifies" even as it interprets it (*AN* 256). Thus I argue that it is because of their activity as readers of stories that the centers of consciousness experience perceptual growth, and thus the characters who embody the central intelligence become acute readers of the situations which they undertake to read. In *The Ambassadors*, Strether not only reads volumes of French literature, but as a result of his desire to comprehend the world of Parisian values, he is well able to read stories in the incidents of the lives of his friends, and of his own. For example he learns to read Chad Newsome's "story," not as authored by Mrs. Newsome, but the one that he finds as a result of his own observations and interpretations.[15] And in *The Golden Bowl*, the Italian Prince Amerigo has even read not simply American fiction, including Poe's "story of the shipwrecked Gordon Pym," but is able to draw connections between this story and certain events of his own life. Consequently, on observing the golden bowl in a Bloomsbury antique-dealer's shop, he even listens to or reads the "story" of the crystal bowl.[16] And Maggie Verver, who has even "read stories of the wild west," knows how to ironically relate one of the stock features of this genre to an episode in her own life (540). Because these imaginative reflectors read stories in the situations they observe, they are able to create meanings, for example, to create purpose, and causal connections, in those situations. Hence they exert narrative authority.

For to read a story, as James shows it through his centers of consciousness, is to learn to make narrative connections between events, that is, between their interpretations of those events. This is why James ponders the significance of "connexion" or "relation" in *The Art of the Novel*: "We are shut up wholly to cross-relations, relations all within the action itself; no part of which is related to anything but some other part - save of course by the relation of the total life" (114). And in the preface to *The Ambassadors*, he writes: "one's bag of adventures ... has been only half-emptied by the mere telling of one's story. It depends so on what one means by that equivocal quantity. There is the story of one's hero, and then, thanks to the intimate connexion of things, the story of one's story itself" (*AN* 313). Clearly, James, the storyteller, is much intrigued by "that equivocal quantity" known as "story". And although much critical attention has been devoted to the centers of consciousness as "artists" and as watchers or readers, not much has been devoted to their preoccupation with reading stories, and therefore to the significance of the "story" within the story for James. Just as there is "the story" within the story in the sense of its origin, so there is "the story" within the story in the sense of the stories that the reflectors read. And what the Jamesian reflectors' ability to read stories signifies is their ability to forge connections. Thus it is for Strether "to establish and carry on" other characters' "coherency" and "relation" to the main action (*AN* 317). Indeed, to make narrative connections is to work for the creation of coherent epistemological patterns. For it is from the center of consciousness that the narrative takes its "pattern" (*AN* 320). This then is why James writes in the concluding sentence of *The Art of the Novel* (in the preface to *The Golden Bowl*), "connexions are employable for finer purposes than mere gaping contrition," that is, than the fear of breaking the accepted literary codes or set of critical rules (*AN* 348). Clearly, these "finer purposes" are associated with the creation of epistemological patterns, patterns which may not be completed, but through which the imaginative consciousness creates meanings.

As James is well aware, these epistemological patterns are never complete. For, as he writes in "The Art of Fiction," "Experience is never limited, and it is never complete; it is an immense sensibility, a kind of huge spider-web of the finest silken threads suspended in the chamber of consciousness".[17] And as "experience consists of impressions," and therefore, as "impressions *are* experience,"[17] the "huge spider-web of the finest silken threads suspended in the chamber of consciousness," which constitutes "Experience," is the never-completed epistemological design (made out of a continual flow of "impressions,") that the Jamesian reflector or register is forever engaged in creating. For example, Strether's continually changing imagination creates continually changing epistemological patterns. Thus even for himself Strether's imagination is associated with "the *growing* rose of observation" (397, my emphasis). It has not finished "growing" and therefore the epistemological pattern it creates continues to develop coherence. This is why for James, "the continuity of things is the whole matter," as he writes in *The Art of the Novel* (5). The "canvas of life" has a "vast expanse of ... surface, [a] *boundless* number of ... distinct perforations" and the "embroiderer" makes his "many-coloured flowers and figures to cover and consume *as many as possible* of the little holes" with his "needle" (*AN* 5, my emphases). Consequently, James points out that as there is no end to confusion or chaos ("perforations" or "holes"), so there is no prearranged design or set of numbers for the metaphorically embroidered flowers with which the storyteller creates an epistemological pattern. The metaphorical embroidery of flowers, then, never ends.

Thus these epistemological patterns, and therefore James's concern for "the close consistency in which parts hang together even as the interweavings of a tapestry," do not indicate obliviousness of the break of consistency within the narrative on his part (*AN* 139). In the preface to *The Ambassadors*, James refers to his understanding of a "complete" scene as having "logical start, logical turn, and logical finish" (*AN* 323). As J. Hillis Miller claims, to maintain a line of logic without a break in the line is out of the question,[18] and James's use of the phrase "logical *turn*" (my emphasis) instead of "logical midpoint" or "growth" indicates his awareness that to maintain an unbroken scenic consistency, and therefore an undisturbed line of continuity of thematic order and unity of purpose is neither possible nor desirable. For an unbroken consistency takes away the dramatic complexities, "the thrilling ups and downs, the intricate ins and outs of the compositional problem" (*AN* 319). Thus the line of logic "turn[s]" and breaks up an undeviating forward movement. And such a "turn" is itself paradoxically "logical" because it shows the center of consciousness, from whom the whole subject-matter takes its "pattern," as a groping mind to which James's readers can relate. Thus in another preface he writes, "to be *too* acute ... would have disconnected ... [the consciousness] and made it superhuman: the beautiful little problem was to keep it connected, connected intimately, with the general human exposure, and thereby bedimmed and befooled and bewildered, anxious, restless, fallible, and yet to endow it with such intelligence that the appearances reflected in it, and constituting together there the situation and the 'story,' should become by that fact intelligible" (*AN* 16). In short, just as the reflectors make intense perceptions, so they make intense mistakes. Thus Strether's growth as a contemplative, imaginative observer, for example, is not consistent, that is, he does not consistently move forward: he moves through "winding passages, through alternations of darkness and light" (*AN* 316).

It is this struggle through these metaphorical "passages" with the aim to create epistemological patterns that makes Strether, like other Jamesian spectators who find themselves perched in a figurative house of fiction, a storyteller, as it were. James describes "the consciousness of the artist" as "the watcher" who observes the "human scene" from "a pierced aperture," which is "at the best" one of the "windows ... perched aloft" in the metaphorical "house of fiction," which does not have any "hinged doors" to connect the artist directly with "life" (*AN* 46). Thus

James describes the storyteller in himself, in another preface, as "being reduced to watching" the subject-matter through the "windows of other people's interest" in it, for he is the author whose "instinct everywhere [is] for the *indirect* presentation of his main image" (*AN* 306). The consciousness itself, for James then, is a metaphorical window, a window that signifies his interpretive and thus creative imagination. Like the "master-builder" who literally composes narratives, his deputies, for example, Strether, Maggie, and Brydon, look out from an aperture in the metaphorical "house of fiction" and compose figurative narratives as they interpret "the human scene" in their own particular ways: "[T]he affair of the painter is not the immediate, it is the reflected field of life, the realm not of application but of *appreciation* ... My report of people's experience - my report as the 'story-teller' - is essentially my appreciation of it" (*AN* 65). The storyteller, then, depends on his interpretive imagination not only to be a reader of stories but, consequently, to be a creative composer of narratives. My reading of the narrative concerns of the center of consciousness has grown out of Sheila Teahan's argument that in *The Golden Bowl*, Maggie translates as she constructs Amerigo's and Charlotte's consciousness, and in effect becomes a Jamesian narrator.[19] And it has also grown from Millicent Bell's argument that "[t]he labors of the Jamesian consciousness are narratological."[20] But for Bell, these labors lead only to partial success with regard to the arrangement of events to make a story and with regard to "the discovery of meaning in this story."[20] As I read "The Jolly Corner," *The Golden Bowl*, and *The Ambassadors*, just as the reflectors read stories in their surroundings, that is, as they watch their surroundings, so they compose little stories successfully, although they do not literally write them. For, as James writes in a preface, "[t]he teller of a story is primarily ... the listener to it, the reader of it, too" (*AN* 63). The "listener" or "reader" develops into the composer or "teller" of stories as the center of consciousness's imagination continues to grow in refinement.

To some extent, then, my reading of the center of consciousness as a storyteller has also grown out of Carren Kaston's argument that Maggie Verver is the character of consciousness that launches into "independent fiction-making," that is, into creating design in the materials of her life, and thus living her own fiction, because she possesses the Jamesian "imagination in *predominance*".[21] But as I see the central consciousness's involvement with stories, the absence of "imagination in *predominance*" does not prevent the reflectors from composing stories, for they possess "imagination galore" (*AN* 310). Nor do I see James as conceiving any of his centers of consciousness as having "imagination in *predominance*": "So particular a luxury - some occasion, that is, for study of the high gift in *supreme* command of a case of a career - would still doubtless come on the day I should be ready to pay for it" (*AN* 310). As James wrote the prefaces after he wrote *The Golden Bowl*, it is obvious that he did not conceive Maggie as having "imagination in *predominance*". For what is significant to James is the drama of the imaginative consciousness's struggle to compose a design, and therefore a tortuous journey rather than a straightforward progress, and the question of the dramatic struggle to create a design does not arise for a character whose imagination is in predominance or in supreme command. As the Jamesian reflectors possess "imagination galore," they are equipped to become "register[s] of impressions" (*AN* 142). Consequently the action is reflected by (contemplated), and therefore reflected through (mirrored, imaged), the centers of consciousness.

The centers of consciousness, then, seem to present their impressions through images. James's "irrepressible ideal," that is, his goal as storyteller, he writes in the preface to *The Golden Bowl*, is "the process and the effect of representation" (*AN* 328). Thus he calls the storyteller a "painter of life," and states that "the most interesting question the artist has to consider" is how to "give the image and the sense of certain things" (*AN* 14). And as he writes in the preface to *The Golden Bowl*, "The essence of any representational work is of course to bristle with immediate images" (*AN* 331). I argue that James's reflectors, who are acute readers of stories, then, usually develop into tellers of stories because of their ability to compose vivid and well-developed pictures. My reading has partly grown out of Edgar Dryden's discussion of "the painted image" as "James's model for his idea of representation": "Representation ... is a constructive, interpretive act that derives from an 'impression of life'".[22] Extending Dryden's observation about James to the reflector, I see this interpreting center of consciousness as developing a story out of a picture, for it is "a picture," James writes in a preface, that shows "arrangement" (*AN* 101). Thus my reading of the Jamesian reflector has also grown out of Susan Griffin's argument that "[t]o perceive in James's fictions is to compose reality into pictures."[23] The picture, that is, the image, reveals the reflector's ability to arrange impressions. Because Spencer Brydon arranges his impressions of what he might have been if he had never left New York, his imagination is able to personify them as an "image" of "some strange figure".[24] And as these impressions continue to grow, the "image" continues to grow, and consequently the figure of what he might have been grows into the figure of his other self, and into the figure of a fictional narrative of what he might have been, which he reads in the "margin" of the door, and which is therefore also a figurative margin of the pages of his figurative narrative (187). Thus the figure of his other self, which is also the figure of his narrative of what he might have been, manifests itself as a vivid picture: "No portrait by a great modern master could have presented him with more intensity, thrust him out of his frame with more art, as if there had been 'treatment,' of the consummate sort, in his every shade and salience" (187).

But how are we to figure out exactly what parts the central consciousness and the narrator respectively play in the construction of these images? For the development of my concerns about the relationship between the central consciousness and the narrator, I am indebted to Teahan, who discusses the Jamesian center of consciousness as a rhetorical structure, and argues, "indirect discourse, of which the Jamesian reflector is a technical variation, notoriously precludes any absolute rhetorical distinction between the language attributed to the central intelligence and the narrator's own third-person discourse." Thus Teahan goes on to claim that the conception of the center of consciousness as "a representational ground" is at once "a necessity and an impossibility."[25] Indeed, it is absolutely impossible to figure out exactly what role the center of consciousness plays in representation and figuration. But it also seems to me that there are several instances where James suggests that the image is the reflector's. Thus in the passage of Brydon's image of "some strange figure" mentioned above, James begins the paragraph with, "It had begun to be present to him [Brydon] ... it met him there - and this was the image under which he himself judged the matter ...The quaint analogy quite hauntingly remained with him" (165). As I read this example, it shows the reflector's ability to represent his ideas through images for which he does not require to depend on the narrator. It exemplifies Bell's point that, by endowing "the perceiving *character* ...[with] more than common powers of observation and understanding," James "reduce[s] the authority of the narrator".[26] And there are instances where James suggests that the image is the narrator's. Thus in *The Golden Bowl* when Amerigo contemplates a financially fulfilling future with his imminent marriage, and we are given the image of the aromatic bath, the narrator adds, "we thus represent him" (48). This "we," which may indicate the narrator's partnership with the author in the act of "represent[ing]," marks a clear separation from the "him" which indicates the designated center of consciousness of the first volume. But despite this separation James points out that there is a connection between the two that is not broken. For the center of consciousness depends on the narrator to represent his thoughts through an image that he later incorporates into his own system of representation, and thus this dependence proves to be efficacious for Amerigo. But as James also points out in regards to this center of consciousness, late in the novel Amerigo creates images without assistance from the narrator. And through these images James draws a separation between the narrator and the reflector, which indicates this reflector's problems in the exertion of narrative authority. But, as he suggests in the case of the reflector of the second volume, it is the narrator who is eager to form an interdependent relation with Maggie, and thus the narrator who forges an inseparable connection between his images and hers. And in *The Ambassadors*, James suggests how the reflector, who early in the novel depends on the narrator for the construction of his images, and therefore whose association with the narrator seems to be inseparable at that point, learns to surpass the narrator in his narrational abilities as a result of his ability to create coherent images on his own.

What makes a discussion of figuration also relevant to my argument about the Jamesian reflectors as storytellers is that the images themselves contain scenes, which they connect with other scenes presented through other images to become parts of a story. Thus my argument has also grown out of Phyllis Van Slyck's argument about representation in many of James's novels, particularly in *The Golden Bowl*: "The power to create a portrait - of oneself or another - is, in effect, 'the power to narrate'".[27] As James shows in *The Golden Bowl*, Amerigo creates images of his metaphorical voyage that depict little scenes through which he tells Fanny Assingham the story of frustration in his perceptual quest, and which he develops out of a "story" that he has read (56). And he continues this story of his inactivity with subsequent images of water and ship/ boat. Likewise Maggie creates images, for instance, her image of "dancing," which contain scenes, and thus little stories (330). She even goes a step further than Amerigo in that she picks up his image of her as a panting and resting little dancer, although he never verbally communicates it to her, and makes it a part of the little story of her own inactivity. And with another image of dancing she depicts a new scene - that of her activity. Her images, then, show that in composing a picture, Maggie composes a narrative that moves forward, as it were. "One's work should have composition," James writes in the preface to *The Ambassadors*, "because composition alone is positive beauty" (*AN* 319). The "beauty" of "composition" is the beauty of organization, orchestration, and the construction of purpose. Thus a storyteller, who is a perceiver, thinker, and organizer, demonstrates a well-developed ability to forge connections.

Perched in isolation in his house of fiction the author *creates* his connection, that is, relation, with the life he watches and interprets. For James, as he writes in the preface to "The Jolly Corner," a story ultimately "fails" if it "stops short for want of connexions ... in the sense of further statement, ...[and] of our own further relation to the elements, which hang in the void" (*AN* 257). According to Kaston, most of the centers of consciousness renounce material experience, withdraw from "personal feeling," and become "failed imaginers of a self," and thus they become "failed authors".[28] But, perched in their own houses of fiction, these centers of consciousness realize their isolation, and create their connection with their surroundings, and consequently give their "stories" the connections in the sense of their own "relation to the elements": "The painter's subject consist[s] ever, obviously, of the related state, to each other, of certain figures and things. To exhibit these relations ... is to treat his idea" (*AN* 5). To relate a story, then, is to establish relations. And establishing a relation between events parallels and figures establishing a relation between people. Therefore, as I see the metaphorical house of fiction, it does not invoke the tyrannical "parentally authored structures" from which a "parent-artist ... dominate[s] and discipline[s] the material" that Kaston sees in them,[28] but rather it enables these isolated observers to realize the need to establish connections with their surroundings. For as readers and tellers of stories their aim is to make their own lives purposeful and meaningful in as many ways as they can.

Notes

1. Henry James, The Art of the Novel, ed. R. W. B. Lewis (1934; rpr. Boston: Northeastern University Press, 1984) 15. Cited parenthetically as AN.

2. For a discussion of the entrepreneurial implications of the authorial authority in James and his association of the author with the civil engineer, see Stuart Culver's "Representing the Author: Henry James, Intellectual Property and the Work of Writing," in Henry James: Fiction as History ed. Ian F. A. Bell (Totowa: Vision and Barnes and Noble, 1984). Culver argues that James's analogy between the author and the civil engineer "serves ultimately to underscore a crisis in the author's authority"(122).

3. Vivienne Rundle, "Defining Frames: The Prefaces of Henry James and Joseph Conrad," The Henry James Review 16.1 (1995): 72.

4. Mark Seltzer, Henry James and the Art of Power (Ithaca: Cornell University Press, 1984) 14,87-88. Seltzer's argument looks forward to Edward Said's argument about narrative and power in Culture and Imperialism (New York: Alfred A. Knopf, 1993): "The power to narrate, or to block other narratives from forming and emerging, is very important to culture and imperialism, and constitutes one of the main connections between them" (xiii).

5. As Jonathan Auerbach, in The Romance of Failure: First Person Fictions of Poe, Hawthorne, and James (New York: Oxford University Press, 1989)

observes, James identifies "his own procreative labors with the passions and labors of his characters" (129). Thus Auerbach implies that, in effect, James bestows upon his centers of consciousness these "procreative labors".

6. Laurence Bedwell Holland, The Expense of Vision: Essays on the Craft of Henry James (Princeton, New Jersey: Princeton University Press, 1964) 165,119.

7. Tony Tanner, The Reign of Wonder: Naivety and Reality in American Literature (Cambridge: Cambridge University Press, 1965) 318.

8. Ora Segal, The Lucid Reflector: The Observer in Henry James' Fiction (New Haven and London: Yale University Press, 1969) x,xii.

9. Carolyn Porter, Seeing and Being: The Plight of the Participant Observer in Emerson, James, and Faulkner (Middletown: Wesleyan University Press, 1981) 122.

10. Paul Armstrong, The Phenomenology of Henry James. (Chapel Hill: University of North Carolina Press, 1983) 63,64.

11. Sharon Cameron, Thinking in Henry James (Chicago and London: University of Chicago Press, 1989) 42.

12. Daniel Mark Fogel, Henry James and the Structure of the Romantic Imagination (Baton Rouge and London: Louisiana State University Press, 1981) 25.

13. William Goetz, Henry James and the Darkest Abyss of Romance (Baton Rouge and London: Louisiana State University Press, 1986) 207.

14. Henry James, In the Cage, In the Cage and Other Stories (Middlesex: Penguin Books Ltd., 1972) 15,21,23.

15. Henry James, The Ambassadors (1903; London: Penguin Books, 1986) 179.

16. Henry James, The Golden Bowl (1904; London: Penguin Books, 1985) 56,123.

17. Henry James. "The Art of Fiction," The Art of Fiction and Other Essays (New York: Oxford University Press, 1948) 10,11.

18. J. Hillis Miller, "Line," Ariadne's Thread (New Haven and London: Yale University Press, 1992) 6.

19. Sheila Teahan, The Rhetorical Logic of Henry James (Baton Rouge and London: Louisiana State University Press, 1995) 137.

20. Millicent Bell, Meaning in Henry James (Cambridge and London: Harvard University Press, 1991) 33.

21. Carren Kaston, Imagination and Desire in the Novels of Henry James (New Brunswick: Rutgers University Press, 1984) 10.

22. Edgar Dryden, "The Image in the Mirror: James's Portrait and the Economy of Romance," The Form of American Romance (Baltimore and London: Johns Hopkins University Press, 1988) 125.

23. Susan M. Griffin, "The Selfish Eye: Strether's Principles of Psychology," American Literature: A Journal of Literary History, Criticism, and Bibliography 56.3 (1984): 401.

24. Henry James, "The Jolly Corner," The Jolly Corner and Other Tales (London: Penguin Books, 1990) 165.

25. Teahan, 2,11.

26. Bell, 14.

27. Phyllis Van Slyck, "'An innate preference for the represented subject': Portraiture and Knowledge in The Golden Bowl," The Henry James Review 15.2 (1994): 180. As her quotation reveals, Van Slyck, in turn, has been influenced by Edward Said's Culture and Imperialism.

28. Kaston, 3,7-8.

Chapter 1

In the Cage of Commonness

In his preface to *In the Cage*, James reveals his interest in "the question of what it might 'mean,' wherever the admirable service [of a postal-telegraph office] was installed, for confined and cramped and yet considerably tutored young officials of either sex to be made free, intellectually, of a range of experience otherwise closed to them".[1] This intellectual freedom to mull over "a range of experience" in confinement that James allows his telegraphist, enables her to make narrative connections among the bits and pieces of information about upper class life that she receives by way of the telegrams which pass through her hands. By allowing her to make interpretations and analyses, and consequently to read parts of the story of the Captain's romantic life, which is prompted by her desire to bring refinement into her stifled life, James shows that his protagonist exerts narrative authority as a reader. She even creates romantic narratives about the Captain's intimate relationship with Lady Bradeen and about her own imaginary intimacy with him. But these narrative projects prove to be unsuccessful, and therefore remain incomplete. It seems as though James suggests that the reader who develops into a teller of stories does not experience consistent growth. Thus even when her narrative projects come to a standstill, she exerts narrative authority as a reader that enables her ultimately to move beyond reading or constructing sentimental fiction. According to Duncan Aswell, who has no sympathy for the reflector of this novella, "the last laugh is always at the expense of the girl herself" whose intelligence or sophistication is merely her delusion.[2] And even for Jean Blackall, who clearly has some sympathy for the protagonist, James only ironizes her in that he shows her ingenuity or clearsightedness and then undercuts it by "his insistence on ...[her] limitations".[3] But I would like to show that, although James presents his protagonist in an ironic light by depicting her "limitations," this irony, which is delicate and mild, and the product of a profoundly acute imagination, is not simply meant to insist on her limitations, or to produce "the last laugh" at her expense. For if with his irony James shows the telegraphist's limitations in the form of her indulgence in sentimental, that is, maudlin fiction, and thus as the teller of a story, then with a turn of the screw of irony he points out her ultimate rejection of the corpus of sentimental narratives.

In the first paragraph of this novella, James describes the protagonist's work as a telegraphist, and in so doing he gives his readers the circumstances - her constant handling of "words" - that provoke her to read stories:

> Her function was to sit there with two young men - the other telegraphist and the counter-clerk; to mind the 'sounder', which was always going, to dole out stamps and postal-orders, weigh letters, answer stupid questions, give difficult change and, more than anything else, count words as numberless as the sands of the sea, the words of the telegrams thrust, from morning till night...[4]

This image of the sands and the sea which represents the reflector's impressions of an overwhelming sense of frustration and privation, and which is the first of a series of images about water, may either be the narrator's or the joint product of the narrator's and the reflector's. But it seems to me that when James wants his readers to comprehend the reflector's system of representation he clearly indicates, even at the novella's beginning, that the image is either the telegraphist's or one she shares with the narrator in the making.[5] But for this image of water and sands, James gives no such indication. He, then, implicitly suggests that this image and several other similar images are the narrator's rather than the reflector's. It shows that when the center of consciousness first takes upon herself to read "stories," she often depends on the narrator's system of representation to give expression to her thoughts and feelings. Words, when she begins work as a telegraphist, are merely an endless succession of numbers that reveals no design. For to count words as "numberless as the sands of the sea" is to be threatened by or immersed in a sea of incoherence. Exposed and enigmatic, words in a telegram give her curious glimpses of a mysterious private world made as public as the "sands of the sea". They stretch continually and defy her to discover a meaning and purpose or to mold them into meaningfulness and purposefulness. In other words, they defy her to connect the perpetually increasing, puzzling, slippery fragments and read "stories and meanings without end" (23). As James himself writes in the preface, "the small local [postal-telegraph] office of one's immediate neighbourhood ...had ever had, to my sense so much of London to give out, so much of its huge perpetual story to tell that any momentary wait there seemed to take place in a strong social draught, the stiffest possible breeze of the human comedy" (*AN* 154).

And for James's unnamed protagonist, who works long hours in the post office, the "social draught" is so strong that she responds to it by reading stories about those people from whose lives her own is completely isolated.[6] Although (or perhaps because) she belongs to the lower class, the telegraphist finds it necessary to "cultivate ...[the] legend" of being a "lady" in the class-conscious world of London (26). Her introduction into the world of telegrams has been a shock to her because her customers generally are upper class people who wire "even their expensive feelings" (18). She is sadly confounded by "the revelation of the golden shower flying about without a gleam of gold for herself" (23). Blown away from the beau monde by "the cold breath of disinheritance" to the cramped space where she works as a public servant in return for a meager wage, the telegraphist conceives the little telegraph office as her "cage" (27). As in it she is reminded of "the great differences of the human condition" (49), this cage, as Jennifer Gribble observes, is a social and economic cage.[7] Because it is a socioeconomic cage for the disgruntled telegraphist, it is the cage of commonality, that is, the cage of common people where she is only an indistinguishable part of the multitude, and thus a nameless representative of it. But her interest in upper class people is not simply because of the indigent person's astonished and painful curiosity of "the profligate rich [who] scatter[] about them, in extravagant chatter ...an amount of money that would have held the stricken household of her frightened childhood ... together for a lifetime" (21-22).

The sensitive telegraphist is irresistibly drawn to deciphering the mysterious details of aristocratic people's lives, and thus to reading the stories of their lives, particularly because of her idea that they exhibit "a play of refinement and subtlety" (22). As Philip Sicker observes, she "sees no logical relationship between her own intellectual superiority and the economic state to which fate has reduced her."[8] Her economic state frustrates the telegraphist because it imposes restraints upon her quest for "refinement and subtlety". As her image of the "golden shower" suggests,[9] wealth to her signifies the feel of the fine stream of delicacy. Splendor, for her, as James ironically suggests, is the balmy touch that cleanses and sublimates (as it illuminates) the upper class world.

> Her conceit, her baffled vanity were possibly monstrous; she certainly threw herself into a defiant conviction that she would have done the whole thing much better. But her greatest comfort, on the whole, was her comparative vision of the men; by whom I mean the unmistakable gentlemen, for she had no interest in the spurious or the shabby, and no mercy at all for the poor... her fancy, in some directions so alert, had never a throb for any sign of the sordid. (23)

James's ironic mirth at the expense of the telegraphist is completely explicit. This, I suspect, is also why the third-person narrator makes a first-person intrusion in this passage. It seems as though the narrator finds it necessary to mark here (and in two preceding chapters) a separation from the center of consciousness, that is, as though James marks a break in the indeterminate relation between the narrator and the reflector. In addition, the narrative voice even mentions "we" once, which plural pronoun presumably suggests the narrator's partnership with the narratee in opposition to partnership with the center of consciousness: "What may not, we can only moralize, take place in the quickened, muffled perception of a girl of a certain kind of soul" (45). For her "fancy" becomes dull or empty when it encounters the sign of poverty, and yet it teems with "vision" when it encounters the sign of wealth in members of the opposite sex. As Ralf Norrman observes, the telegraphist's goal is to rise socially.[10] But, as James also points out despite all his irony, such a goal is guided by her profound concern for refinement. Although she is well aware that there are "places commoner still than Cocker's," it does not relieve her own impression of the coarse, plebeian "picture of servitude and promiscuity that she must present to the eye of comparative freedom" as she sits confined in the post office, her cage of commonness (29). Her obsessive desire to connect the "clues" she keeps by way of the telegrams, and thus to read stories of upper class life, even as she sits in her cage, is reflective of her desire to create refinement in her own coarse and stifled life (14). Thus she turns to two representatives of the upper class, Lady Bradeen and Captain Everard, and to a perusal of their telegrams. For the idealizing little telegraphist, these adulterous lovers are the flowers of aristocracy: Their beauty is meaningful because of their refinement. Lady Bradeen is exquisite because of the extreme refinement of her "manner that, even at bad moments, was a magnificent habit and of the very essence of innumerable things"(15). A subtle play of refinement seemingly saturates her entire being, for it has soaked her highly polished surface - the "light" of her eyes and the "colour" of her hair - with "splendour" (15). To the idealizing telegraphist, this subtle play of refinement is so spontaneous that its possessor exhibits complete unconsciousness of it. Likewise, Captain Everard is fascinatingly handsome because, with his "awfully good manners," he seems to represent

> people of that class...These manners were for everybody...What he did take for granted was all sorts of facility; and his high pleasantness, ...his unconscious bestowal of opportunities, of boons, of blessings, were all a part of his magnificent security... He was, somehow, at once very bright and very grave, very young and immensely complete; and whatever he was at any moment, it was always so much as all the rest the mere bloom of his beatitude. (20)

If the telegraphist's devotion for this apparently dashing specimen of the upper class finds expression in devotional excrescence ("beatitude"), then, at this stage, her readings seem to reveal nothing more than puerility. It seems to her that the Captain's radiance grows on him like an exquisite flower. As James ironizes the telegraphist's idealized view, the Captain's radiance signifies the spontaneous "bloom" of his confidence and ease. Thus her aristocratic couple's refinement, for the telegraphist, leads to their "happi[ness]" (19). For in refined manners she reads the story of "magnificent security".

In the refinement of manners the telegraphist reads the story of a "complete" sense of self. She begins to connect the different elements of Captain Everard's appearance and attempts to draw a sketch of his character by grasping his type. He is "complete," and therefore, for the telegraphist, the happy possessor of a public identity, which comes from her view of his social status and his occupation, as well as a private or "personal identity," which comes from her view of his individual distinction (20). Likewise, Lady Bradeen with all her delicate and distinct beauty, and with her title, has a private and a public identity. What Lady Bradeen "couldn't have got rid of ...if she had wished" comes from her manners, which in turn have become possible because of her social class, and gives her a distinctive appearance (15). Her refined manners give the telegraphist a sense of the aristocratic woman's "innumerable things - her beauty, her birth, her father and mother, her cousins, and all her ancestors" (15). Thus her manners tell the story of the influence of heritage on a particular member of her family. And when the telegraphist starts reading the story of a social world of personal relationships, the meaning she gleans is that the people with refined manners have a private identity because of their social identity. It seems to the telegraphist that upper class people's social life helps them to be recognized as distinct individuals. Thus the telegraphist is struck by a luxurious profusion of personal names in Lady Bradeen's telegrams, the names of her friends: "Agnes," "Fritz," and "Gussy" (14). This accumulation of personal names extends to the writer of the telegrams herself: "Cissy" and "Mary" (14). Certainly the telegraphist is well aware that the abundance of personal names demonstrates the promiscuous practice of blurring and disguising a person's identity. Thus she connects the phenomenon of Cissy Bradeen's use of a pseudonym with the phenomenon of "ladies wiring to different persons under different names" (14). But the interpretation she is much preoccupied with is that the plurality of names illustrates a wealth of social and personal "relation[s] of elegant privacy" (29).[11] Thus, through the telegraphist's memory of a particular incident in this connection, James points out how she reads the story of protective friendship: "There had once been one [lady] ...who without winking, sent off five [telegrams] over five different signatures. Perhaps these represented five different *friends*" (14, my emphasis). What this copiousness of names suggests to the telegraphist, then, as James ironizes her, is not so much the upper class people's impenetrability,[12] as their active social life that enables them to be recognized as distinct persons. Thus, in the case of Captain Everard too, she is struck by a luxuriance of personal names. It does not matter to her that she cannot locate Everard's private identity because of all his pseudonyms and titles. For it seems to her that his friends certainly can. It seems almost as if all his different appellations constitute different parts of his distinct being for the infatuated young telegraphist. They point out his immense social contacts for her. Therefore they point out all his individual relationships with different people. And thus all these different names point out to her "whatever he ...[is] and probably whatever he ...[isn't]" (21). For the telegraphist, whatever he is not seems to help her in finding out whatever he is. But to James's readers, whatever he is and whatever he is not point out his elusiveness. As Tzvetan Todorov asserts, the "essence" of Captain Everard's character is ungraspable.[13] And as Joel Salzburg observes, Everard "appears to have lost an authentic self among his social masks".[14] I would add that James, with his penchant for irony - "whatever he was" - also makes a proleptic allusion through the plethora of the Captain's personal names to the professional deceit he practices and that catches up with him late in the novella.

But even in the midst of his ironic portrayal of the telegraphist, James points out that she turns to reflect on her own life, and what she reads is the absence of a personal identity and therefore the story not of happy relations but of frustration in personal relationships. She yearns to have "a personal identity" for the Captain, and to have a personal relationship with him: "the thing in all [that Captain Everard experiences in the little post office] that she would have liked most unspeakably to put to the test was the possibility of her having for him a personal identity that might in a particular way appeal" (20). To conduct this "test" is to create a personal relationship with him. She suffers enormously from her sense of a lack of social relations, and therefore of personal relations in "the intense publicity of her profession" (11). It seems to her that she is enclosed in a public world with no scope for private relations, and therefore for a personal identity:

> It had occurred to her early in her position - that of a young person spending, in framed and wired confinement, the life of a guinea-pig or a magpie - she should know a great many persons without their recognizing the acquaintance. That made it an emotion the more lively - though singularly rare and always, even then, with opportunity still very much smothered - to see any one come in whom she knew, as she called it, outside, and who could add something to the poor identity of her function. (9).

Even with the first lines of his novella, then, James points out his protagonist's vexation at her public life which shows an absence of a personal identity. To be "recogniz[ed]" is for her to have a personal identity for, and thus a personal relationship with, the person who does the recognizing. James gives expression to the center of consciousness's own absence of a self-identity by giving her only a professional "identity" and never a name. She even strips herself (and her fellow-workers) of a human identity, as the images of confinement - birds and animals - reveal. And as her impressions reveal, this absence of a personal identity is linked with a deficiency in personal relations. Her need of personal relations is not simply confined to a need of romantic love.[15] With her alcoholic mother she has such a strained relationship that all she can do is smolder in vain with "the rage at moments of not knowing" how she gets hold of alcohol (13). The two women live under the same roof with hardly any communication it seems. Even with the ones she does have communication, it seems she can at best have only acquaintances. Thus Mrs. Jordan, for the telegraphist, is more of an "acquaintance" than a friend (29). And with her fiance, Mr. Mudge, she has such a starchy relationship that she thinks of him only in terms of his surname. The thought of marrying Mr. Mudge is not at all exciting to her because, as James points out with his bantering tone, it suggests the conspicuous absence of the dynamic and vital story of a romantic bond: "after her consent to their engagement, she had often asked herself what it was that marriage would be able to add to a familiarity so final" (10). What irritates her most about Mr. Mudge is that for him she has no personal identity: "There were times when she wondered how in the world she could bear him, how she could bear any man so smugly unconscious of the immensity of her difference. It was just for this difference that, if she was to be liked at all, she wanted to be liked" (33). But as James points out with his subtle play of irony, she herself often neglects to recognize "the immensity" of her difference from others, and only barely recognizes a "human" identity in Mudge (33).

As Mr. Mudge does not possess a personal identity as far as the center of consciousness is concerned, so he does not have the ability to read or create a story of success in his personal relationship. The success Mr. Mudge has achieved is in acquiring an occupational identity: "His very beauty was the beauty of a grocer, and the finest future would offer it none too much room to expand. She had engaged herself, in short, to the perfection of a type" (34). His only identity is his professional identity: that of a typical English grocer. Thus the causal connections he follows, and consequently the story he comprehends, is only in his professional world: "the exuberance of the aristocracy was the advantage of trade, and everything was knit together in a richness of pattern that it was good to follow with one's finger-tips" (37). In this "perfection of a type," his fiancee does not read the possibility of a distinct individual character, and thus of a personal identity. For where there is "none too much room [for him] to expand" is in his personal world. Consequently, when it comes to the story of his personal relationship, there is only frustration. During their vacation at Bournemouth, Mr. Mudge's "resources" of amusement, which are a world apart from the telegraphist's, include the "perpetual counting of the figures" on the pier (65). For the telegraphist, who sits in her cage and lives "the life of a guinea-pig or a magpie," it has been necessary to attempt to convert words that are "as numberless as the sands of the sea," and therefore that are an endless succession of mere numbers, into stories about upper class people's private lives. Now James points out how her fiance sits by the literal sea and, far from reading any story of personal relationships, converts people into mere numbers. Indeed, they themselves have become "close-packed items in terrific totals of enjoyment" (64). Unlike his fiancee, he does not even attempt to read a story about other people's personal relationships; but like her he falls into self-objectification, for like her, he cannot read the story of success in his own personal relationship. After having to swallow his fiancee's admission (which he tries to do with the aid of a "chocolate cream[]") that she is willing to do "anything" which means "everything" for a gentleman customer, poor Mr. Mudge is reduced to identifying himself as the man who is in "danger" from the woman he loves, and therefore the man in a "funk" (68,69). The telegraphist even frustrates his attempt to divert her attention from the aristocratic male customer who has become the center of her thoughts:

> "....I must just keep on as long as he may want me."
> "Want you to sit with him in the Park?"
> "He may want me for that - but ...I can do better for him in another manner."
> "And what manner, pray?"
> "Well, elsewhere."
> 'Elsewhere? - I *say*!"
> ......"You needn't 'say' - there's nothing to be said. And yet you ought perhaps to know." (68)

Alarmed by the vague "want" she mentions - what does her customer "want" his fiancee for? - Mr. Mudge tries to gibe and thus to reduce the serious implication of that word: "Want you to sit with him in the Park?" But his fiancee resists his attempt to take control of the situation with her own unruffled superciliousness: "He may want me for that ..." Further, she firmly suppresses his attempt to "*say*" anything. To frustrate Mudge's attempt to "*say*" is to frustrate his attempt to assert his relationship with the telegraphist. In effect, it is to stop him from telling the story of a successful relationship with the telegraphist: "You needn't 'say' - there's nothing to be said." Instead he is admonished by his fiancee to listen to ("know") the story of her potential relationship with one of her gentlemen customers.

As in the case of Mr. Mudge, so in the case of Mrs. Jordan, the novella suggests the absence of a personal identity, and consequently her inability to create a story of success in personal relationships. Thus Mrs. Jordan, the struggling widow of a clergyman, too is referred to only by a surname, which is not even her own. As an imaginative reader, who at this stage has become familiar with the act of reading stories of other people's lives, the telegraphist responds to Mrs. Jordan's "discourse" by creating her own image to represent her impressions of the latter's past: "This small domain, which her young friend had never seen, bloomed in Mrs. Jordan's discourse like a new Eden, and she converted the past into a bank of violets by the tone in which she said, 'Of course you always knew my one passion!'" (25). The story of the "new Eden" then, is the story of the past, of brief bliss and transient happiness, of an unrealizable dream of a perfect union between man and woman, and it is also the story of the fall of that union. Although the widow in the present has taken up the profession of floral arrangements in the "real homes of luxury," these symbolical flowers are not her own. For her own "Eden" is irretrievably lost. And all she can do is delude herself about "liv[ing] again with one's own people" (26). As Salzburg observes, "James uses a mock-religious language" to expose Mrs. Jordan as a false savior: "Mrs Jordan's name, for instance, carries the implication of a passage to a promised land, but in the extent of her own powers the woman proves to be no more than a fairy-godmother manquee."[16] Her name implies that the promised land is the home of luxury she herself appears to be progressing towards and hopes to reach. Her journey towards the promised land, the sumptuous home where she apparently belongs, never ends. For the "single step ...[that] would socially, would absolutely introduce her" is always beyond her (12). Despite all her "personal calculations" with regard to upper class people, her personal and therefore social relationships are always frustrated (32):

> "But does one personally *know* them?" our young lady went on, since that was the way to speak. "I mean socially, don't you know? - as you know *me*."
> "They're not so nice as you!" Mrs Jordan charmingly cried. "But I *shall* see more and more of them."
> Ah, this was the old story. "But how soon?"
> "Why, almost any day...." (28)

Mrs. Jordan, despite all her "ideas" and "the practice of her beautiful art," fails to create progression in her "story" (28,26). Her "old" story is the story of the unreachable past. This story does not change and therefore does not grow, just as her professional relation does not change and does not grow into a personal relation. And in the "pages on pages" that contain "drawings and plans" which Lord Rye writes to Mrs. Jordan, who dreams about marrying her way into society, the telegraphist does not read a version of the Cinderella story that the widow wants her to read or that she hopes to effectuate (30). This dream is so persistent that even when Mrs. Jordan engages herself to Lord Rye's butler, she cannot make herself identify him as a butler but as his lordship's "great and trusted friend. Almost - I may say - a loved friend" (90). As it turns out, then, the more time that Mrs. Jordan spends professionally in the "homes of luxury," the more thorough becomes her social isolation from them.

The more thorough the protagonist's own isolation from this world of refinement and delicacy, the more intolerable appears the cage of commonness in which the she is immured, and consequently, the more ardent is her search for reprieve. The more aggravating the rudeness of Mr. Buckton's "cunning hostility," the indelicacy of the counterclerk's "importunate sympathy," the banality and tediousness of Mr. Mudge's "daily, deadly, flourishy letter" and, most particularly, the vulgarity of her mother's "caps and conversation, ... and ... whisky," which happens to be "the most haunting of her worries,"[17] the more ardently she seeks solace in the world of imagination (13,11). And the result of this immersion in "fancy" is her "vision" of "silver threads and moonbeams" (23). This vision represents her imaginative pattern or design of delicacy and finesse in a romantic world. Thus through the telegraphist, James depicts a reader who aims at "keeping the clues and finding her way in the tangle," that is, at consciously creating a pattern of refinement in the stories of upper class romantic relationships (23).

But clearly, as the "margin" of the emblematic telegraph cage is "absent," her difficulties are enormous: "She was so boxed up with her young men, and anything like a margin so absent, that it needed more art than she could ever possess to pretend in the least to compass" (29). For Jennifer Wicke, the telegraphist's cage is "the iron cage of Weber's incipient social bureaucratization" where social relations stop. It is also the cage of words that the telegraph office necessitates. Consequently, for Wicke, the absence of margin signifies that the cage "forbids that zone of free relation, whether writerly or social." It also signifies the absence of "a surplus margin above and beyond a speculative exchange."[18] But as it is also possible to see, the "absent" margin in the telegraph cage is James's comment on the restrictions that his center of consciousness confronts within the pages of "the romance" that she tries to read through Lady Bradeen's telegrams to the Captain (19). To escape her cage of commonness she reads a narrative about an aristocrat's romantic life. But as soon as she launches into this project she finds that the cage of the telegraph office becomes the cage of romance,[19] for she finds herself confined by "allusions" in the telegrams that are "tangled in a complexity of questions" (19). The absence of margin, then, is associated with an absence of explanations of the continual flow of mysterious elements in which the telegrams, her texts, abound. Thus the absence of margin indicates the actual absence of a coherent design indicating purpose and causality within the romance. For this narrative is about a social class that is alien to her, and it comes as unconnected bits and pieces made of haphazard facts and figures. Further, it has already begun when the telegraphist first notices Lady Bradeen and her three telegrams. There is also an absence of margin in the narrative because, although the facts and figures that the telegraphist collects are limited and mysterious, the figurative page of the romance is cluttered by several different materials for several different stories. The "perpetual" story that James mentions in his preface is perpetual because it is made up of several different individual stories that the sensitive, creative reader becomes conscious of.

But with her active imagination the telegraphist can hardly be expected to accept the condition of an absent margin.[20] As she creates a "margin" for herself in her relation with Mr. Mudge, so she creates a margin in the narrative of the Captain's liaison with Lady Bradeen (35). For, ever since her confinement in the cage of romance, she looks for ways to read dramatic elements in it: "Most of the elements swam straight away, lost themselves in the bottomless common, and by so doing really kept the page clear. On the clearness, therefore, what she did retain stood sharply out; she nipped and caught it, turned it over and interwove it" (24). As Naomi Schor observes, this passage points out how the telegraphist pieces together the fragments by "adding something of her own" to the meager material she finds: She is not interested in "finding the figure in the carpet, but in weaving the whole cloth".[21] I would also suggest that the telegraphist attempts to erase the disorderliness from the pages of the romance by reading a dramatic pattern of passion and adventure with the "margin" of her imagination. She brings narrative connections to the elements she "retain[s,]" and clears the page of elements that do not contribute to the dramatic pattern of passion and adventure. And the elements that she nips and catches, turns over and interweaves into material for dramatic scenes with imaginative fervor, are material she picks up specifically with regard to Captain Everard:

> The want of margin in the cage, when he peeped through the bars, wholly ceased to be appreciable. It was a drawback only in superficial commerce. With Captain Everard she had simply the margin of the universe. It may be imagined, therefore, how their unuttered reference to all she knew about him could, in this immensity, play at its ease. (39-40)

When the dashing, young, charming and handsome Everard peeps through the bars of the cage, there is drama in the air for the telegraphist. It seems she conceives the imagination itself as the "universe" with Everard in the post office. For Captain Everard passionately inspires and stimulates the telegraphist's imagination, and she is ready to supply her own notion of his character into the pages of her romance in the absence of the character she does not grasp. The "unuttered reference" can "play at its ease" because with "the margin of the universe" she makes free use of her imagination in speculating about the Captain's romantic life.

Specifically, she attempts to fill the gaps of this romance by reading sentimental narratives. At lunch time when it is "rather quiet" at Cocker's, she amuses herself by reading "novels, very greasy, in fine print and all about fine folks," which she borrows from the circulating library, "at a ha'penny a day" (11). These ha'penny novels are her only means of entering the impervious world of "fine folks". And when she commences her project of converting the terse texts, the telegrams, into readable stories, these sentimental novels prove to be her only interpretive tool. They become the notes, as it were, that she can refer to in finding her way about the telegraphs' complex, compressed texts. Her dependence on her ha'penny novels is considerable because they introduce her to some of the mysterious nuances of upper class lifestyles. A faithful student of sentimental novels, she is ready to settle her theory about "Everard's type" and to dismiss his name as merely a disguise (17). As such a student she eagerly paints Lady Bradeen as the majestic Juno - despite all the inherent irony of an adulterous Juno - and, consequently, "all" that surrounds her as "certainly Olympian" (19). With the unstable foundation of her "ha'penny worths," the telegraphist, in indomitable bursts of self-confidence, finds herself "piec[ing] together all sorts of mysteries" (14).

But if James directs his amused irony at his protagonist, then, with another turn of the screw of irony he points out that the telegraphist's efforts at reading the story of the Captain's romantic life, despite her melodramatic approach, prove to be rewarding enough in that she is able to perceive and predict the Captain's and Lady Bradeen's danger:

> Didn't she catch in his face, at times, even through his smile and his happy habit, the gleam of that pale glare with which a bewildered victim appeals, as he passes, to some pair of pitying eyes? He perhaps didn't even know how scared he was; but *she* knew. They were in danger, they were in danger, Captain Everard and Lady Bradeen: it beat every novel in the shop. She thought of Mr Mudge and his safe sentiment; she thought of herself and blushed even more for her tepid response to it. (43)

As James demonstrates through her sense of "a sharp taste of something ... in her mouth before she knew it," at the early stage of her growth as reader of stories, the telegraphist reveals a capacity for instinctive awareness (15). But as James also points out through her reaction at her first sight of Captain Everard as he walks into the post office with Lady Bradeen, her instincts are not always reliable: "She had been sure she should see the lady again; ... But for him it was totally different; she should never, never see him... Well, she saw him the very next day" (18). But these instincts show some signs of development as she continues to read the story of Everard's romantic life. Hence, "even through his smile and his happy habit," she reads his "danger". And, despite her attraction for maudlin elements, the telegraphist has developed her analytical abilities enough to look for parallels and contrasts. Further, despite her self-absorbed tendencies, she even makes an effort at self-analysis. Interestingly, at this point in the novella, the telegraphist is also beginning to depend less and less on her ha'penny novels. This is why her apprehension about the aristocratic couple's danger, which she interpretively brings into the narrative, makes this romance "beat every novel in the shop."

This suggests that her response towards sentimental novels is becoming complex in that, even as she feels stimulated by them, she has begun to develop a condescending and critical attitude towards them. If the romance she reads is superior to the novels in the "shop," then James wants his readers to notice that his protagonist is no longer ready to confer narrative supremacy on these ha'penny novels. Her decreasing dependence on such novels is also noticeable in her awareness that *most* of the social codes recorded in her ha'pennyworths are inaccurate: "if the ha'penny novels were *not all wrong*..." (45, my emphasis). As her reliance on ha'penny novels decreases so her reliance on the telegrams as texts increases: "She had never seen a boudoir, but there had been lots of boudoirs in the telegrams" (58). And as her conversation with Mr. Mudge on the subject of the Captain indicates, she is acute enough to realize that Captain Everard is "not only afraid of the lady - he's afraid of other things" (69). Although she is circumscribed by her naivety, in her obsessive desire to read a story of passion, and by the tenuousness of her facts and figures, she shows a vague awareness of "things" in the Captain's life that are "other" than his romantic relationship with Lady Bradeen. Thus, although she faces limitations, she shows a certain ability to minimize those limitations.

For as a reader of stories she learns to look for narrative connections, and thus learns to see "picture[s]" (44). And because these pictures show her ability to read scenes that are connected, "a picture" even becomes "a panorama":

> As the weeks went on there she lived more and more into the world of whiffs and glimpses, and found her divinations work faster and stretch further. It was a prodigious view as the pressure heightened, a panorama fed with facts and figures, flushed with a torrent of colour and accompanied with wondrous world-music. What it mainly came to at this period was a picture of how London could amuse itself. (21)

Such a "panorama" suggests the development of an artistic sensibility, the ability to see narrative connections between causes and effects, to create a meaningful sequence out of random or incomplete images. The telegraphist's "picture of how London could amuse itself" - a picture that has the potential to grow into a comedy of manners - is a "panorama" because it is a detailed picture that is made up of several connected scenes. Later, even with the unrefined Mr. Mudge at Bournemouth, despite all her condescension at his crude entertainment of watching "dreadful women in particular, usually fat and in men's caps and white shoes," her sense of a "panorama" is so strong that she muses about his sense of "the panorama" around him (65,66). Because of her own sense of panorama, she connects elements of his character to read a consistent story about his "latent force": It is the same "latent force" that earlier enables him to subdue the drunken soldier at Cocker's and that now enables him to refrain from announcing "the great news" (that he is now solvent enough to marry) until he disposes of "other matters" (66). At this point the telegraphist's ability to read a temporal narrative in a single picture has become so significant that she is able to create coherence even in material that strikes her as "a far-away story": "[S]he got back her money by seeing many things, the things of the past year, fall together and connect themselves, undergo the happy relegation that transforms melancholy and misery, passion and effort, into experience and knowledge" (65). The "panorama" begins with the telegraphist's sense of "connect[ions]" or "relations" between people (19,20), and develops into a comprehensive vision of a series of events, her sense of stringing events together, with her "divinations," to form continuity (51). The image of the panorama, then, is suggestive of the "picture" of "the whole experience" (67). The scenes may be diverse and unfamiliar, but as the image of the "wondrous world-music" suggests, she has begun to develop the ability to yoke diversity and unfamiliarity into producing the coherence of "a vista in a painted picture," even if it is only a fictitious coherence (51). She may be "reduced to merely picturing that miraculous meeting ...[with the Captain]," but just as in the case of her ridiculous circuit on the way home, she finds a way to "miraculous[ly]" transform the mere pictures, and actually meet the Captain beyond the cage.

Thus, as the first scene of the Dolman telegram suggests, despite his amused irony at the telegraphist, James points out that she acquires narrative authority as a reader. When Lady Bradeen authors this telegram, which for the telegraphist is another part of the narrative she reads about the Captain's romantic life, her ladyship realizes that she has made a mistake. Her exclamation that she "must alter a word" clearly indicates that Lady Bradeen has no intention of authoring a text with a hidden meaning in order to ensure its protection if it falls into the wrong hands of an interceptor (47). The only reason the troubled writer fails to make the revision is that she simply does not remember the numbers she earlier receives from somebody else or conceives on her own. Thus she does not know how to revise her own text: "she recovered her telegram and looked over it again; but she had a new, obvious trouble, and studied it without deciding" (47). It is at this point that the "author" who fails to read her own text is vanquished by the reader who intrudes and makes a revision:

> It was as if she had bodily leaped - cleared the top of the cage and alighted on her interlocutress. ..... Our young friend smiled, meeting the other's eyes, and, having made Juno blush, proceeded to patronize her. "*I'll do it*" - she put out a competent hand. Her ladyship only submitted, confused and bewildered, all presence of mind quite gone; and the next moment the telegram was in the cage again and its author out of the shop. Then quickly, boldly, under all the eyes that might have witnessed her tampering, the extraordinary little person at Cocker's made the proper change. (48).

In this scene of "[h]er ladyship['s] submi[ssion]," James, then, shows that the "author" guiltily and hastily surrenders her narrative authority to the reader without realizing that the telegraphist refers to her mistake of her own (that is, Lady Bradeen's) address for Dolman, and not to the mistake in the numbers or any other part of the message in the telegram. Consequently, at this moment the telegraphist breaks out of her cage of commonality and experiences the delight of soaring triumph. But, as James ironically suggests, if she soars up, she also comes down ("alight[s]"). For she is an intrusive ("tampering"), impertinent "little" person who "patronize[s]" another person. She is, in her self-objectified status, like a bird, and because of her intrusive hand and bold speech, here James makes the reader recall the "magpie" of the first sentence of this novella. As Tony Tanner asserts, through the image of the magpie, James depicts the telegraphist as someone who has a predilection for seizing and hoarding precious things in which the outcast - excluded from participation - finds consolation.[22] Further, with her mawkish insistence on conceiving Lady Bradeen as "Juno," the telegraphist creates the amusingly ludicrous picture of herself as Juno's bird, the peacock! Thus, by "clear[ing] the top of the cage and alight[ing] on her interlocutress,"[23] the young woman only commits herself to her ladyship's service. But if James ironically calls her an "extraordinary" person, then with further irony he also points out in the same passage that she is a remarkably careful reader whose revising "hand" is "competent" enough to make a "proper" alteration on the basis of her past reading: "she put out a competent hand... Then quickly, boldly ... made the proper change." According to Norrman, this "change" presumably increases the couple's danger by exposing their "secret system of communication".[24] But because of the telegraphist's intrusive narrative authority, the "confused, and bewildered" Lady Bradeen terminates her search for the mistake. It is not utterly improbable that if this search were longer, the author of the telegram would ultimately have found the right numbers and corrected her mistake, which correction would have led to dire consequences for her lover and herself. And because of this intrusive narrative authority the telegraphist, with the "change" of address she makes, helps to make the telegram appear authentic and not deliberately misleading to the interceptor(s). The telegraphist's interfering, patronizing, criticizing hand shows how she has developed an "intense ... vision" (and consequently enhanced her memory) by way of the romance she reads (45). Thus James writes in the preface, "To criticise is to appreciate, to appropriate, to take intellectual possession, to establish in fine a relation with the criticised thing [that is, Lady Bradeen's text, the Dolman telegram] and make it one's [that is, the imaginative telegraphist's] own" (*AN* 154).

Indeed, the imaginative telegraphist develops narrative authority as reader to such an extent that she even goes on to absorb the narrator's imagery of water into her own system of representation. The narrator builds a series of water images after the first image of the sands and sea, which represent the wondering reflector's oppressive sense of bewilderment. For example, the bustling and buoyant upper-class world of fashion and the extravagant activities of its airy members, who have awakened with the spring, pose such a challenge and a tantalizing torment for the telegraphist, who staggers laboriously under the weight of the lower classes, that the narrator represents her impressions through images of the stormy "waves of fashion" (13), "a returning tide," (15) "a sea of other allusions" (19), and "ladies submerged, floundering, panting, swimming for their lives" (26). The image of water represents her emotionally charged impressions of the fluid, unstable, slippery and uncontrollable world of elegance and luxury. And in the hot and dry days of summer, as she sits in "her stuffy corner" in the cage of commonness she is distressed by her bewildered impressions of fashionable resorts: "the names - Eastbourne, Folkstone, Cromer, Scarborough, Whitby - tormented her with something of the sound of the plash of water that haunts the traveller in the desert" (49). To be overwhelmed and tormented by the unreachable and uncontrollable world of elegance and luxury is to be frustrated and tormented by the overwhelming and uncontrollable world of penury and privation, and thus by Mr. Mudge's economical plans for their vacation at Bournemouth: "he had flooded their talk with wild waves of calculation" (49). In all these images James never makes any suggestion that the reflector is involved in the creation of these images. At Bournemouth, however, he shows that the reflector literalizes the narrator's metaphors. For, just as James never metaphorically depicts her as enjoying the uncontrollable or unreachable water, so at Bournemouth he never depicts her in the act of literally entering and thus enjoying the water. She puts a noticeable distance between herself and the water as she sits on the pier, on the cliffs, on the decks of steamers, or at the far end of the beach. Her literal association is with the sands of the beach just as her metaphorical association is with "the sand on the floor" (40), or with words that are like "sands of the sea," or with "the desert." Sitting on the beach, she prefers to observe and contemplate. Because she is an "intense observer," her "muffled perception" develops into "perception," and her perception evokes "reflection" (47,45,46). And her reflections, even as she sits in the beach, enable her to read a "far-away story" in "a picture" (65). Through the literalization of the narrator's metaphors, then, James shows how the reflector absorbs the metaphors. Thus she subsequently goes on to create her own images of water to represent her impressions of uncontrollable bewilderment. For example, as she realizes through her verbal exchanges with the helpless Captain that her memory is in complete possession of the contents of Lady Bradeen's Dolman telegram, her "emotion was such a flood that she had to press it back with all her force" (83). The telegraphist, then, feels the metaphorical "flood," just as she does a little later in the same exchanges with the Captain: "Heavens! what was he going to say? - flooding poor Paddington with wild betrayals!" (84). As James implies despite his ironic mirth at her anxious concern for the Captain,[25] the reflector has developed the narrator's ability of representation.

The telegraphist's interest in the Captain grows so steadily that she even attempts to create a dramatic story about the adulterous couple. For, clearly, she takes hardly any interest in flat and passionless ("prosaic and coarse") stories (49):

> It was just the talk - so profuse sometimes that she wondered what was left for their real meetings - of the happiest people of the world... If the girl, missing the answers, her ladyship's own outpourings, sometimes wished that Cocker's had only been one of the bigger offices where telegrams arrived as well as departed, there were yet ways in which, on the whole,

she pressed the romance closer by reason of the very quantity of imagination that it demanded. (19)

As James suggests, his protagonist even in the beginning has begun to be carried away by the liaison between Lady Bradeen and Captain Everard. And one of the "ways" by which she tries to overcome the problem of limited information in the romance she reads through the telegrams is by attempting to create a romantic comedy about her aristocratic lovers. This is why their profuse "talk," as James subtly suggests, for his protagonist, has begun to be associated with the dramatic dialogue (in the actual absence of proper dialogues) of "the happiest people in the world." She has decided, because of her own infatuation with the dashing and handsome Captain Everard, to "take a pure and noble account of such an infatuation [as the one that governs his affair with Lady Bradeen] and even of such impropriety" (40). And this desire to take a "noble account" shows her inclination to make not just a romantic comedy but also a high comedy out of the Captain's romantic life. For she interprets their "large and complicated game" which has a "fine, soundless pulse," as "their high encounter with life" (17). Such an exalted view corresponds with her aversion to "vulgar plays" (33).

But as the focus of her narrative exploits is Captain Everard himself, the telegraphist herself has begun to supplant Lady Bradeen as the heroine of a new romantic or high comedy. More specifically, her romantic comedy about the Captain's affair with Lady Bradeen gives way to a romantic or high comedy about her own imaginary personal relationship with him. Thus she has begun to picture a new dramatic episode with herself as the heroine and the Captain as the hero. The farther she moves away from the constraints imposed by the romance the easier it becomes for her to indulge in fanciful flights. Consequently, as James announces with ironic amusement, even the heroic stature of the Captain increases dramatically in her eyes: whatever "spot" he stands on is "sanctif[ied]" by his presence (46). In the actual Captain Everard she hopes to find the character of her dramatic narrative: he is "the object of her homage" (46). With her vigorously active imagination she finds a way out of the disappointment of not playing an interesting and noble role herself. Thus, although she receives "the sharpest impression" of "the unattainable plains of heaven," as Lady Bradeen comes with her unguessable thoughts to author her Dolman telegram, these unguessable thoughts also cause her "to thrill with a sense of the high company she did somehow keep" (46). In short, these unguessable thoughts help her to supplant Lady Bradeen in the role of heroine.

Susan Winnett argues that at the point the telegraphist "crosses the street" to walk towards the Captain's residence, she crosses "into the frame of the text of manners and violates the frames that separate art from life and her life from the upper classes".[26] As a result of her circular walk home, she has already begun to devise the "ideal setting for the ideal speech" (44). And when she sees her opportunity to make her dramatic entry, she jumps into the "stage" (literally she starts to cross the street to the Captain's side of it) "for the small momentary drama" (52). And once she is on this "stage," she launches straight into the climactic scene with her version of "the ideal speech":

> "I've known perfectly that you knew I took trouble for you; and that knowledge has been for me, and I seemed to see it was for you, as if there were something - I don't know what to call it! - between us. I mean something unusual and good - something not a bit horrid or vulgar." (57)

And to this outburst she emphatically adds, "I'd do anything for you. I'd do anything for you" (58). This is the "high and fine ... brave[] and magnificent[]" "truth" that governs her present action (58). This is the "truth" that is the essence of her dramatic narrative. Her insistence on refined manners and refined environments is so emphatic that even as she enacts her dramatic scene, she adds fresh details to her "ideal setting". Consequently, the bench in the Park becomes "a satin sofa in a boudoir" (58).

As James's ironic tone makes clear, the telegraphist's attempt at constructing a romantic comedy proves to be too "small" and "momentary". No dialogue of noble sentiments ensues from her ardent declaration. Her hero is only embarrassed by her impassioned speech. And the "ideal setting" proves to be too transient in the "impossible" situation made up of "obscure and ambiguous" and therefore "impossible" activity among other couples occupying other benches in the Park (55). Consequently, she fails to create a personal, that is, a romantic relation with the Captain. As Winnett argues, through this scene, James demonstrates the telegraphist's delusion, and "enforces the barrier between the girl's sphere and that of the Captain".[26] And instead of a romantically fulfilling denouement, the happy ending of a romantic comedy, the telegraphist conceives a bitter-sweet scene of star-crossed love that aspires to the tone of tragedy: "I thank and acquit and release you. Our lives take us. I don't know much - though I have really been interested - about yours" (80).

Thus both her projects for a romantic comedy remain incomplete. According to Gribble, the telegraphist weaves stories or "pieces together" a "romance,"[27] but as I see her narrative projects, as the teller of a story the telegraphist creates only a few scenes that do not contain a complete story. When she launches into her "small momentary drama" in the Park, that is, when she attempts to create the dramatic narrative about her own personal relationship with the Captain, we realize that she launches into it without providing a denouement for the dramatic narrative about Lady Bradeen's relationship with the Captain: "The chapter wasn't in the least closed" (78). Just as she intrudes into Lady Bradeen's Dolman telegram, so she intrudes into her narrative project about her ladyship's personal relationship with the Captain. It seems as though as a teller of stories, the margin she creates for herself proves to be too "brave" (72). This creates the problem of a beginning for her new dramatic narrative about her own personal relationship with him. After meeting him in front of his residence, she tells him, "Oh, I don't take walks at night! I'm going home after my work" (52). But instead of going home, she walks and sits in the Park with the Captain, and has no idea about how such action comes about. Thus she has no idea about how she launches into the drama of her personal relationship with him: "She never knew afterwards quite what she had done to settle ["the question of the degree of properness" that enabled her to walk and sit with him in the Park]" (52). Not to know quite what she has done to settle the question of proper form is, in this context, not to know how this new dramatic narrative begins. Perhaps the problem she faces as the teller of a story is simply because, even though she has "gaps in her learning," she chooses to focus on people of the upper class. And therefore perhaps the problem is the result of her naive confidence in her knowledge: "How much *I* know - how much *I* know!" (47).[28]

Another problem with her efforts at creating romantic comedies seems to be with the hero of these dramatic projects. Her desire is to conceive a romantic and noble, urbane and genteel hero, and to do so she turns to the actual Captain Everard. But in his "wonderful face" all she catches is a glimpse of the "old story" of the "Scandal" and shame of adultery (86). She has wanted to replace the "old story" of the scandal and shame of adultery by conceiving a new dramatic story of noble passion once with Lady Bradeen as the heroine and once with herself as the heroine. But her strange and portentous fear of the hero who practically proposes "supper" (76) every time he looks at her after her "small momentary drama" with him in the Park poses problems for both her versions of the dramatic story of noble passion. And the "old story" finds expression only as a courtroom scene she "[en]vision[s]" in her impression of "a picture" within the Captain's eyes, a scene in which she is reduced to being the "*alibi*" of an adulterous man with a tarnished reputation. If the romantically inclined telegraphist's image for the Captain's implied offer of a sexual relationship with her is merely "supper," then it signifies that his offer as she conceives it is a mundane and prosaic, emotionless and unimaginative, cliched and routine matter. In a certain manner, then, it parallels Mr. Mudge's "daily" letter. Certainly James suggests, as critics have pointed out, the telegraphist's sexual repressions and inhibitions.[29] According to Stuart Hutchinson, her fear is of sexual experience itself and "it is a prime cause of her romanticism": It is her fear of the intrusion of the real into the imagined, the idealized, and it motivates her to take refuge in the "cage of her imagination" which is also the state of virginity.[30] But it is also possible to see that the telegraphist's fear of sexuality that is no more than "supper" is her fear of meaningless sexuality, her fear of a vulgar fling. James plainly suggests that his protagonist craves the distinct, individual, delicate touch. Her interpretation of the Captain's looks as a proposition of entertaining himself with sexuality that can neither be the outcome of nor lead to noble sentiments thus clashes violently with her project of creating meaning, that is, a life of sensitiveness and discrimination. Hence it poses a serious problem for the vitality of her projects for romantic comedy. The telegraphist's fear, for Aswell, is her panic at losing control over Captain Everard who steps out of the dramatic role she assigns to him. According to Aswell, the roles she creates and plays are "solipsistic," and her delusional imagination makes her "increasingly ... unaware of the world around her."[31] But by turning the screw of irony James points out that the "solipsistic" telegraphist's goal is not simply to control meaning but also to create refinement in her own life of coarseness. Thus when the hero is reduced to "fidget[ing] and flounder[ing,]" to displaying "futil[ity]" and the "want of power" (78), that is, to the indelicacy of unheroic, ignoble passivity, her projects for romantic comedies tumble into "incoherence" (77).

Consequently, although she looks for heroic material to uphold her theme of refinement, what she finds herself ultimately peering into is an appalling abyss of antiheroic material as becomes obvious in her last conversation with Mrs. Jordan:

> The girl met [Mrs Jordan's] eyes a minute, then quite surrendered. "What was there else about it?"
>
> "Why don't you know?" - Mrs Jordan was almost compassionate.
>
> Her interlocutress had, in the cage, sounded depths, but there was a suggestion here somehow of an abyss quite measureless. "Of course I know that she would never let him alone."
>
> "How *could* she - fancy! - when he had so compromised her?"

> The most artless cry they had ever uttered broke, at this, from the younger pair of lips. "*Had* he so -?
> "Why, don't you know the scandal?" (99)

Indeed, the "abyss" of this passage, in the context of the paucity of the telegraphist's "know[ledge,]" is a direct reference to an abyss of unknowability. But the abyss of unknowability, whose "depths" she has already "sounded" when the Captain makes his last appearance in the post office, now shows itself to be "measureless" because it reveals that all she has not known and has not wanted to know is the abysmally bathetic and anticlimactic material that does not in any way fit into her narrative projects of a romantic comedy. The abyss of unknowability has become "measureless" because it has become an abyss of mockery. Instead of one comprehensive and final glance at a dashing and adventurous person's noble exploits, she finds herself peering into a fearful and measureless abyss of sordid and cheap, bleak and petty action. This is the consequence of her having fallen into "that deepest abyss of all the wonderments" that breaks out for her as she imputes to the Captain, despite her awareness of his scant imagination, "the critical impulse and the acuter vision" (*AN* 155). Thus, instead of the romantic comedy she has been trying to construct, she finds herself reading some kind of a satirical comedy. Indeed, the moral question always erupts to the surface for the telegraphist with uncontrollable and unfaltering regularity. It takes the form either of the upper class people's "silly, guilty secrets" (22), or of "their little games and secrets and vices" (31), or of their flexible idea of "infidelity" (53), or of their selfish, extravagant, immoral "horrors" (61). She tries to suppress the moral question behind the Captain's "debts" with all the art she can muster in order to tell a story of noble passion: "As she didn't speak frankly she only said: 'His debts are nothing - when she so adores him'" (98). But, as her "artless cry" signifies, all the art with which she has produced little dramatic scenes crumbles irremediably when she makes the narrative connection between the Captain's "debts" and "the scandal". By grasping the causal relationship between "debts" and "scandal," she now reads the story of his financial dishonesty. If she earlier manages to cover the problem of the Captain's adultery with the warm, bright colors of romantic love, she now finds that his adultery has not been the only moral issue. There is yet another moral weakness, one for which she cannot summon an excuse.

As James points out with his penchant for mild and subtle irony, despite all the problems she faces as a teller of stories, the telegraphist continues to exercise narrative authority as an acute reader of stories. Thus, although Mrs. Jordan attempts to offer her a story of passion and deliverance with Lady Bradeen as the heroine, and the heroine as the main character, James's "heroine" refuses to read such a story in the material she receives, as her hesitation to explain anything reveals:

> "A good servant," said Mrs Jordan, now thoroughly superior and proportionately sententious, doesn't need to be told! Her ladyship saved - as a woman so often saves! - the man she loves."
> This time our heroine took longer to recover herself, but she found a voice at last, "Ah well - of course I don't know! The great thing was that he got off. They seem then, in a manner," she added, "to have done a great deal for each other."
> "Well, it's she that has done most. She has him tight."
> "I see, I see. Goodbye."........
> "And didn't he want to [marry Lady Bradeen]?"
> "Not before."
> Not before she recovered the telegram?"
> Mrs Jordan pulled up a little. "Was it a telegram?"
> The girl hesitated. "I thought you said so. I mean whatever it was."
> (100-101)

James draws a narrative connection between what his protagonist "hesitate[s]" to say and what she accidentally discloses, and thus reveals that although she experiences a break as storyteller, she continues to be a reader of stories. What the telegraphist has now begun to read is that the adulterous lovers only "seem" to have done "a great deal for each other." As a result of her experience in the surprising hazards of interpretation, then, the telegraphist has come a long way from her confident view of "the high reality, the bristling truth" that "float[s] through the bars of the cage" early in the novella (15). What has "floated through the bars of the cage" of the romance lately is her growing impression of the "black darkness" of unknowability (82). And it culminates with "Ah well - of course I don't know!" She now realizes that appearances are not as readable as she has fancied in the past.

Thus she seems to realize, though she is careful not to provoke the "thoroughly superior and proportionately sententious" Mrs. Jordan with this realization, that what these lovers "in a manner" "have done ... for each other" has not simply been to aid each other in a mysterious and scandalous personal affair, but also to abet each other in a mysterious and scandalous impersonal affair. If Mrs. Jordan realizes that the Captain has done "[s]omething bad" (100), then the telegraphist, who is well aware that Lady Bradeen "would never let him alone" (99), realizes that her ladyship has been connected with him in this "bad" deed. This is what she subtly and indirectly reveals when she states,

"They seem then, in a manner, to have done a great deal for each other." Heroes and heroines indeed! The telegraphist's realization and her subtle manner of revealing that realization demonstrate that the refinement she acquires is not what she finds *in* the story of the aristocracy but something she develops as a reader *of* that story.

Thus this passage suggests that as our telegraphist listens to the story that has grown out of and about the Captain's and Lady Bradeen's scandals, she becomes aware of the common but insatiable thirst for creating sentimental narratives. Raising her narrative on the foundation of the maudlin narratives, early in the novella, the telegraphist composes "a scene better than many in her ha'penny novels," in which she plays the role of a seductive blackmailer[32] and Captain Everard that of a seductive, mischief-making victim (42). Indeed, she has exhibited an unflagging interest in constructing scenes that belong in sentimental narratives: "She literally fancied once or twice that, projected as ...[the Captain] was toward his doom, her own eyes struck him, while the air roared in his ears, as the one pitying pair in the crowd" (43). But she realizes at the end of the novella that within the bars of the cage of commonness she has only been constructing sentimental narratives. Thus what she reveals as, with Mrs. Jordan, she declines to divulge her own role in providing immediate relief to the Captain, is her own refusal to take any kind of part - and certainly not that of a heroine - in any kind of sentimental narrative. This is why, James seems to suggest, his protagonist refuses to be the teller of a story. What she now becomes aware of as she listens to Mrs. Jordan's eulogy of Lady Bradeen, the new employer of Mr. Drake, the butler, is the tendency of the prospective bride of the butler to fill in the blanks of the story of her ladyship's adventures (particularly those blanks which have to do with Lady Bradeen as Captain Everard's accomplice in the scandal of his nonromantic affairs) with acts of heroism. Thus the telegraphist turns quietly away from this new sentimental narrative (a successor of *Picciola*, say, that struggles for its life even as the frail and feeble "picciola" in *Picciola*) that Mrs. Jordan, the faithful bride of the faithful servant, is eager to promote. Carren Kaston argues that the telegraphist has been caged in melodramatic fiction by the cage of her consciousness, and that at the end of the novella she is "rescued" from this cage. For Kaston, it is "[Mudge's] collaborative presence [that] helps her out of the cage of consciousness and the imagination of sexual melodrama".[33] And for Salzburg, Mr. Mudge redeems the telegraphist from "her own solipsistic imagination".[34] As I see this change in the end, the telegraphist's evolving imagination now enables her to *see* that she has been merely reading and therefore constructing sentimental narratives in the cage of commonness, and thus, it is not so much her "rescue" from melodramatic fiction as her rejection of it. Indeed, it is her own realization that redeems her from her "solipsistic imagination". As James writes in the preface, "the catastrophe" and "the solution" depend on the telegraphist's "winged wit" (*AN* 157). It is her imaginative consciousness that causes the "catastrophe" to her romantic projects, that is, she now realizes that these romantic projects have only been sentimental projects; and thus, with her imaginative consciousness she also changes, that is, brings a "solution" to her problem of sentimentalizing. The telegraphist's "Good-bye" to Mrs. Jordan signifies her abdication of the domain of sentimental narratives. Her freedom from the corpus of sentimental narratives and her decision to marry Mr. Mudge[35] and hence to move into Chalk Farm, show that even though she cannot escape the cage of class consciousness, she breaks out of the cage of commonness, that is, of coarseness. James may not have desired his protagonist to exercise authority as a sophisticated storyteller, but as he suggests through the context of sentimental narratives, there seems to be a reason for it. This seems to be the case particularly because, despite this break in storytelling, she continues to exercise narrative authority. For she becomes increasingly an acute reader.

In the middle of the concluding paragraph of this novella James offers a comparison between the narrator of his story and the center of consciousness. Through this comparison he seems to suggest that the point of view slips from the center of consciousness: "A policeman, while she remained [close to the parapet], strolled past her; then, going away a little further and half lost in the atmosphere, paused and watched her. But she was *quite unaware* - she was full of her thoughts" (101, my emphasis). James seems to suggest here that what the narrator shows awareness of is beyond what the center of consciousness shows awareness of. And therefore, by suggesting a difference between what the narrator manages to do and what the center of consciousness does not, James seems to imply that the narrator has an advantage over the center of consciousness. But by the same token, he ironically suggests that what the narrator gains over the center of consciousness is questionable. As James suggests, the narrator is not quite certain about the reflector's actions: "Distinguishing vaguely what the low parapet enclosed, she stopped close to it and stood a while, very intently, but *perhaps* still sightlessly, looking down on it" (101, my emphasis). She looks at the waters of the Paddington canal, and not only is there no sudden resurgence of the narrator's water imagery, and therefore of the need of the narrator's representational skills, which show that the reflector now exerts the narrative authority that the narrator exerts, but there is no need of the reflector's own water imagery either. For, as

James implies, she is no longer flooded by emotions. As the reference to the telegraphist's "thoughts" implies, clearly she has now become more involved with "thoughts" than with uncontrollable emotions. Although she has "now for ever lost" the opportunity to be in touch with the Captain, and thus has "lost" the Captain himself, she does not brood over the loss (99). Further, as James implies, perhaps the narrator cannot keep up with all of the protagonist's "thoughts": "They were too numerous to find a place just here, but two of the number may at least be mentioned" (101). Indeed the narrator's voice reveals the narrative virtues of economy and relevance here. But perhaps it also reveals that the narrator gives us "two" of the telegraphist's thoughts presumably because the only connection that the narrator has mastered is between these two thoughts. Of these two thoughts, however, the second is worth studying particularly because it gives a specific example of the protagonist's freedom from sentimental narratives.

This freedom is clearly exemplified in the ironic vision she directs at herself in the concluding sentence of the novella: "it was strange that such a matter [as her decision to marry Mr Mudge immediately] should be at last settled for her by Mr Drake" (102). For Dale Bauer and Andrew Lakritz, this signifies her amazement at finding her marriage to be "contingent upon no more nobler things and persons than butlers" and that she is "ruthlessly reduced to her insignificance in the end".[36] But as James points out through his ironic use of the subtle and indefinite adjective "strange," his protagonist is capable not simply of being amazed at "her insignificance," but also of turning an ironic eye at herself for her own arrogance. If the telegraphist directs her ironic vision at the pathetically pretentious Mrs. Jordan via Mr. Drake, the butler, then she also directs a rather dry ironic vision at her own pathetically pretentious self that cannot rise above prejudice against her own socioeconomic class. This is her indirect, ironic reference to her own snobbery. It is her ironic reference to her own "strange" self that does not have the ability to settle such a matter as marriage by the consideration of love but by that of convenience. It is "strange" and ironic that despite all her notions about the powerlessness of the lower classes, a representative of the lower classes exercises the power to settle the matter of her imminent marriage. And by extension it is "strange" and ironic that despite all her notions about the powerlessness of the lower classes, Mr. Drake comes up with the power to open the door of a satirical comedy and close that of the sentimental narratives for herself even as he opens it for his prospective bride. Thus even in the concluding sentence of the novella James illustrates his protagonist's narrative authority as an acute reader in that she has begun to develop an ironic eye. She may not have completed a romantic comedy but the attempt to compose a dramatic narrative leads her to develop her abilities as a reader and to develop an essential attribute of the comic spirit. Perhaps, then, the telegraphist's unfinished narrative is not so much an indication of her failure as a storyteller as of the complicated process of storytelling, which involves breakage and inconsistencies.

Notes

1. Henry James, The Art of the Novel (Boston: Northeastern University Press, 1984) 154. Cited parenthetically as AN.
2. Duncan Aswell, "James's In the Cage: The Telegraphist as Artist," in Texas Studies in Literature and Language: A Journal of the Humanities 8.3 (1966): 376. For Aswell, the telegraphist's "art" is expressive of her self-deception (376). In a similar vein, Charles Thomas Samuels, in The Ambiguity of Henry James (Urbana: University of Illinois Press), finds the telegraphist invincibly petty, and the novella "a gay, pitiless satire" (154).
3. Jean Blackall, "James's In the Cage: An Approach through the Figurative Language," University of Toronto Quarterly 31.2 (1962): 177. In this essay on In the Cage, Blackall discusses the images of the cage, money, darkness and light, and animals. For Blackall, the cage is "a place of confinement," but more importantly, it is "a line of demarcation between two worlds" (164). And it is a study of the telegraphist's "various relationships" to this central image that enables Blackall to "trace the progress of the girl's adventure" (167).
4. Henry James, In the Cage and Other Stories (Middlesex, England: Penguin Books Ltd, 1972) 9.
5. For this image neither does James preamble it with "It had occurred to her early that in her position" (or something similar) as he does in the case of the image of the cage, which suggests that the image may be the product of both the narrator's and the reflector's imagination, nor with "our fatigued friend had sufficient store of mythological comparison" to see "Juno" in Lady Bradeen, (or with something similar) which leaves no doubt in the reader's mind as to the origin of the image (9,16).
6. For Leon Edel in Henry James: The Treacherous Years 1895-1901 (Philadelphia and New York: J. B. Lipincott Company, 1969), In the Cage exemplifies James's own alienation from London. Edel argues that this novella shows James as assuming "the disguise of a young adolescent girl" who feels abandoned by the environment to which she directs her curious eye (248). According to Edel, it shows how James gathers himself up after his painful disappointment with the world of the theater.
7. Jennifer Gribble, "Cages," The Critical Review 24 (1982): 112. Gribble argues that James shows through the telegraphist's creative quest "the experience of creative imagination," though it has its limitations, in the

"process of perception" (114). But, according to Gribble, it is because the telegraphist is excluded from "a 'larger life'" that it becomes possible for her to experience "the delight of catching impressions of it and weaving them into 'stories'" (111). And for Maqbool Aziz in "How Long is Long; How Short Short! Henry James and the Small Circular Frame," in A Companion to Henry James Studies, ed. Daniel Mark Fogel (Westport, Connecticut and London: Greenwood Press, 1993), the cage is the cage of the telegraphist's past and present predicaments. But for Aziz, it is also the cage of her fantasies with regard to Captain Everard, and the cage of the Victorian civilization at its final phase with its "injustices now fortified with a machinery" (218).

8. Philip Sicker, Love and the Quest for Identity in the Fiction of Henry James (Princeton, New Jersey: Princeton University Press, 1980) 79. For Sicker, the telegraphist's cage is "a window of subjective perception," and more importantly "a studio for self-conscious artistic creation" (80). It is the barrier she imposes against and the distance she maintains from chaos, the world of flux. Sicker argues that by showing the telegraphist as eliminating this barrier, James depicts "the artistic imagination gone wild" (81).

9. For Aziz this image telescopes "the myriads of tensions" within the telegraphist's soul (224): She is "both attracted and repelled by the 'golden shower' that will not rain on her" (223). According to Aziz, the "essence" of the story of the telegraphist in her cage is her "double life" which fills her with an anguished awareness, for she is tempted by the glitter but is also "blessed by the vision of the terrors of social and actual reality" (221).

10. Ralf Norrman, Techniques of Ambiguity in the Fiction of Henry James (Abo: Abo Akademi, 1977) 133. Norrman also claims that James uses ambiguity to protect the suggestiveness of his prose against the onslaughts of the particular.

11. Andrew Moody in "'The Harmless Pleasures of Knowing': Privacy in the Telegraph Office and Henry James's 'In the Cage,' in The Henry James Review 16.1 (1995), argues that through the telegraphist's ineffectual attempt to comprehend the private details of the Captain's life, James's novella represents, at a time when telegraph workers posed "a potential threat of blackmail and a threat to privacy" (65), a system of communication that "does not threaten upper class privacy" (55). Moody maintains that although the telegraphist's interest in the upper class goes beyond the harmless pleasure of knowing, through her Paddington impersonality, she returns "to the ethics of treating the public with anonymity" (64), and thus through "a nameless part of the great postal mechanism" within the cage (65), James shows that "employees serve best when they maintain official distance" (61).

12. Priscilla Walton, in The Disruption of the Feminine in Henry James (Toronto: University of Toronto Press, 1992) argues that the names and the absences of names in this novella "signify unknowability" (97). According to Walton, the fictions the telegraphist creates are multiple interpretations

engendered from "absence," and therefore they are "not factual Realist representations" (93).

13. Tzvetan Todorov, The Poetics of Prose (Ithaca, New York: Cornell University Press, 1971) 148. Todorov argues that James's use of the line of narrative movement corresponds to a vertical spiral which always leads us back to "the same figure in the carpet," that is, there is always the pursuit of knowledge, and thus the "presence of the quest," and always the "absence of its object" (153).

14. Joel Salzburg, "Mr Mudge as Redemptive Fate: Juxtaposition in James's In the Cage," Studies in the Novel 11.1 (1979): 71. Salzburg's main point is that it is Mudge who restores the telegraphist from a distorted or incomplete view of reality (70).

15. Sicker, 79. For Sicker, the telegraphist's quest for identity through love is reflective of her "need to establish a point of fixity" by transforming "the changing beloved ... into an unchanging image" (78).

16. Salzburg, 65.

17. William Veeder in "Toxic Mothers, Cultural Criticism: 'In the Cage' and Elsewhere," in The Henry James Review 14.3 (1993), argues that the initial cause of the telegraphist's negative traits is not socioeconomic but psychological: She is the disgusted daughter whose development of a functional self has been hindered by her alcoholic mother. For Veeder, the ultimate source of the telegraphist's rage, envy, self-hate, and her projective penchant, is "an archaic sense of contamination" (267).

18. Jennifer Wicke, "Henry James's Second Wave," The Henry James Review 10.2 (1989): 146,151. According to Wicke, the telegraphist's cage suggests that "the text can never be aloof from its historical enmeshings," and the novella itself highlights "the modern scene of writing - where communication is technologized and words are part of a larger economy" (151).

19. On a different note Muriel Shine, in The Fictional Children of Henry James (Chapel Hill: The University of North Carolina Press, 1968) argues that the cage is a shelter of the creative imagination and that it is "emblematic of a special kind of unreality" which provides a shelter for "the passive observer of men and manners... from threatening experiences" (143). Shine's main point about In the Cage is that it focuses on "the process of growing up" (145): The growth of the adolescent telegraphist who is maturing into adulthood, is metaphorical of "the growth of the artist" (142).

20. For Walton, "margin" on the one hand betokens the telegraphist's confinement in the post office and on the other liberty and power (94). Thus Walton argues that the telegraphist "creates the inside of her text" from "the outside or the margin," yet this text only reinforces her "marginalization from her creation" (95). Creativity, Walton argues, "derives from the space of the Feminine Other," and therefore does not engender "Masculine Knowledge"

(99). And for Richard Hocks, in Henry James: A Study of the Short Fiction (Boston: Twayne Publishers, 1990), the telegraphist's "margin" ultimately signifies marginalization: "she decides ... at the conclusion just how severely marginalized she herself is" (58).

21. Naomi Schor, "Fiction as Interpretation or Interpretation as Fiction," The Reader in the text: Essays on Audience and Interpretation eds. Susan Suleiman and Inge Crosman (Princeton, New Jersey: Princeton University Press, 1980) 171. Schor, for whom the act of interpretation constitutes the whole of the action of this novella, argues that the telegraphist is "an exemplary interpretant," that is, "the interpreting character" (170,168), and that her "hermeneutic hyperactivity" is synonymous with creative, imaginative activity (171).

22. Tony Tanner, The Reign of Wonder: Naivety and Reality in American Literature (Cambridge: Cambridge University Press, 1965) 312. Tanner claims that James's focus in In the Cage is on "the wondering imagination," and the telegraphist's cage is the cage of her isolated imagination" (312). For Tanner, the unnamed protagonist represents a principle more than an identity, a principle that James uses to represent "the predicament and function of the artist" (318).

23. Janet Gabler-Hover in "The Ethics of Determinism in Henry James's 'In the Cage,'" in The Henry James Review 13.3 (1992) argues that this figurative leap signifies "the fitful surfacing" of the telegraphist's unconscious desires prompted by envy and ambition and it expresses her "ambivalence about the upper class" (263). According to Gabler-Hover, the telegraphist's consciousness prevents her from intentionally indulging in unethical considerations, and therefore she "escapes into the unconscious" where action can take the form of accident (263) and where she can give free expression to her animal instincts or desires, including the desire for sexuality and revenge. In her unconscious adventures, then, for Gabler-Hover, James's protagonist is "a vampire" (266). But, Gabler-Hover further argues, through her attempt to transform desire, that is, "through her imagination of higher ethical values" she engages in the "artistic project of creating meaning and duration" (269,272).

24. Norrman, "The Intercepted Telegram Plot in Henry James's 'In the Cage,' Notes and Queries 24.5 (1977) 427. In this essay Norrman focuses on the intercepted telegram plot to argue that in the novella the main theme is the question of the relationship between the subjective and objective realities: If on the one hand the romantic imagination is free to create subjective reality then on the other hand objective reality imposes constraints on that freedom. Thus Norrman concludes that the telegraphist's "speculations go wrong" (427). But we must keep in mind that all of her speculations do not go wrong. For instance, it turns out that the Captain does live close at hand, or that the lovers are in danger, or that Lady Bradeen is more eager about her lover than he about her, or that he does have "other things" worrying him apart from an adulterous

relationship. Certainly James shows, as Norrman claims, making many mistakes, but she is not, as Norrman also claims, "wrong about everything" (425)..

25. Heath Moon in "More Royalist Than the King: the Governess, the Telegraphist, and Mrs Gracedew," in Criticism 24.1 (1982), argues that the telegraphist acts in the capacity of a "protectress" towards Captain Everard because of her loyalty, her sense of duty, to the aristocracy (32). And for Moon, in this sense the telegraphist is a parallel of the governess of The Turn of the Screw and Mrs Gracedew of "Covering End".

26. Susan Winnett, Terrible Sociability: The Text of Manners in Laclos, Goethe, and James. (Stanford: Stanford University Press, 1993) 179,175,180. Winnett argues that it is the telegraphist's caged perspective and therefore her distance from the upper classes that enable her to read a competent romance: "Her [generic] competence is impaired when she leaves her cage and undertakes to act in the world" (181).

27. Gribble, 108.

28 Eric Savoy in "'In the Cage' and the Queer Effects of Gay History," in Novel: A Forum on Fiction 28.3 (1995), argues that the telegraphist's "knowledge," which is "a queer mixture of fact and fancy," produces certain effects which in turn produce queerness (286). And queerness, for Savoy, which is produced by James's displacement of sexual and class scandal-related panics of the 1890s, has double referents, and signifies the displaced, the uncanny, and the oblique. And Walton argues that in her attempt to "appropriate" and "know," the telegraphist engages in "Masculine Realist activity" which ultimately impedes her imaginative activity (92).

29. For Gribble, the telegraphist's cage also signifies" emotional and sexual" barriers (112). And for Darshan Singh Maini, in Henry James: the Indirect Vision (Ann Arbor or London: U. M. I. Research Press, 1988) the telegraphist's cage is the cage of her "sexual inhibitions and fantasies" (13). Maini maintains that In the Cage is among a group of James's fiction that depicts "emotional erosion and subversion" (13), and gives indirect expression to James's "sexual miseries" (172) and "suppressed puritanism" (97).

30. Stuart Hutchinson, "James's In the Cage: A New Interpretation," Studies in Short Fiction 19.1 (1982): 24, 22. For Hutchinson, Mudge and Everard, although dissimilar characters, are similar in that they "embody an identical threat" for the telegraphist (24).

31. Aswell, 378,384.

32. Savoy observes that this particular fancy of the telegraphist's "signifies the cash nexus in which blackmail was comparable to and might accompany prostitution, and it demonstrates the contingent power that accrued to the working class servant" when the public medium of telegraphy caused the circulation of the secrets of the upper class people's private lives (292).

33. Carren Kaston, Imagination and Desire in the Novels of Henry James (New Brunswick, New Jersey: Rutgers University Press. 1984) 118. For Kaston, the cage is the cage of the telegraphist's imagination or consciousness, and in it she has maintained a genteel separation from experience

34. Salzburg, 63.

35. Her decision to marry Mudge immediately illustrates that a glimpse into the foibles of the hitherto idealized Captain brings out an appreciation of her fiance's virtues for the telegraphist.

36. Dale M. Bauer and Andrew Lakritz, "Language, Class, and Sexuality in Henry James's 'In the Cage,'" New Orleans Review 14.3 (1987): 69. Bauer and Lakritz argue that the telegraphist's decision to marry Mudge immediately is because her knowledge of Everard's destitution awakens her to an apprehension of the material, sexual damage that she herself suffers through her association with him. She realizes, according to Bauer and Lakritz, that she "cannot interpret her way out of her social position any more than she can transcend the limits of her imagination or class," and therefore she is "scared into marriage" (69). For, trapped "in the cage of language, class, and sexuality," she sees marriage as her "only security" (69).

Chapter 2

Spencer Brydon's Aesthetic Quest in the "Human Actual Social" World

As we find out from the preface to "The Jolly Corner," to James the author who writes this tale for his "love of 'a story as a story,'" the subject of "representation" is of utmost importance: "[B]eauty" is inseparably connected with "r*epresentation*" because "One's [that is, the storyteller's] working of the spell is of course - decently and effectively - but by the represented thing, and the grace of the more or less closely represented state is the measure of any success".[1] Like his creator, the aesthetically inclined center of consciousness of "The Jolly Corner," Spencer Brydon, is deeply involved in creating images - personification, metaphors, similes, and the like - because of his deep interest in the subject of "represent[ation,]" and thereby in creating beauty.[2] Also, like his creator, for whom the "love of 'a story as a story'" is "the vital flame at the heart of any sincere attempt to lay a scene and launch a drama," Brydon shows his love of a story as a story when he attempts to lay a scene and launch a drama in his old empty house on the jolly corner (*AN* 252-253). Thus Brydon begins to exert narrative authority in that he is in a manner a storyteller who begins to compose a narrative about "what he personally might have been" if he had never left his home (169). His quest for what he might have been is his quest for a fictional narrative through which he seeks self-fulfillment. Indeed, at one level, the figure of Brydon's alter-ego represents the narrative of what he might have been. Brydon attempts to figuratively create a narrative of what he might have been because it is through such a fiction that he hopes to create a purposeful life. If

James turns to "art," as he writes in another preface, because "life persistently blunders and deviates, and loses herself in the sand," and therefore is full of "confusion," then his fictional creation, Brydon, turns to "art," as it were, because he seems to understand that his own life shows blunders, and confusion (*AN* 120). As in his life he does not read a coherent story about his aesthetic quest, and thus, as he does not find aesthetic fulfillment in that story, he hopes to find it through a fiction of meaningful, purposeful, well-ordered sequence of events. But Brydon's self-imposed isolation from the "human actual social" world creates a problem for his narrative authority (176). Likewise, it is when he rejects or renounces his self-imposed isolation that he reasserts his narrative authority. It is the "human actual social" world, say in the form of Alice Staverton, that contributes to Brydon's narrative of what he might have been, and thus that enables him to make a beginning of his fiction. And it is Alice Staverton's contribution that ultimately enables Brydon to find fulfillment in his aesthetic quest.

As the tale begins, James suggests that, despite Brydon's thirty-three years of life in Europe, his aesthetic pursuits remain unsuccessful. He has "lived his life" in Europe with his "back ... turned" to such materialistic concerns as the money-making scheme of house-building, which he conceives as "vulgar and sordid," and his "face addressed to those of so different an order" that evidently they have been contrary to those "vulgar and sordid" materialistic concerns (163). Indeed, working to make money does not seem to have been a concern for the expatriate at all, for while in Europe, his rented property at home has provided him with his income. Living comfortably without even the slightest worry about a steady flow of capital, Brydon had turned his attention to the life of "pleasure," and thus it appears, to the enjoyment of beauty and refinement, as is evident from his sensitivity to "all delicate things" and "sweetnesses" (164), or from his consternation at "the monstrosities" of the swelling city of New York (162). But the "sweetnesses" that the "wander[ing]" Brydon had hoped to bring into his life, while in Europe, have "fail[ed] him (164). Thus he confesses to his old friend, Alice Staverton,

> "I've not been edifying - I believe I'm thought in a hundred quarters to have been barely decent. I've followed strange paths and worshipped strange gods; it must have come to you again and again - in fact you've admitted to me as much - that I was leading at any time these thirty years, a selfish frivolous scandalous life. And you see what it has made of me."(171)

If he has "not been edifying" this means that he has turned out to be a great moral disappointment to himself. And to have been a moral disappointment to himself is to have been unsatisfied in his aesthetic quest, as Brydon suggests through the word "decent." The "paths" he has "followed" and the "gods" he has "worshipped" turn out to have been "strange" because they have not fulfilled his aesthetic quest. As a result he feels the conspicuous absence of self-fulfillment, for he suffers from the sense of a failure to effectuate the "development of ...[his] own nature" (170). He cannot contradict the general opinion that he has lived "a selfish frivolous scandalous life" because of his own gnawing sense of having lived a purposeless and unformed life. And Staverton firmly believes that Brydon has not lived up to his potential: He is "[f]ar from it" (171). As Brydon looks back it seems to him that the only possibility of a "full-blown flower," his image for the attainment of beauty within himself, has been in the past, that is, before he uproots himself from his home; and that, instead of working towards the blossoming of his potential into a culminating point of development in Europe, he has only "blighted" the possibility of the blossoming (170). It is his shocked awakening into this confusion and failure of his morally fulfilling aesthetic quest that prompts Brydon's interest in a specific form of art,[3] that is, in composing a narrative (though not literally) other than the one that tells about his actual life.

And it is Brydon's shocked awakening into the confusion of his aesthetic quest that finds expression in his sense of self-division regarding New York. James depicts Brydon's self-division even near the beginning of the tale. On the one hand he is clearly charmed by his burgeoning "capacity for business and ... sense for construction" and dismisses his own involvement in "vulgar[ity]" and "sordid[ness]," and on the other he is appalled by the vulgarity of the displayed products of New York's entrepreneurial activity (163). As Annette Benert describes Brydon, he is an embodiment of "all the contradictions of the heroic age of capitalism."[4] With glaring inconsistency Brydon finds the products of the environment's entrepreneurial activity distasteful to his aesthetic sensibility. Thus to go to Staverton's small house he has to pick his way through

> the dreadful multiplied numberings which seem[ ] to him to reduce the whole place to some vast ledgerpage, overgrown, fantastic, of ruled and criss-crossed lines and figures - ...the vast wilderness of the wholesale, ... through the mere gross generalization of wealth and force and success ... (163-164).

His image of the "criss-crossed lines and figures" through which he intends to give expression to the disorderliness and inharmoniousness of the "gross" modern American milieu of "wealth and force and success" and which ends up by giving expression to the marks made in his own mind by contrary lines of thinking, is unambiguously Brydon's own image. For, as the narrator points out, the "numberings ... *seemed to him* to reduce the whole place to some vast ledgerpage ..." (my emphasis). Brydon tries to make a pattern out of the crossed lines of his thinking, keep account of it all in a "ledgerpage" as it were, but the relatively simple additions and subtractions have become complex multiplication and divisions - multiplication of his confusions and divisions of his values. It seems to him that he has betrayed his aesthetic, moral, emotional, and spiritual values with his newly surfacing penchant for materialistic values: "There are values other than the beastly rent-values, and in short, in short -!" he exclaims in exasperation during one of his conversations with Staverton (167). With his return to what has now become the thoroughly unfamiliar environment of his native New York, Brydon becomes so distressingly aware of the frustration of his aesthetic pursuits that he finds all his "[p]roportions and values ...upside down" (162). Brydon claims to cherish his house on the "jolly corner," which again the narrator clearly points out to be the center of consciousness's term ("he usually ... described it"), because of all the moral, emotional, and spiritual values that it signifies for him. But instead of giving life to these intangible values by living in this house, he chooses to live in a hotel and ironically let the "jolly" corner stand in the dolorous solemnity of conspicuous desolation (162). Indeed, he cannot live on the jolly corner with his return to America because his contrary impulses have not intersected to merge into a harmonious whole. It seems to him that his only hope of unity has been in the past when his "*alter ego*" "had" been "within" him (170). Thus it seems to him that only in the past has there been a dialectic between his ego and alter ego, a chance at the exquisite synthesis that he envisions in his metaphor of "the full-blown flower". But as James points out through this metaphor of the flower, Brydon is so confused at this point that even as he implicitly suggests the union of his ego and alter ego through the metaphor, he explicitly situates the full-blown flower in the alter ego alone.

Nevertheless, Brydon's image of the full-blown flower is one of several images he creates that are worth noticing because of the part they play in his efforts to read or create order and meaning through aesthetic means. Brydon's deep involvement with literary concerns, for example, his concern for "irony" and "imagination" or for literary "terms" and "comparisons," and consequently, his creative turn with images, reveals the process through which he exerts narrative authority (167, 175). The first of these images is his interpretation of Alice

Staverton's small house: "the charm of his having encountered and recognized, in the vast wilderness of the wholesale, ...a small still scene where ... economy hung about like the scent of a garden" (164). As James points out through the narrator's voice, then, this image too is unambiguously Brydon's own, that is, an image the center of consciousness does not share with the narrator. Staverton has brought such order into her frugal home that the aesthetically inclined Brydon is thoroughly charmed by it and therefore attempts to articulate his impression through a simile. He does not wish to limit himself to the visual image of "a garden" because he is particularly struck by the subtlety and delicacy of Staverton's home, and so he goes on to create an olfactory image as well. This shows his concern for careful and clear expression. The desire to steer clear of a "cloud of words" and to create word pictures that suggest and represent ideas and feelings and that communicate meaning with refinement and beauty is what Brydon's representational tendency reveals (168).

And representational skills, as "The Jolly Corner" suggests, are the effect of the faculty of wonder. To wonder is to continue to ponder, inquire, and speculate, that is, to watch and interpret. Also, to wonder is to feel awe, astonishment, and admiration. And James is emphatic about Brydon's ability to wonder: he is always "wonder[ing,]" either about his "situation" or about a "fact" (180), either about an idea or about an emotion. It is because he wonders that he comes to possess "the most wonderful hour" late in the tale (189). To wonder is to guess and to make thought productive. To wonder, then, is to enhance the imaginative faculty. Thus it is Brydon's "wonderment" that leads him early in the tale to conceive his "image" of what he might have been as "some strange figure" (165). And it is because Brydon "keep[s] for ever wondering" that his image expands to a narrative (169-170). In his ability to wonder, then, James's protagonist is like James the storyteller. For, in the preface to this tale, the author points out that his "love of 'a story as a story,'" and consequently, his "attempt to lay a scene and launch a drama" is inseparable from his "appeal to wonder" (*AN* 252-253). He refers to the "blest faculty of wonder" as the "star" under which the author "will ... gather in what he shall most seek to represent" (*AN* 253,254). It then is the guiding light that James the author depends upon to illuminate his images. For it is what James wonders most about that he "seek[s] to represent" (*AN* 254).

Hence it is Brydon's personified "image" of what he might have been, that is the product of his "wanton wonderment," with which James clearly illustrates how his protagonist begins to exert narrative authority:

> It had begun to be present to him after the first fortnight, it had broken out with the oddest abruptness, this particular wanton wonderment: it met him there - and this was the image under which he himself judged the matter, or at least, not a little, thrilled and flushed with it - very much as he might have been met by some strange figure, some unexpected occupant, at a turn of one of the dim passages of an empty house. The quaint analogy quite hauntingly remained with him, when he didn't indeed rather improve it by a still intenser form: that of his opening a door behind which he would have made sure of finding nothing, a door into a room shuttered and void, and yet so coming, with a great suppressed start, on some quite erect confronting presence, something planted in the middle of the place and facing him through the dusk. (165)

Clearly, at this point, Brydon develops his metaphors so that they reveal the beginning of his grasp over narrative connections. For his "image" in this passage reveals how he begins to create a fictitious shadowy character, a setting, and scenes in a narrative fiction. Hence he conceives the "image" of "dim passages of an empty house" and of "some strange figure" that has become an "unexpected occupant" in that empty house, which he develops into a scene of suspense with his meeting this strange occupant "at a turn of one of the dim passages". Brydon even moves on to "improve" his "quaint analogy" by changing the scene in which he meets the strange occupant from the dim passages of an empty house to "a room shuttered and void". Further, the "unexpected occupant" in this scene develops into an "erect confronting presence," which looms up in the dark and empty room. He also develops the scene in that he adds to the dramatic "intens[ity]" by sketching the element of emotion ("a great suppressed start") at the unexpected encounter.

And Brydon continues to develop this element of emotion as he continues to concentrate on his conception of the figure that represents what he might have been:

> He had always caught the first effect of the steel point of his stick on the old marble of the hall pavement... This effect was the dim reverberating tinkle as of some far-off bell hung .. in the depths of the house, of the past, of that mystical other world that might have flourished for him... On this impression he ... put his stick noiselessly away ... feeling the place once more in the likeness of some great glass bowl, all precious concave crystal, set delicately humming by the play of a moist finger round its edge. The concave crystal held ... this mystical other world, and the indescribably fine murmur of its rim was the sigh there, the scarce audible pathetic wail to his strained ear, of all the old baffled forsworn possibilities. (174)

The jolly corner, the setting of his narrative fiction of what he might have been, seems to fill with "the slow opening bars of some rich music" (174). This image of an aesthetically pleasing, melodious, and powerful instrumental music represents for Brydon the development of meaning and purpose, and of his strong sense of harmony, or his strong belief in the construction of a purposeful world of fiction. It therefore is comparable to the "rich music" of a delightful concerto. But the image of instrumental sounds is an overture that heralds the image of human sounds. Indeed, Brydon carefully continues to build his sense of "the conscious human resonance" (167). Thus, as his stick touches the marble squares of his childhood and his youth, the "rich music" gradually diminishes into "the dim reverberating tinkle ...of some far-off bell". It is as though Brydon is preparing the stage for the human drama to begin. Therefore the instrumental music gives way to a "humming" sound. And as the drama increases, the hum is replaced by a "murmur" followed by "sigh," and a "pathetic wail". It is as though, like his creator, who writes in his preface that the "excitement, ... amusement, ... thrill and ...suspense" of a "story" is in the development of "the human emotion," the reflector understands the drama of human emotion (*AN* 257). The suggestion here is that Brydon's conception of his personified figure of what he might have been continues to develop the human element so persistently that not only does the image of instrumental music give way to the image of human sounds, but the sounds themselves show Brydon's increasing awareness of the drama of human emotion. For, at this point, his "old baffled forsworn possibilities" have increasingly begun to take a human form.

Brydon then has developed his image of the personified figure, the vague and dim "presence" that represents "all the old baffled forsworn possibilities" of his life, to give them one specific "Form" based on "verisimilitude" (174,175). His conception of the image of one full-blown flower, or "a small still scene" (164), or "some great glass bowl, all precious concave crystal,"[5] or one concerto of "rich music" clearly illustrates his desire to harness all his contradictory impulses and create a harmonious whole for himself (174). And the form under which he thinks he has united "all" his "old baffled forsworn possibilities" is the figure of his "*alter ego*," the other self he could or would have become if he had stayed at home (175).[6] Brydon even goes on to "wake" all his old and rejected unexplored potential "into such measure of ghostly life as they might still enjoy" (174). He does not conceive several separate narratives for his several rejected and unexplored "possibilities," but one narrative fiction of a particular kind for all of them. In effect, then, to live one "ghostly life" is for all those possibilities to come together, to cohere and connect, and to become a ghostly alter ego that represents one imaginary life, and consequently, that represents one narrative fiction. Brydon hopes to visualize the apparition "telescopically," at the "far end" of a clear vista, framed within an open door, for this is how he projects "into it always a refinement of beauty" (181). Thus his idea is to create an aesthetically pleasing work of art that consistently preserves a romantic aura of mystery, and therefore to study it from a distance but without frustrating the illusion of nearness, even as though the object were natural or real, and not artificial or imaginary. Brydon's interest in clear "vistas" reveals his interest in conceiving a comprehensive view in which the elements of his picture, and consequently a succession of events of a probable past, fall into sequential order. Thus his idea is to create a work of art that tells a story about an adventure, a quest, and a discovery. More specifically, his "odd pastime" turns out to be the construction of a narrative that he creates without literally writing it, but that is nevertheless a narrative whose author is particular about "verisimilitude": "This was the essence of his vision - which was all rank folly, if one would, while he was out of the house and otherwise occupied, but which took on the last verisimilitude as soon as he was placed and posted" (174-175). Unhappy with the actual story of his life, he conceives a different story, an imaginary but plausible one, raised on the foundation of his remote but actual past, that is, he conceives the fiction of what might have been. He has "like[d]" to open shutters of the upper room windows through which "the flare of the street-lamps below" or the "hard silver of the autumn stars" above would enter and light up his world of fiction with verisimilitude (176). Perhaps it is because of this concern for plausibility that, for Walter Shear, James's protagonist comes to believe that the image of what "he would have become had he remained in America will yield him a sense of the historical reality in which the image might have lived,"[7] and for Smythe, that protagonist is writing an autobiographical story.[8] Further, for Bell, who points out James's use of the homonymous pun through "storey," Brydon, like many other characters in James, possesses a literary consciousness, by which the Jamesian character "duplicate[s] the actions of the author himself ... when he is said to be searching for a 'form' from storey to storey (or story to story)".[9] As I read this passage, however, it is not so much that James's protagonist moves from story to story as that he moves from one part of his narrative fiction to another.

As James indicates, for a time Brydon even succeeds in moving on with the creation of a narrative fiction of his unexplored possibilities on the jolly corner. The ground floor of the jolly corner, with its marble squares of Brydon's "childhood" and his "youth," represents Brydon's remote but actual past (186,189). And each of the upper "storey[s]" that he wanders from and into represents each of the parts of the plot of the story that Brydon constructs on this symbolical foundation of the remote but actual past (174). Just as there are four upper floors, so Brydon's narrative about his relationship with his other self, that is, with the self that he might have been, is structured into four parts of a plot. The first part of the plot, which shows how Brydon begins with a stable situation, is about how he hunts this other self from storey to storey. Through this part of the plot Brydon establishes that the conflict or problem of the story he conceives is with regard to discovering the "ineffable identity" (178). For the second part of the plot, the rising action, the situation moves from stability to instability as he develops the action as well as the character of the other self: he is cautious, shifty, and roams restlessly, like Brydon himself. Thus, at this point in Brydon's narrative of what might have been, the problem of discovering the "ineffable identity" becomes deeper. And by the third part of the plot, the crisis, this problem culminates. Thus Brydon develops the thrill of suspense in his narrative:

> the conviction of its probable, in fact its already quite sensible, quite audible evasion of pursuit grew for him from night to night, laying on him finally a rigour to which nothing in his life had been comparable... he had tasted of no pleasure so fine as his actual tension ... (175).

In the climactic part of Brydon's narrative, then, the tension in his fiction rises to a peak. For the character he creates becomes a worthy opponent who is adept at "evasion of pursuit".

But as Brydon moves to the fourth part of the plot of his narrative, and correspondingly, as he reaches the door of the fourth room of the fourth floor, James points out how he creates a problem for his narrative authority. As the "evasion of pursuit" continues to grow, the problem of *discovering* the "ineffable identity" slips out of it and becomes replaced by the problem of *alienating* that "ineffable identity" without Brydon's intending such a change. Through his own clear structuring of the tale into three parts, James marks a clear separation here between himself as fiction-maker and his representation of a fiction-maker. Brydon creates a problem in the fourth part of his fiction because, instead of executing a falling action and denouement, and thus of moving the situation from instability towards the formation of a new stability, he finds himself overwhelmed by a peripeteia that is directed at himself and not at the other self. This means that it seems to Brydon it is he himself, and not the other self, who experiences a sudden reversal of fortune in the sense of a fall. For, in the fourth part of his fiction, Brydon's narrative loses coherence for him.

Brydon gives expression to this problem of narrative control in the image "of a man slipping and slipping on some awful incline" (179).[10] It seems as though his images have begun to take a turn of their own against his intentions. Thus the image of the hunted becomes concretized as the image of the hunter. And yet, to him, "the strangest moment of his adventure perhaps, the most memorable or really most interesting" moment is this moment at which he begins to lose control over his narrative (179). For his failure to exercise control over his fictional plan signifies for him the uncanny repetition of his failure to bring fulfillment and completion in the story of his actual life. Instead of accomplishing the falling action that he anticipates for his fictional character he finds that he is himself experiencing a fall. Although he tries to distance himself from his fiction with the image of "a man" on an "awful incline," this image of a man is Brydon's picture of himself as not already fallen into an abyss but as "slipping and slipping" into one, and thus, as gradually losing control in an abyss of unforeseen turns in his narrative about the unexplored possibilities of his life.

Consequently, it is at this point in the tale that the narrator first makes an intrusion in the first person: "He had made, *as I have said*, to create a baseless sense of a reprieve," and a little later, "[t]here came to him, *as I say* - but determined by an influence beyond my notation" (177,178, my emphases). With these intrusions the narrator consciously separates himself from the center of consciousness, and points out that he wants the narratee to notice the separation. As the point of view is the center of consciousness's, James does not require the narrator to make his presence felt usually. Therefore when he does make the narrator speak with an "I," it becomes noticeable. For Deborah Esch this intrusion is "to emphasize the decisiveness of Brydon's coming-to-terms".[11] As I see it, however, through this separation from the center of consciousness the narrator indicates the reflector's problem of narrative authority. Thus, at the point in the tale where Brydon fails to open the door of the fourth room on the fourth floor, and tries to deceive himself with his idea of his own "Discretion,"[12] that is, at the precise point in the tale that Brydon breaks the continuity of his narrative and thus creates a problem for his narrative authority, the narrator once again makes his emphatic intrusion: "When I say he 'jumped' at it I feel the consonance of this term with the fact that - at the end of I know not how long - he did move again, he crossed straight to the door" (182). The narrator here juxtaposes what he has accomplished with what the protagonist has failed to accomplish.

As a result, into Brydon's world of realistic fiction the world of romance[13] makes a stealthy invasion. The romantic images, as James points out, fail to become a part of Brydon's realistic fiction where his glimmering candle fails to figure the light of knowledge. The glimmering light therefore "would have to figure his sword" (180). To indicate the incongruity between Brydon's romantic images and his realistic fiction-making, James points out how, for the protagonist, his dignities seem to be more of a burden than a joy: "What he mainly felt now was that, since he hadn't originally scuttled, he had his dignities - which had never in his life seemed so many - all to preserve and to carry aloft" (180). As James indicates with adroit irony, Brydon's name itself suggests the word "burden," particularly if one remembers the Old English root, "brythen". Brydon's load is heavy indeed. This, James implies, would not be the case in "an age of greater romance" (180). According to Brydon, the only difference between his own and "the heroic time" is that he does not have a sword in one hand and his dignities concretized and documented in "a parchment scroll" (180). But he overlooks the significance of this difference. Whereas in the heroic age the literal would be given a figurative turn, the tangible object an intangible context, and the focus (as the allegorical narratives of the age of greater romance reveal) would be on the intangible values, in Brydon's age of materialism the opposite, James suggests, seems to be the case: Intangible values are conceived of in tangible terms and the focus is on tangible objects. Thus Brydon takes his abstractions and gives them a literal, bodily or "physical" form (180). It is not a story of dignities that he can visualize at this point but the physical object in which such a story may be recorded: the parchment scroll. He conceives of his intangible dignities in tangible terms - a parchment scroll - whereas the tangible parchment scroll in the heroic time, James implies, would be conceived of as the intangible dignities. Brydon conceives of "brandishing" his dignities and "proceed[ing] downstairs with a drawn sword in his other grasp" and not of proceeding with his dignities in one grasp and brandishing his sword in the other. Clearly he would like to direct his aesthetic values toward the incorporeal joys of a "mystical other world" and has a distaste for a corporeal world of mere "sensation[s]," but is ambivalently attracted by this corporeal world, and his values are often sensually evoked (178). (The attraction and the sensualism, presumably, are the effects of his environment.) It is not surprising, then, that his dignities shrink dramatically into "dignity" despite his desperate clutch at "Discretion," and even this shrunken dignity is on the verge of extinction: "The pretext that wouldn't have been too silly or too compromising, the explanation that would have saved his dignity and kept his name, in such a case, out of the papers, was not definite to him" (183).

Thus the narrative that goes beyond Brydon's control makes a mockery of his aesthetic quest:

> He was kept in sight while remaining himself - as regards the essence of his position - sightless, and his only recourse then was in abrupt turns ...It was indeed true that his fully dislocalized thought of these manoeuvres recalled to him Pantaloon, at the Christmas farce, buffeted and tricked from behind by ubiquitous Harlequin ... (177)

If there is irony in the hunter's becoming the hunted, there is further irony in that Brydon, the author of his fiction, or who has been the author of his fiction at the beginning of the adventure, suddenly seems to have become a character in the fiction, and a stock character, a "Pantaloon" for that matter, that is a conspicuous affront to the aesthetic sensibility (177). On the other hand, for Brydon, the character of his fiction becomes elevated from the status of a "creature" (however "subtle") to a "ubiquitous Harlequin" (175,177). Brydon's realistic fiction, then, shrinks into a harlequinade for him, and the harlequinade turns out to be nothing other than a "farce". Further, such a reduction results in the extinction of his authorial role: He is reduced to envisioning himself simply as one of the characters (the completely grotesque one) in a harlequinade. Consequently he envisions the other self as the principal character of the harlequinade. Therefore the latter's ascent from the status of a fictional character to an actual "somebody," and ultimately to the status of author is, as James demonstrates, a gradual progression that reveals all the ironic possibilities that Brydon has not thought out in the construction of his fiction. And as such all the irony within the narrative that unfolds by way of Brydon's adventure points at the confused Brydon who separates himself from his alter ego.

Clearly, then, the fourth part of the plot of Brydon's narrative fiction moves out of his control because of the obvious confusion in it regarding the protagonist. Brydon takes the subject of his unexplored possibilities and personifies them into a character, which, as the unexplored possibilities are the subject of his narrative, is to be assumed as the likely protagonist of the narrative, but then he moves on to conceiving himself as the protagonist. As the fiction is about Brydon himself this move itself does not constitute the problem, but as he sees a complete division between his present self and his potential self, he creates confusion in his narrative. Thus the figure of the "forsworn possibilities" which he turns into the self he might have been goes on to take a "sinister" aspect (174). Instead of giving expression to Brydon's unified sense of self it becomes the "alter ego". Thus for Smythe, Brydon's failure is his failure to read, which in turn, is his "failure to recognize the principle of difference within identity" because of a "predisposition toward a unified identity".[14] As the self-absorbed Brydon has not developed a sense of otherness, the other self becomes the alien, the adversary. Brydon then turns from seeing his potential self as the protagonist into seeing this self as the antagonist. For he creates an image but does not know how to connect it to and make it a part of himself. And this constitutes the problem in Brydon's narrative. For if the potential self is the antagonist why then does Brydon yearn for those potentials that in his actual life he has failed to realize? It, then, is this fourth part of Brydon's story that is "the one least suited to his book" because it is here, by an ironic reversal of roles, that the hunted becomes the hunter, and the potential victimizer becomes the potential victim (177).

For the self-divided Brydon, then, the hunted is divided from the hunter. Even though the hunted *becomes* the hunter and the hunter *becomes* the hunted, the other self is separated into "another agent" (181). Ralf Norrman argues that the reversal of roles "reveals the typical uncertainty as to roles," and also that there is "not a whit of difference" between Brydon and his specter.[15] I would suggest that one way in which James points out a lack of difference is by indicating that the hunter is also the hunted. But Brydon fails to see that the victim is also the victimizer. Thus, as he fails to open the door of the fourth room on the fourth floor, he fails to see the self in the other or the other in the self. At this point Brydon insists, as his single eye-glass and his single light illustrate, on his need to overcome all duality and achieve oneness. Thus, although the "black-and-white" marble squares are always *together* as the pattern of the hall pavement, and make a pattern because they are together, for the self-divided Brydon these black and white squares are separated as distinct opposites (174).

The self-divided Brydon's problem reveals that if on the one hand he turns to the "human" and "social" world, then on the other hand he turns away from it. It is because he is drawn to human society that he dines out, visits his club regularly, and even lives in a hotel, but it is because he is also repulsed by it that he is dismissive of it:

> He circulated, talked, renewed, loosely and pleasantly, old relations - met indeed, so far as he could, new expectations and seemed to make out on the whole that in spite of the career, of such different contacts, which he had spoken of to Miss Staverton as ministering so little, for those who might

have watched it, to edification, he was positively rather liked than not. He was a dim secondary social success - and all with people who had truly not an idea of him. It was all mere surface sound, this murmur of their welcome, this popping of their corks - just as his gestures of response were the extravagant shadows emphatic in proportion as they meant little, of some game of *ombres chinoises*. (173-174)

He may be "the welcomed member of New York society," as Benert observes,[16] and enjoys it too, but nevertheless he finds his social exchanges almost meaningless. Brydon's problem is with "Every one," that is, with the community: "'Every one asks me what I think of everything,' said Spencer Brydon; 'and I make answer as I can - begging or dodging the question, putting them off with any nonsense'" (161). As William Freedman points out, the first sentence in James almost always "carries special weight." For Freedman the weight is in Brydon's intuitive awareness that "'everything' is some sort of self-knowledge": "the final specific definition of 'everything' and 'everyone' of the first sentence is having Alice and being himself - as he is."[17] It is also possible to see through this sentence how, from the beginning, James points out Brydon's problem of joining and separating himself from the community, which is the "everything" made up of "[e]veryone" (including Staverton). Brydon feels compelled to beg, dodge, or make answer as he can because he is deeply concerned about and involved with "Every one," but at the same time he is unconcerned and isolated enough to serve up "nonsense" to his society. Consequently he isolates himself from the social scene just as much as he seeks it out. According to Shear, Brydon returns to New York with the idea of the environment as home, but soon finds the environment to be "the source of conflict," and this results in his obvious alienation from the environment.[18] But James tells us that even in the remote past Brydon has had "few social flowers" (162). And he leaves home "almost in the teeth of my father's curse" (170). As Donna Przybylowicz observes, Brydon's "memories are filled with fear and guilt".[19] His environment, then, cannot have become the source of his conflict *now*, that is, with his return. And he returns with his aesthetically inclined consciousness expecting to be mortified by "the ugly things of his far-away youth" that earlier have provoked his voluntary exile (162). Also, he returns to New York not to look at his *home* but to look at his "*property*," "his *house* on the jolly corner" (162, my emphasis). Thus, as he does not come with the idea of "'wanting' to live in New York," he cannot have come with the idea of the environment as home (168). On the contrary, he comes with the idea of being an alien in his environment. Brydon is not always in touch with the stories of his remote past, stories about "his parents and his favourite sister, ...[and] of other kin, ...[who] had run their course and met their end ... [on the jolly corner]" (169). As Mary Doyle Springer observes, Brydon sees his life only as pieces, and not as "a coherent picture."[20] I would add that, consequently, in his reference to his childhood, there is often no story, or reference to a story. Thus in his phrase, "overschooled boyhood," there is only a title instead of the story; and for the years that follow his childhood Brydon again has no story to offer, but an even more daunting and somber label: "chilled adolescence" (162).

As Brydon does not always keep in touch with the stories of his remote past, so he often moves away from what is happening around and to him in the actual present: "[T]he 'swagger' things, the modern, the monstrous, the famous things ...were exactly his sources of dismay" (162). The "newnesses" that assault his vision are too distasteful to Brydon's aesthetic palate:

> It would have taken a century, he repeatedly said to himself, and said also to Alice Staverton, it would have taken a longer absence and a more averted mind than those even of which he had been guilty, to pile up the differences, the newnesses, the queernesses, above all the bignesses, for the better or the worse, that at present assaulted his vision wherever he looked. (161)

Brydon attempts to minimize his own sense of guilt by emphasizing the grotesqueness of the modern American scene. What assaults his vision is so grotesque that he cannot order "the differences, the newnesses, the queernesses, above all the bignesses" in the present scene of tumultuous proliferation around him into any kind of coherence, purposefulness, meaningfulness, and therefore can think only of "pil[ing]" them up. In general, then, there are no stories for him to read in this new American scene but only grotesque confusion. He is even appalled and petrified by modern mechanical contrivances such as street-cars: They are "the terrible things that people scrambled for as the panic-stricken at sea scramble for the boats" (164). Once again, then, for Brydon the modern American scene is mostly a petrifying confusion of scenes, a frightful hotch-potch of affairs which can be "pile[d]" up, but which cannot be organized into a coherent whole made up of connected parts.

Thus, if on the one hand Brydon's narrative fiction concerning his vision of the other self reveals his interest in the actual human drama, then on the other hand it reveals how he isolates himself from it. If, like his creator, Brydon is interested in the drama of "human emotion," as I have discussed earlier, then, unlike his creator, he is not always mindful of the "human attestation, the clustering human conditions" that "make the story - in the sense that the story is our excitement, our amusement, our thrill and our suspense" (*AN* 257). Hence the personified figure of Brydon's other self becomes, in his narrative fiction, "a creature" to be "stalk[ed,]" "more formidable than any beast of the forest," but nevertheless a creature in isolation (175). His shrinking response to the emotional makeup of this personified figure seems to be in proportion with his shrinking response to the emotional Alice Staverton who asks him, "How should I not have liked you?" and who, a little later in the same conversation laments, "you don't care for anything but yourself" (171,172).[21] The human emotion projected by Brydon's personified figure of his other self seems to diminish even as his own sense of alienation from the self he might have been seems to increase, and as his own isolation from the "human actual social" world seems to increase. Indeed, Brydon takes refuge from society in his narrative fiction: "He projected himself all day, in thought, straight over the bristling line of hard unconscious heads and into the other, the real, the waiting life; the life that, as soon as he had heard behind him the click of his great house-door, began for him, on the jolly corner" (174). It is isolation that finds expression in his narrative fiction about the "stalking of a creature ... more formidable, than any beast of the forest." And it has disconnected his imagination from his world of verisimilitude. As James writes in the preface to *The American*, "The balloon of experience is ... tied to the earth, and under that necessity we swing, thanks to a rope of remarkable length, in the more or less commodious car of the imagination; but it is by the rope we know where we are, and from the moment that cable is cut we are at large and unrelated: we swing apart from the globe" (*AN* 33-34). It is this problem of self-isolation that causes problem to the progression in Brydon's narrative fiction. Clearly, Brydon's narrative progresses as long as he keeps connection, on the uppermost floors, with the "human actual social" world as his symbolical action of opening windows and letting the light of the street lamps and the stars enter into the jolly corner reveals. But on this particular evening, after "a calculated absence of three nights" (177), Brydon is full of the sense of his having "hunted ...[the alter ego] till he has 'turned,'" and conceives himself as having "come ... 'to stay'" (178). The quoted phrase "to stay" is of special significance because it illustrates Brydon's extreme obsession with his narrative fiction and consequently, a deep sense of separation or isolation from society. "He had stiffened his will against going" (179), that is, against reestablishing relations with the "human actual social" world. And all he does this night is to roam around on the fourth floor ("still at the top") and keep track of the inner doors, particularly the door of the fourth room on the fourth floor, which has been closed by the other self (179). And he never opens a window until after he "retire[s]" and "renounce[s]" the pursuit of his alter ego (183).

But, as James suggests with supreme irony, it is only when Brydon retires and renounces his pursuit that the alter ego, and consequently, the narrative over which he earlier loses control, comes, as it were, to him. Thus, as Brydon comes down the stairs to go out of the jolly corner, he notices "a figure" that stands "as still as some image" within the penumbra, and consequently, within the "semicircular margin," of the outer door (187). With the use of an "image" as a simile, James points out to his readers the need to see the "figure" of the alter ego as a representation. And with the use of the image of the "margin" - a word he emphasizes through repetition - James indicates the context in which the "figure" may be interpreted. It is the narrative that Brydon earlier has been searching and composing: "He saw, in its great glimmering margin, the central vagueness diminish, and he felt it to be taking the very form toward which, for so many days, the passion of his curiosity had yearned" (187). Within the clearly outlined margin then is the text that becomes more and more clear to his vision:

> So Brydon ... took him in; with every fact of him now, in the higher light, hard and acute - his planted stillness, his vivid truth, his grizzled bent head and white masking hands, his queer actuality of evening-dress, of dangling double eye-glass, of gleaming silk lappet and white linen, of pearl button and gold watch-guard and polished shoe. No portrait by a great modern master could have presented him with more intensity, thrust him out of his frame with more art, as if there had been 'treatment,' of the consummate sort, in his every shade and salience...[H]e could but gape at his other self in this other anguish, gape as proof that *he* standing there for the achieved, the enjoyed, the triumphant life, couldn't be faced in his triumph. Wasn't it proof in the splendid covering hands, ...[one of which] had lost two fingers, which were reduced to stumps as if accidentally shot away...The hands as he looked again, began to move, to open; ...Horror with the sight, had leaped into Brydon's throat ... (187-188)

If Brydon takes in "every fact" of the figure of the other self, that is, the figure of the self that he might have been, then he now reads the whole narrative and takes "in" the whole plot of the narrative at the fourth part of which, earlier in the tale, he becomes stuck. For to consciously align the figure of the other self, not simply with "margin" but also with "art," and with the language of "art,"[22] as James does here, is to consciously point out that this "portrait" reveals an entire narrative, that of the singular American billionaire Brydon might have been if he had stayed at home, a billionaire with a singular "anguish," whose materialistic "triumph" produces the exact opposite of a moral triumph. Thus through this image, this "portrait," or metaphorically painted picture, and thus this triumph of representation, James suggests that his center of consciousness has constructed a short story. For "a short story," as he writes in the preface to *The Spoils of Poynton*, has to choose between being either an anecdote or a picture ... I rejoice in the anecdote, but I revel in the picture" (*AN* 139). As he is emphatic about the "portrait" that Brydon visualizes with his interpretive and creative imagination, James seems to revel in this character's ability to paint a picture, and thus compose a complete narrative, as it were. And the reflector receives his grasp of the whole narrative only now because it is now that he stops running after it.

For at this point Brydon has finally realized how he has isolated himself from the "human actual social" world. In his memoirs of Henry James, Desmond MacCarthy writes about an exchange with the former at a luncheon party regarding writing and isolation that is of particular relevance to us here:

> We happened to be drinking coffee together while the rest of the party had moved on to the verandah, "What a charming picture they make," he [James] said, with his great head aslant... There was nothing in his words, anybody might have spoken them; but in his attitude, in his voice, in his whole being at that moment, I divined such complete detachment, that I was startled into speaking out of myself: "I can't bear to look at life like that," I blurted out, "I want to be in everything. Perhaps that is why I cannot write, it makes me feel absolutely alone..." The effect of this confession upon him was instantaneous and surprising. He leant forward and grasped my arm excitedly: "Yes, it is solitude. If it runs after you and catches you, well and good. But for heaven's sake don't run after it. It is absolute solitude." And he got up hurriedly and joined the others. [23]

Brydon's quondam problem as an artist reveals that he has been obsessively "run[ning] after," as it were, his narrative fiction, and in the process, envelops himself in the "absolute solitude" of isolation. The Jamesian artist, like James himself in this passage, always understands the need to form relations with the world around him or her, but also always makes that understanding by watching in isolation. Thus Brydon, who now suffers acutely from his self-isolation, opens his window, and yearns to "get into relation" with the world around him:

> The empty street - its other life so marked even by the great lamplit vacancy - was within call, within touch; he stayed there as to be in it again, high above it though he was still perched; he watched as for some comforting common fact, some vulgar human note, the passage of a scavenger or a thief, some night-bird however base. He would have blessed that sign of life; he would have welcomed positively the slow approach of his friend the policeman, whom he had hitherto only sought to avoid, and was not sure that if the patrol had come into sight he mightn't have felt the impulse to get into relation with it, to hail it, on some pretext, from his fourth floor. (183)

Nothing in the human world now is too "common" or "base," or too "vulgar" for Brydon. He now longs for human society, or for some kind of representative of the actual world because he now comprehends his problem of self-alienation. It is his desperate desire to establish contact with the actual human world that makes him ponder a failure on his part: "Had they ever, he asked himself, the hard-faced houses, which had begun to look livid in the dim dawn, had they ever spoken so little to any need of his spirit?" (184). The houses are "hard-faced" because he has failed to establish contact with them. It is his "spirit," the sensitive soul, his whole consciousness, that craves for the signs of actual life as he looks out his open window. Like other Jamesian watchers from other windows in the house of fiction, Brydon now looks to see the "human actual social" world as he looks out of his window in his house on the jolly corner. Earlier in the tale, Brydon regularly wanders around the house with his "glimmering light," that is, an artificial light, preparing himself for "a considerable vigil" (173). But if in those times he has "known fifty times the start of a perception," then he has "fifty times" also known that "perception" to have "dropped" (181). Now, however, he has become the acute watcher who takes in "every fact" of his potential self, and thus exerts control over every detail of his narrative of what he might have been.

Indeed, the house on the jolly corner is Brydon's house of fiction. Finally the jolly corner lives up to its name by becoming a completely successful house of fiction. For now Brydon finally understands the problem which earlier stops his narrative fiction from moving forward. He "believe[s]" in his fiction (187). Like the author who writes in his preface that to "begin to wonder" it is necessary to "begin to believe" (*AN* 254-255), Brydon "believe[s]," and as a result, wonders with his whole consciousness, that is, makes the utmost use of his creative faculty of imagination. As a consequence, the whole empty house on the jolly corner seems to be flooded with the influence of the fiction of what Brydon might have been, as his images of the "sea," and "some watery under-world" signify (186). And if the reflector receives his complete vision of the figure of what he might have been on the ground floor, and if this figure, who wears a double eye-glass and has "two fingers" missing,[24] stands on the black-and-white slabs, then James suggests how Brydon is ready to overcome his self-absorption and comprehend the other within himself, and has finally overcome his conflicting response to the past and the present. If earlier the "jolly corner" is a name conspicuous for ironic effect, now at the tale's conclusion it is a name that suggests the intersection between the past and the present. This house that stands in the corner of an "Avenue" and a street which show the influence of the past and the influence of the present respectively, suggests the dual presence of the "comparatively conservative" self and the "dishonoured and disfigured" other in Brydon. Earlier this house has symbolically suggested Brydon's emptiness, but now it suggests his ability to connect the present with the past, and the self with the other, and thus suggests the reassertion of his narrative authority (165). If the ground floor is filled with "an illumination of its own," then it is because Brydon successfully connects the actual with the imaginary world in a clear vision of what he might have been (186). The fluid medium of fiction has immersed the jolly corner and made it a house of fiction because the windows in this house of fiction bring in the "gleam of street-lamps," that is, the influence of the "human actual social" world which Brydon has been watching from his perch (186).

Indeed, the "human actual social" world around him has contributed persistently to the growth of Brydon's narrative fiction. James illustrates this even from the beginning of his tale, through Alice Staverton's and even through Mrs. Muldoon's remarks. Mrs. Muldoon's remark of "what one *might* see," in "thim top storeys in the ayvil hours" evokes "a gruesome vision" in Brydon's consciousness (166). She makes him "grave" with her comment for it makes an unnervingly deep impression on him (166). The impression is so deep that later Brydon finds her "right, absolutely, with her figure of their 'craping'" (175). It is her image of "craping" that seems to have acted as the famous "germ," the "small seed as minute and wind-blown" as the "casual hint ... dropped unwittingly by ...[James's] neighbour[s], a mere floating particle in the stream of talk," acts for James himself (*AN* 119). For it is this image of "craping" in the "ayvil hours" that seems ultimately to grow into Brydon's picture of a "cautious" and "shifty" and "sinister" alter ego.[25] And it is this intriguing, "sinister" alter ego that ultimately develops into the morally disappointing character that Brydon might have been. Mrs. Muldoon's image, then, plays a relevant part in

Brydon's conception of the figure of his alter ego. But if Mrs. Muldoon, who represents the common world, contributes considerably to Brydon's growing sense of his image, then Staverton, who represents the refined section of society, plays a most significant role.

For it is her image of "the inventor of the sky-scraper" that greatly influences the wondering Brydon who has started to contemplate what he might have been if he had stayed at home (165). Her image about the profusely inventive, business-minded, and profit-making architect (the potential Brydon whose continual productivity leads him to enormous wealth) creates such an impression on Brydon that it blends harmoniously into his own "wonderment" regarding what might have been: "He was to remember ...[Staverton's] words ...for the small silver ring they had sounded over the queerest and deepest of his own lately most disguised and most muffled vibrations" (165). Her words, even more than Mrs. Muldoon's, are a significant version of the celebrated "germ," "the vague echo," at touch of which the storyteller's "imagination winces" (*AN* 119). For they positively blend with, and therefore become part of, his own impressions and thoughts. His "vibrations" develop into his "wonderment" and ultimately into a personified "image" because of the effect of Staverton's meaning-making imagination on them (165). And his image continues to develop after Staverton mentions that she has seen his other self twice in a dream: "It was after this that there was most of a virtue for him, most of a cultivated charm, most of a preposterous secret thrill, in the particular form of surrender to his obsession" (172). Clearly, what she communicates leads to the productivity of his own imagination.

Staverton's image of the entrepreneurial inventor is especially worth discussing because it contains a miniature but complete narrative. Observing the present Brydon's flair for architecture and business, she points out with wit, humor, and "mild irony" the likely development of an aptitude that would be the likely product of its environment (167):

> [S]he had ... said to him (though to a slightly greater effect of irony [than of sympathy]) that he had clearly for too many years neglected a real gift. If he had but stayed at home he would have anticipated the inventor of the sky-scraper. If he had but stayed at home he would have discovered his genius in time really to start some new variety of awful architectural hare and run it till it burrowed in a goldmine. (165)

Through her image of the "goldmine" she creates a lively picture of the bustling modern American economy. And through her image of an "architectural hare" she creates a delightfully quaint picture of buildings that rise as rapidly as scurrying hare, and of the mood of vigorous activity. Also, through her picture of the "awful" architectural hare that makes a burrow, Staverton creates an amusing, and not sarcastic, picture of the environment's confident and accelerated thrust towards artificial products, a thrust that culminates in distorting views of nature as well as in aesthetic anomalies. With her abundant imagination she connects the image of modern buildings and machines with objects that are as diverse as gold mine and hare. And through her pictures she creates a succession of connected scenes in a drama of pursuit that is crowned by temporal success. Her images then have come together to produce a miniature narrative. Her little narrative, which shows her grasp over causal relationships, is expressive of her awareness of the connection between Brydon's actual present and his potential present. It is Staverton, then, who makes a concise narrative about what Brydon might have been if he had stayed at home even before Brydon does, and whose narrative influences his own. As Russell Reising observes, Staverton's comment about Brydon as the inventor of the skyscraper advances her friend's search for the alternate self.[26] I would also point out that Brydon's search for his alternate self which results in his narrative fiction, is the result of the narrative embedded in Staverton's comment. Bell calls Staverton "the perceiving reader," and Smythe calls her "the model reader".[27] I would add that as the "perceiving" or "model" reader Staverton is also a creator. As Brydon himself is well aware, she scatters "no cloud of words" (168). Because her words are not confusing but reveal meaning and purpose, her images develop into a narrative. She tells a story about the potential Brydon based on her observation of the present Brydon. Clearly, then, Staverton does not separate the Brydon of the present from the Brydon of the potential present. She tells a story about the potential Brydon's pursuit of his creation, a pursuit that culminates in his acquisition of temporal power. In Staverton's miniature but distinctly formed narrative there is the clear construction of a protagonist who successfully triumphs over the object of his pursuit. In her narrative, then, there is a distinct denouement. Thus Staverton goes "a little further" than the Brydon who breaks the continuity of his narrative fiction at the fourth part of his plot (168). Also, she goes further than that Brydon because of her clear depiction of the potential Brydon as the protagonist of her minuscule narrative.

Because Staverton is a storyteller of sorts, her "memories" are *organized* into "histories" - stories of the past (164). She has her little place fitted out with the "relics," the emblems of her past, and she literally keeps contact with these relics: "His old friend ... herself dusted her relics and trimmed her lamps and polished her silver"

(164).[28] Brydon's own interest in stories makes him appreciative of her references to "memories and histories into which he could enter" (164). He is particularly interested in her ability to narrate the stories of their past, and therefore at making the past meaningful (164). She even conceives of Spencer Brydon's life in Europe, his experience as a man or as a wanderer, in the form of stories, of which certain "passages" are "strange and dim to her, ...but still unobscured" (164). Her ability to talk to Brydon about their "antediluvian social period and order" is her ability to articulate a meaningful story of the past (164). In her own home she has preserved and brought the past into the present. Her "delicate things," that signify how she values her past, are perfectly congruous with the present: "[they have] kept the sharpness of the notes of a high voice perfectly trained" (164). For Brydon, then, Staverton's relics make a charming performance that produces aesthetic success. And this performance, which strikes the note of harmony for Brydon, illustrates how Staverton has not isolated the past from the present. Her home is a "still scene," as Brydon observes, because of her ability to harmonize the past with the present (164).

As she connects the past with the present so she connects her own narrative with Brydon's. As she figures out what has happened to Brydon, who fails to keep his appointment with her, she connects her third dream with his encounter of the other self, and thus she connects her own narrative with his:

> She met it, the wonder she had stirred. "In the cold dim dawn, you say? Well, in the cold dim dawn of this morning I too saw you."
> "Saw *me* -?"
> "Saw *him*," said Alice Staverton. "It must have been at the same moment."
> He lay an instant taking it in - as if he wished to be quite reasonable. "At the same moment?"
> "Yes - in my dream again, the same one I've named to you. He came back to me. Then I knew it for a sign. He had come to you." (192).

With her third dream Staverton comprehends that Brydon has finally received his complete vision of what he might have been, and that consequently, he has completed his narrative fiction. With her third dream, then, she reads the significance of Brydon's narrative fiction and points out the connection between Brydon and his other self. Thus, as Staverton literally "support[s]" him, so she strengthens his narrative and protects it from falling apart, or helps to hold it from flooding out, much as the first part of her name "[s]tave" indicates (193). Although she sees the other self in a dream, her dream of Brydon's other self is her own narrative fiction of his other self, the self that he might have been.[29] But because her acuteness of vision matches his own, and also because she contributes to his narrative through her image of the entrepreneurial architect, the character she depicts coincides exactly with that which Brydon depicts. The figure that "advance[s]" towards Brydon does not advance "for aggression" but "*as for* aggression," that is, it only seems *as if* it advances aggressively (188, my emphasis). As Staverton realizes, the figure advances for union. If the alter ego comes to Staverton with a "sign," then at last, after all the tension and suspense, the confusion and mystification, he proves to be no antagonist or adversary. "And when this morning I again saw I knew it would be because you had - and also then, from the first moment, because you somehow wanted me. *He* seemed to tell me of that" (193). This third dream, then, is not an exact repetition of the dream she has seen twice over. It is an extension that is intricately connected with Brydon's narrative of what he might have been, the purpose of which is to connect Brydon's other self with him.

Because Staverton connects her own narrative fiction of what Brydon might have been with Brydon's own, she helps him to accept the connection between himself and his other self. She helps him to understand that his "denial" of the other self is not so much his failure to comprehend his relation with the other self, as it is his "dismay" (188). This is why James couples denial with dismay, or why he writes of Brydon, "the horror *within him* a horror" (188, my emphasis). Staverton understands that Brydon's "denial" is "the passion of his protest" and outrage, his sense of intense "horror" and "shock" at the "hideous," "odious," or "vulgar" "stranger" within himself (188). It is this understanding that is the "meaning blurred" by her smile: "No, thank heaven," she tells him, "it's not you! Of course it wasn't meant to have been," which makes Brydon gently insist, "Ah but it *was*" (191). Thus she takes him to the point where she can ask "Isn't the whole point that you'd have been different?" which question has "the breath of infallibility" for him (192). Indeed, Brydon's "horror" shows that he is no longer as self-absorbed as he has been, and therefore that he does receive a glimpse of the other in himself. For, clearly, there would have been no great "horror" for Brydon if he could have conceived the other self as a "stranger". Staverton then helps him to overcome his denial, a denial that shows his initial grudge and resentment at having to accept the other in himself. He may find it difficult,[30] but he gradually learns to accept the connection:

> But though it all brought for him ...a dim light, "You 'pitied' him?" he grudgingly, resentfully asked.
> "He has been unhappy, he has been ravaged," she said.
> "And haven't I been unhappy? Am not I - you've only to look at me! - ravaged?"
> "Ah I don't say I like him *better*,' she granted after a thought. 'But he's grim, he's worn - and things have happened to him. He doesn't make shift, for sight, with your charming monocle."
> "No"- it struck Brydon: "I couldn't have sported mine 'downtown.' They'd have guyed me there." (193)

Brydon gradually begins to see "a dim light" when she tells him of her pity for the character she envisions in her dream, that is, for the character in her own narrative. For if she can pity the odious and the vulgar, then Brydon certainly is not going to be a source of disappointment and disillusion for her. The "dim light" that is suggestive of Brydon's gradual acceptance of his connection with the other self is James's way of pointing out that what Brydon grudges and resents is his own connection to the odious and the vulgar. The "dim light" is also James's way of illuminating for his readers the parallels that Brydon draws between himself and his other self: Like the other self he is "unhappy" and "ravaged".[31] Further, he goes on to picture himself in the other self's position "downtown." And when Brydon "wince[s] - whether for his proved identity or for his lost fingers," James implies in his subtle, ironic, indirect way Brydon's awareness of the "horror" and the other within himself (193). I, however, do not mean to imply that there is no ambiguity in the text regarding the issue of Brydon's identity with the other self. As Tzvetan Todorov argues, it is indeed uncertain whether Brydon is identified with or different from the other self: "The Other is and is not himself."[32] And like Todorov, Donald Burleson asserts that James leaves his readers in hermeneutic uncertainty as to whether or not Brydon is conflated with his other self.[33] But even when James leaves his readers in uncertainty regarding Brydon's identity with or difference from the other self, he still suggests Brydon's empathic awareness of the "lost fingers." Brydon may either wince "for his proved identity" with the other self then, or because, with his sympathetic imagination, he himself feels the pain of the loss of fingers.[34] And that is enough to suggest that he has begun to accept otherness or the other in himself. And this acceptance is the result of the connection between Brydon's narrative fiction with Staverton's.

As James implies, then, Brydon's meaning-making activities, and consequently his exercise of narrative authority, are inextricably connected with the "human actual social" world. Thus on regaining consciousness it seems to Brydon that he has been "picked up ...[from] the uttermost end of an interminable grey passage" (189). The "interminable grey passage" represents, at one level, the concluding passage, the denouement of moral desolation and the doom of isolation that he reads in his narrative fiction of what he might have been. If Staverton picks him up from this "grey passage" where the shocked and overwhelmed Brydon loses consciousness then it is because she understands Brydon's shock and bewilderment at the odious, lonely, and vulgar stranger within himself. The grey passage illustrates the emptiness of isolation from which Staverton relieves him by "pick[ing]" him up into her arms. As Benert observes, Staverton encourages Brydon to outgrow "a fantasy of male isolation" that he "seems determined to enact".[35] I would go further and say that Staverton's emphasis on togetherness, that is, her emphasis on "*their* common ... social period and order" expresses her awareness that meaning-making activities cannot occur in isolation (164). As he depends on her for comprehension - 'As I didn't turn up you came straight -?" so she depends on him for the same - "In the cold dim dawn, you say?" Together they try to make sense of their experiences. And together they connect Brydon's loss of consciousness with the return of his consciousness. With Staverton at his side, Brydon is confident that he will be able to read meaning where he has failed to, for he feels "a treasure of intelligence waiting all round him for quiet appropriation" (189).

Thus it is because of the connection between his own narrative fiction with Staverton's that Brydon ultimately moves away from apparitions and an apparitional world into the "human actual social" world of fact where he gives and receives love to and from the other (Staverton). The creation of his fictional narrative yields Brydon his particular human individuality, his self-identity, the identity which cannot be limited to that of the "grim" and "worn" other self (193). And Staverton confirms it when she murmurs, "And he isn't - no, he isn't - *you*!" (193). As Carren Kaston observes, Staverton seems to offer Brydon "a freeing identification in the belief that Brydon is whole now, rather than a ghostly part."[36] Indeed, the alter ego acts in the capacity of synecdoche, and Staverton's comment, "he isn't ... *you*" is indicative of her solution to the problem of the literalization of synecdoche. As the last exchange between Brydon and Staverton in the end of the tale seems to signify, the other self is only a part and not the whole of Brydon. Thus, although readers like Stein may argue that "Brydon has accomplished little, either in the world of art or intellect or in terms of his human relations," James shows quite the opposite. [37] Brydon has learned to "piec[e] together the parts" of his narrative fiction about what he might have been with Staverton's, and as a result, finds the relation of love (191).

Consequently, it is through the making of a narrative fiction, which helps him to forge a meaningful relation with Staverton, that Brydon finally fulfills his aesthetic quest. As James points out in the denouement of his fiction, with the return of his consciousness the protagonist experiences "the most wonderful hour, little by little, that he had ever known" (189). Now as he "wonder[s]" he finds a wonderful subject to wonder about: despite his fall he finds himself "all so wondrously without bruise or gash," and "as much at peace as if he had had food and drink" (190). For he has at last found "the beauty of his state" which "resemble[s] more and more that of a man who has gone to sleep on some news of a great inheritance, and then, after dreaming it away, ... has waked up again to serenity of certitude" (189). Thus now for Brydon physical, tangible objects are no longer a source of confusion.[38] Corporeal values have ultimately become the vehicles to represent incorporeal values. Tangible property now represents intangible love. Indeed he has risen far above the self-absorbed and corporeal frame of mind in which he objectifies Staverton "as some pale pressed flower" that, "failing other sweetnesses," is "a sufficient reward for his effort" (164). Thus now Staverton's "look ...[is] more beautiful to him than the things of this world" (192). According to Tuveson, at the tale's conclusion Brydon moves to a "better spiritual condition than he has experienced before."[39] I would also suggest that at the tale's conclusion aesthetic fulfillment becomes one with spiritual fulfillment for Brydon. Finally Brydon has found a morally satisfying aesthetic fulfillment. For in Staverton's look he finds the fusion of the aesthetic and the spiritual worlds. Clearly, because he exerts narrative authority in connection with the "human actual social" world, Brydon ultimately effects the connection between aesthetic and spiritual attainment. It is not this world itself that fulfills his aesthetic quest, but the connections he learns to make as a result of the narrative authority in, or in conjunction with, this "human actual social" world that brings fulfillment to Brydon. Thus if earlier through Brydon's name James suggests the word "burden," now he goes on to suggest the word "bridoon" (or the French "bridon") as it is associated with the word "bride," and thus with the language of needlework, in that Brydon is now able to make the link that joins the pieces of a pattern. Brydon further demonstrates his ability to create effective connections by making a smooth transition from the denouement of his fictional narrative to the denouement of his life's narrative: "'He has a million a year,' ... 'But he hasn't you'" (193).

Notes

1. Henry James, The Art of the Novel (Boston: Northeastern University Press, 1984) 252,254. Cited parenthetically as AN.
2. Henry James, The Jolly Corner and Other Tales (London: Penguin Books, 1990) 168.
3. According to J. U. Jacobs, in "The Alter-Ego: The Artist as American in 'The Jolly Corner,'" in Theoria 58 (1982), Brydon has had a "successful artistic career in Europe" (52). But clearly, it is because it has been unsuccessful in Europe that he resumes his aesthetic quest, and consequently develops an interest in a fictional narrative, in America. Further, a "successful" artistic career would hardly require Brydon to depend on his rent-values. As Jacobs himself states, Brydon's "[a]esthetic values are supported by living realities" (54). For Jacobs, Brydon has a "schizoid personality" and his consciousness is divided into "a world of fancy and a world of fact" (54). Consequently, he argues that Brydon is the self that represents the "European man of fancy," while the other self, which is a figment of the man of fancy, represents the "American man of fact," and that both these representations are "examples of the distortion of the self" that results from a failure to "reconcile the imagination with reality in a fully integrated consciousness" (58).
4. Annette Benert, "Dialogical Discourse in 'The Jolly Corner': The Entrepreneur as Language and Image," The Henry James Review 8.2 (1987): 122. Benert argues that the "jangle of voices" in Brydon - the intersecting languages of psychology, commerce, romance, and sport - reveal Brydon's conflictual worldview which is "a romantic view that the structure of the tale implicitly questions" (122,116).
5. For a discussion on the image of the "concave crystal" bowl see Lynda S. Boren's, Euridice Reclaimed: Language, Gender, and Voice in Henry James (Ann Arbor: U. M. I. Research Press, 1989). For Boren, the image of the bowl "serves as an icon for Brydon's felt sense of his past," and signifies that James's telling of the story reaches its "crescendo of lyricism" (13,14).
6. For Sharon Cameron in Thinking in Henry James (Chicago and London: University of Chicago Press, 1989) the alter ego is the incarnation or "reification" of Brydon's "private thought" of what he might have been (135n). For Millicent Bell in Meaning in Henry James (Cambridge, Massachusetts: Harvard University Press, 1991) this figure is a poetic expression of "psychic reality" through which vehicle becomes tenor (278). Bell argues that Brydon works as "a writer of fiction [in] that he sees how analogy and metaphor ...assist the process by which the hypothetical acquires living form" (288). And

for Karen Smythe in "Imaging and Imagining: 'The Jolly Corner' and Self-Construction," in Dalhousie Review 70.3 (1990), this figure is "an unacknowledged synecdoche of Brydon's unrepresentable subjectivity" (381). Smythe argues that 'The Jolly Corner' can be read as an "allegory of autobiography" (375). According to Smythe, this tale is about a character who is preoccupied with imagining and not imaging through which James implies that it is futile to write about oneself because "it is impossible to represent the self with any combination of pronouns" (378-379).

7. Walter Shear, "Cultural Fate and Social Freedom in Three American Short Stories," Studies in Short Fiction 29.4 (1992): 544. According to Shear, although Brydon has his imaginative anticipations and suspicions regarding the image's "monstrous nature," these anticipations and suspicions fall short of "the shocking force of historical cumulation and the accrued, apparently total, social commitment" that the alter ego represents (544). Thus, for Shear, it is history that "orchestrates ...the drama" in Brydon's boyhood home and Brydon realizes that he is "the game in the drama of time" (546).

8. Smythe, 375.

9. Bell, 282.

10. For Walter F. Wright in The Madness of Art: A Study of Henry James (Lincoln: University of Nebraska Press, 1962), this image suggests how introspection leads "the mind at first haltingly and then swiftly" to disengage its grasp of "the inadequate, though hitherto apparently safe, world it has always known when a new, even though forbidding world opens before it" (203).

11. Deborah Esch, "A Jamesian About-Face: Notes on 'The Jolly Corner,'" ELH 50.3 (1983): 592. Esch's argument is that Brydon turns the tables on his own figures so as to "fix their significance" and thus Brydon engages himself in "an ongoing activity of literalization" (594). According to Esch, Brydon is so eager to confront his other self that he confuses his figures in the process (595).

12. T. J. Lustig, in Henry James and the Ghostly (Cambridge: Cambridge University Press, 1994), reads in this scene Brydon's turning away from "the explosive contents of Pandora's box" and consequently, his avoidance of disfigurement and defeat (222). Lustig argues that in "The Jolly Corner" James endows the figure of the American businessman "with the metaphors of romance" (223).

13. See Benert for a discussion of Brydon's use of the language of romance and his "heroic quest" to tell his story. The language of romance, according to Benert, is also a means to represent "a reaction against the rational capitalism of New York" (121). And for Benert, the alter ego itself is "a male collective shadow lengthening over America during the golden age of capitalism" (118).

14. Smythe, 376. And according to Esch, Brydon cannot read the figure because he "cannot tell (or admit) the difference between its literal and figurative senses" (595). As a counter-stroke to Esch's argument, Russell

Reising in "Figuring Himself Out: Spencer Brydon, 'The Jolly Corner,' and Cultural Change," in The Journal of Narrative Technique 19.1 (1989), argues that Brydon loses control over his figures of speech because they are meant to postpone if not displace, his increasingly troubled sense of his complicity in an economic world he disdains" (125). Reising sees a dialogue between a rhetorical use and an economic use of the term "figure".

15. Ralf Norrman, The Insecure World of Henry James's Fiction: Intensity and Ambiguity (London and Basingstoke: The Macmillan Press Ltd., 1982) 146.

16. Benert, 119.

17. William A. Freedman, "Universality in 'The Jolly Corner,'" Texas Studies in Literature and Language 4.1 (1962): 12,13. Freedman argues that through the "constant references to 'all,' 'everyone,' 'everything,' and the like," James produces "a sense of universality" with regard to Brydon's curiosity about what he might have been (14).

18. Shear, 544. For Shear, the root of Brydon's interest in business and construction is his "idea of environment as home," but as I see it, the root lies in his being a product of that environment.

19. Donna Przybylowicz, in Desire and Repression in the Dialectic Self and Other in the Late Works of Henry James (Alabama: University of Alabama Press, 1986) 115. Przybylowicz argues that because of a constant conflict between "a distant past ... and a familiar present, [Brydon] returns to the jolly corner in order to relive his childhood and to undergo some kind of expiation for his rejection of America by searching for his alternate self and attempting to capture a synchronic, hypothetical present" (116).

20. Mary Doyle Springer, A Rhetoric of Literary Characters: Some Women of Henry James (Chicago and London: University of Chicago Press, 1978) 121. Springer focuses on the significant role that Staverton plays in helping Brydon "to get a framing distance" on the disjointed pieces of his life so that he can order these pieces into a "coherent picture" (121). For Springer, Staverton is no mere frame for she helps Brydon try to discover his identity.

21. For a reading of Staverton's implied offer of love to Brydon, and of the latter's evasion of that offer, see John Byers's "Alice Staverton's Redemption of Spencer Brydon in 'The Jolly Corner,'" in South Atlantic Bulletin 41.2 (1976). Byers argues that Staverton brings redemption to Brydon and she does it by pursuing him just as he pursues his alter ego.

22. For a discussion on James's interest in the art of "painting" and the portraiture of mutilation, see Bell (284-285).

23. Desmond MacCarthy, Portraits (New York: Oxford University Press, 1955) 154.

24. For Ernest Tuveson in "'The Jolly Corner': A Fable of Redemption," in Studies in Short Fiction 12.3 (1975), the missing fingers symbolize the "suppressed personality" (277). Tuveson argues that James depicts many selves

of the mind of which Brydon represents the conscious self and the alter ego represents the unconscious, the "subliminal, primal self," and that the conflict between the selves results in the protagonist's experience of the "loss of a secure sense of identity" (275,273). And for Joan Delfattore in "The Other Spencer Brydon," in The Arizona Quarterly 35.4 (1979), the two missing fingers represent Brydon's ineffectuality for they imply a "lack of completeness and an inability to take hold or grasp" (339). Also, for Delfattore, the double eyeglass represents Brydon's psychological blindness. Delfattore argues that Brydon remains immature, passive, and ineffective because of "his failure to recognize and to integrate ...[his] hidden self" (335).

25. I do not, however, mean to over-emphasize the role played by the environment on Brydon's creative faculty. As David Carroll argues in The Subject in Question: The Languages of Theory and the Strategies of Fiction (Chicago and London: The University of Chicago Press, 1982), "The conscious origin is never the ultimate origin. The 'germ' is 'wind-blown' rather than the product of a conscious, intentional, fully controlled act" (62).

26. Russell Reising, "'Doing Good by Stealth': Alice Staverton and Women's Politics in 'The Jolly Corner,'" The Henry James Review 13.1 (1992): 57. Reising argues that Staverton dominates the final scene of the tale and that such a focus reveals not the coherent picture of a particular moment in history" but the flux of "social and cultural change" (51). Thus for Reising, Staverton grasps the interdependent relationship between culture and economics, and consequently is associated not simply with the conventions of Victorian womanhood, but with "a new strategy of feminine politics" (55).

27. Bell, 288. Smythe, 382.

28. For a scriptural reading of "The Jolly Corner," see Jason P. Rosenblatt's "Bridegroom and Bride in 'The Jolly Corner,'" in Studies in Short Fiction 14.3 (1977). For Rosenblatt, "The Jolly Corner" makes several allusions to the 25th chapter of Matthew; for example, Staverton is a wise virgin, the bride who waits for the bridegroom and trims her lamps (282). Thus for Rosenblatt, Brydon is the bridegroom - the Christ figure of the Second Coming.

29. For a reading of Staverton's dreams as supernatural means of communication, see Earl Rovit's "The Ghosts in James's 'The Jolly Corner,'" in Tennessee Studies in Literature 10 (1965). For Rovit the significance of the supernatural is in its translation into the moral by way of allegory. Rovit argues that Brydon's consciousness is composed of three parts, of which Brydon himself represents the self, the alter ego represents the other, and Staverton represents "the conscience, the integrating spirit" (67). Also, for Rovit, Brydon's rebirth signifies the fusion of the "self," the "other," and the "spirit" into "a new union and communion" (68). And Staverton's third dream, for Rovit, is "a direct communication between the 'otherness' of Brydon and the 'spirit' of Brydon" (70).

30. This difficulty is so pronounced that for Allen Stein, in "The Beast in 'The Jolly Corner': Spencer Brydon's Ironic Rebirth," in <u>Studies in Short Fiction</u> 11.1 (1974), Brydon does not change at all. According to Stein, Brydon even "perverts Alice's potentially redemptive love" (63).

31. For Stein this is merely Brydon's self-pity (64). But as I see it, what begins as Brydon's self-pity moves out into an acceptance of what he shares with the other.

32. Tzvetan Todorov, <u>The Poetics of Prose</u> (Ithaca, New York: Cornell University Press, 1977) 160. Todorov asserts that "The Jolly Corner" shows "selfhood" to be as uncertain as "being" (160). He argues that the Jamesian narrative centers around "the quest for an absolute and absent cause" (145). Thus, as long as the alter ego is absent, Brydon's quest for it contributes to his "quest for self-discovery and self-identity" (160). Brydon, Todorov argues, "does not recognize himself" in the alter ego because its presence takes away that contribution (160). Todorov also argues that in this tale "<u>To</u> <u>be</u> is supplanted by <u>to have</u>, <u>I</u> by <u>you</u>" (188).

33. Donald Burleson, "James's 'The Jolly Corner,'" <u>The Explicator</u> 49.2 (1991): 100. Burleson argues that, although for Brydon, Staverton represents a "stabilizing point," she is "the very locus at which the text slyly allegorizes the unreliability of apparently stable structures and the illusoriness of hermeneutic uncertainty" (100).

34. According to Kathryn Cramer, in "Possession and 'The Jolly Corner,'" <u>The New York Review of Science Fiction</u> 65 (1994), Brydon "winces for his lost fingers" (22). Cramer argues that Brydon becomes possessed on the one hand by Staverton who is "perhaps James's most subtle manipulator," and on the other hand by the alter ego who is the narrator of the story (21).

35. Benert, 123.

36. Carren Kaston, <u>Imagination and Desire in the Novels of Henry James</u> (New Brunswick, New Jersey: Rutgers University Press, 1984) 152. Kaston stresses the "romantic bond" between Brydon and Staverton (152). For her the alter ego is associated with "love and sexuality" (152), and therefore Brydon's horror of the other self is his "fear of his repressed self" (151).

37. Stein, 65.

38. For Rosenblatt, however, Brydon's focus has never been on tangible objects. According to him, Brydon's spiritual aspirations are represented by the narrator in material terms. For Rosenblatt, then, there is a "spiritual reality" behind the material symbol" even before the midpoint of the tale (284).

39. Tuveson, 278.

Chapter 3

The Changing of Old Stories in *The Golden Bowl*

In his preface to *The Golden Bowl* James seems to minimize his own narrative authority by "get[ting] down into the arena" of his characters, and shaking off "the muffled majesty of authorship".[1] As a result, he subjects "the whole thing ... to the register, ever so closely kept, of the consciousness of but two characters," the Prince and Maggie in their respective Volumes, who, although they are "actor[s] in the offered play," significantly are the "reporters and critics," that is, the interpreters, and consequently the reflectors of the action (*AN* 329). For these designated reflectors make us "see the things that may most interest us reflected in [their consciousness] as in the clean glass held up to so many of the 'short stories' of our long list" (*AN* 329). The "short stories" James refers to are, I suspect, not simply the short fiction of his New York Edition. Implicit in his reference to his own "short stories" is James's allusion to the "short stories" composed, although not literally, by his centers of consciousness. For as he makes use of his imaginative consciousness to create stories, so his reflector characters make use of theirs. Thus, like Maggie in the second volume, although the Prince "doesn't speak in the first person," he "virtually represents to himself everything that concerns us," and therefore functions as a reader and storyteller in the first volume more than any other character in it (*AN* 329). In effect, then, James "get[s] down into the arena" to allow his centers of consciousness to take control of the "short stories" within this novel, as it were, and thus depicts himself as sharing his narrative authority with them. For if the author conceives his characters as participants in an "arena" he depicts them not so much as characters who perform parts written for them as characters who act as improvisers.

Consequently, the centers of consciousness act in the capacity of storytellers. Their "short" or little stories reveal their ability to make narrative connections in their interpretive efforts, which I will show through a study of their well-developed images. With their images they paint scenes that become parts of other scenes, which they paint in other images. And thus they make narrative connections between their images to form "short stories". Consequently, it is through them that James depicts the study of the narrative authority that a storyteller exercises. I argue that if James, through the Prince in the first volume shows how the center of consciousness makes a beginning in the exertion of narrative authority, then, in the second volume, through the Princess, who "becomes a compositional resource ... of the finest order," the author shows how the center of consciousness learns to develop the exertion of narrative authority (*AN* 329). For it is Maggie, with her intensely contemplative and interpretive imagination, who is able to ponder changes in the stories she reads, and also to change an old story into a new one, and consequently to replace the old equilibrium of the two couples with a new equilibrium. Further, in their exercise of narrative authority we see both Maggie and Amerigo involved with stories regarding the key metaphor of the novel, the golden bowl. If Amerigo reveals his narrative authority as the reader of one short story of the golden bowl then Maggie, whose narrative authority grows beyond Amerigo's, is not simply a reader but also the teller of another short story which comes as a result of his reading of the first one. And it is as the teller of the story of the golden bowl that Maggie enables Amerigo to change from a dilettantish to a serious spectator.

The scene of the Bloomsbury antiquario's shop in which the Prince reads the "story" of the golden bowl, produces an illustration of the early stages of the reflective center's exercise of narrative authority.[2] In this scene James points out both Amerigo's ability as an acute reader in a certain way and his inability in another. As Charlotte realizes, "below a certain social plane, he never *saw*. One kind of shopman was just like another to him - which was oddly inconsequent on the part of a mind that where it did notice noticed so much" (114). Through this odd combination of a heightened perceptiveness in some respects and an appalling imperceptiveness in some other, James indicates why he chooses to portray the Prince as the narrative consciousness in the beginning of the novel. It seems that he emphasizes Amerigo's function as an initiate, in the sense that the reflector of the first volume does not strive to develop his narrative authority and seems to enjoy the stance of an amateur, a dilettante, in the exercise of it. Thus on the one hand James points out Amerigo's analytical shortcomings as his bias against the intelligent Jewish shopkeeper or against lower social classes reveals, and on the other hand he points out Amerigo's acuteness as a listener or reader of the "story" of the golden bowl:

> He continued to look at ... [Charlotte]. "Five pounds?"
> "Five pounds."
> He might have been doubting her word, but he was only, it appeared, gathering emphasis. "It would be dear - to make a gift of - at five shillings. If it had cost you even but fivepence I wouldn't take it from you."
> Then," she asked, "what *is* the matter?"
> "Why it has a crack."
> It sounded, on his lips, so sharp, it had such an authority, that she almost started... It was as if he had been right, though his assurance was wonderful. "You answer for it without having looked?"
> "I did look. I saw the object itself. It told its story. No wonder it's cheap." (123)

As Sheila Teahan argues, through Amerigo's remark - "It told its story" - "James calls attention to the bowl's narrative status," for Amerigo's remark is "fulfilled" when the bowl acts in the capacity of a witness for Maggie after she purchases it.[3] I would add that in calling "attention to the bowl's narrative status," James also calls attention to Amerigo as the listener or reader of the story. For he both launches the bowl's narrative status and connects aspects of the bowl to locate that story. When Amerigo hears the antiquario say that he can part with the exquisite bowl "for less than its value," he quickly figures out one aspect of the story of the bowl: that it is not made of "fine old gold ...[but] of some material once richly gilt" (119,118). To this aspect of the story of the bowl he connects another. For when the Prince figures out that it is not made of old gold he becomes suspicious of this beautiful crystal bowl that the antiquario calls "perfect" even though he also indirectly admits that it has a "joint or ... piecing" and therefore is not cut out of a single crystal (119). And when Charlotte gives him to understand that the old bowl is "cheap," he has read enough of the little story of the "crack" in the golden bowl. The "authority" that Amerigo's "wonderful" assertion reveals then is in a manner his *narrative* authority. For what James illustrates about the Prince is not simply the latter's analytical shortcomings, as his emphasis on superstitions and omens reveals, but also the ability to connect his observations to make a meaning, that is, to interpret a "story." And the narrative authority that Amerigo's creator reveals here is the ability to make this short story an integral part of his whole story. Thus we find an added significance of the "story" of the cracked crystal bowl that Amerigo reads.

For in a manner what Amerigo hints is his vague, instinctive apprehension that the story of the cracked bowl, a short narrative that has come out of the annals of the past, is connected to the story of his own immediate future. To accept a gift with a crack is for Amerigo to make way for a crack in his happiness, his safety, his marriage, in short, a crack in "everything" (123). "[E]verything" is an equivocal word, but what it suggests through its complexity is "everything" that concerns Amerigo's own self. Early in the novel he already shows an acute awareness of the schism between his princely, public identity and his private self in his self-comparison with a gourmet chicken "chopped up and ... cooked down as a *creme de volaille*, with half the parts left out" (46). All that his sophistication and his heritage seem to have done for him in his quasi-penurious state is to chop him up and disconnect one "half" of his attributes, which have gone into constituting his princely, public identity (presumably the "cooked" parts), from the other half of his attributes, which could have constituted his private identity if they had not been "left out." And now, as his instinctive apprehension of the crack suggests, he seems to have received another glimpse of the crack in his whole life. Thus, as he reads the "story" of the golden bowl, Amerigo, in a vague and barely formed manner associates his sense of his own fragmented self with the cracked bowl.

And early in the novel, through his reference to "the story" of the journey of Poe's Gordon Pym, the Prince depicts a scene that gives expression to his own perceptual adventures. In his conversation with Fanny Assingham regarding his desire to comprehend his prospective father-in-law and his bride, and by extension, the American consciousness including that of Fanny, the Prince finds it necessary to reminisce about

> the story of the shipwrecked Gordon Pym, who drifting in a small boat further toward North Pole - or was it the South? - than any one had ever done, found at a given moment before him a thickness of white air that was like a dazzling curtain of light, concealing as darkness conceals, yet of the colour of milk or of snow. There were moments when he felt his own boat move upon some such mystery. The state of mind of his new friends, including Mrs Assingham herself, had resemblances to a great white curtain. (56)

The quasi-pauper Prince, in all his humility, cannot understand, for instance, Fanny's motive - which has become one of his "unanswerable questions" - in bringing about his imminent marriage with the only offspring of an American millionaire, for between his American friends and himself, the advantages effected by this marriage appear vastly to be his own (57). He is immensely mystified by the "seriousness in *them* [his American friends] that made them so take him" (57). Thus in this picture of his journey towards the great curtain the imaginative Prince gives expression to his bewildered state of mind and consequently to his sense of the unknowable element. He cannot figure out the way, in which the American mind works, and therefore conceives himself as a "shipwrecked" voyager. He is as lost as Poe's Gordon Pym, and like Pym, seems to be entering the region of inexplicable mysteries. But in some ways his plight seems to be worse than Pym's, for, unlike Pym, the Prince has confused his "Pole[s]". Therefore Amerigo conceives himself as a voyager in desperate need of direction and guidance. For Daniel Mark Fogel, the metaphorical curtain signifies the Prince's isolation from Adam, isolation that is the result of Adam's "innocence" and of his "closeness to his daughter".[4] And for Paul Armstrong, the curtain signifies the sense of confusion and impenetrability that is expressive of the Prince's disturbing sense of "the Ververs' unfathomable otherness," and its whiteness signifies his sense of their "innocent and unwitting opaqueness".[5] I would also suggest that as Amerigo's metaphor is a white curtain of dazzling light, he conceives the unknowable element as a tantalizing and blinding but alluring surface. As a "dazzling curtain of light," this white veil seems to have been illuminated by a wealth of knowledge that it conceals. Thus it seemingly promises that wealth to his consciousness if he can only give it a twitch. But the problem here is that whereas it is the nature of curtains to mediate and thus to veil the illuminating light, Amerigo's metaphorical curtain is itself the light. And it has become a veil because it is a blinding light. The paradoxical suggestion here is that the light of perception itself is blinding. And although Amerigo may have borrowed his image instead of coining his own, he is, even if in a vague, rudimentary and unformed manner, aware of the paradox.

Further, what is worth noticing here is that Amerigo has begun to develop his own "story" out of someone else's image and "story". For, through his borrowed image, which gives expression to his confused state of mind, Amerigo portrays a scene. Indeed, through this picture of mystification and bafflement he has begun to develop a story. For he depicts himself as a voyager who continues his journey despite severe setbacks. Thus he gives expression to his eager and confident desire to take up the challenge to his faculty of perception through the image of the thick veil of "white air that was like a dazzling curtain of light". He paints himself as a lusty explorer who is not daunted by his "shipwrecked" condition, that is, his economic shipwreck as well as his present failure to probe the American consciousness, but who, on the contrary, makes the best of his adversity. Even his suggestion that perception can only lead to blindness, and thus to the end of his adventures, does not daunt the Prince who conceives himself as a staunch, steady, and perseverant explorer. For, if *Arthur Gordon Pym* is a narrative about how the eponymous protagonist is "nearly overwhelmed" by the mystifying white curtain of inexplicable vapor or powder and by the equally mystifying chasm to which the curtain leads,[6] then the prince's image too contains a narrative about how the reader in Amerigo is nearly but not ultimately overwhelmed by the text (the Verver mind) that he undertakes to read. Thus through his image of his metaphorical voyage, Amerigo depicts himself as an ambitious voyager and connects Poe's "story" of Pym's mysterious voyage with his own story of confusion. He also connects it with his implied story of the success that his famous ancestor of the same name acquires through his literal voyage. The effectiveness of the connection established by this implied story is such that when Fanny discusses with her husband the complication created by Charlotte's unexpected arrival, she goes into the subject of the Prince's "connexion" with the illustrious Amerigo Vespucci (95).

The Prince, a little later in the same conversation with Fanny, goes on to connect the image of his "small boat" with that of his "rigged and appointed" ship, and thus he continues to extend the imagery and hence the story of his metaphorical journey with a subsequent scene:

> "I'm starting on the great voyage - across the unknown sea; my ship's all rigged and appointed, the cargo's stowed away and the company complete. But what seems to be the matter with me is that I can't sail alone; my ship must be one of a pair, must have, in the waste of waters, a - what do you call it? - a consort. I don't ask you to stay on board with me, but I must keep your sail in sight for orientation. I don't in the least myself know, I assure you, the points of the compass." (59)

As he clearly acknowledges, equipped with the Verver wealth, Amerigo's vulnerable little boat has turned into a sturdy, cargo-laden ship. It seems that the connection he forges between the short story of his confused journey and the implied story of the successful journey of his ancestor yields him his own happy tale of pursuit and success: After his "shipwreck[]," he is now ready to embark on "the great voyage," that is, to launch on a grand quest for perception. And Amerigo goes into the details of the connection between his boat image and his ship image by reiterating his desperate need for guidance: Just as he has been bereft of direction in his "small boat," so he is now ignorant of "the points of the compass." And he extends his story by pointing out that the forward movement of the little drifting boat here is followed by the conspicuous absence of any movement at all. For his "rigged and appointed" ship stands absolutely still. After establishing a parallel with the historical Amerigo, then, James's protagonist establishes a significant contrast by depicting himself as suspended on "the waste of waters". He waits impatiently to see, that is, to surround himself with meaning, and consequently to undo the "waste" of his "essential quality and value" that has been generated by his pecuniary embarrassment (56). Amerigo's "unknown sea" then is his metaphor for his unrealized personal identity, his "single self, the unknown ... personal quantity" that he longs to develop (47). He appears to be impatient to create "some new history that should, so far as possible, contradict, and even if need be flatly dishonour, the old" (52). That is, he yearns to create a new narrative of his life, which is about the growth of his private and not his public self. Thus he extends the theme of his journey to comprehend the American mind and connects it with the theme of his quest for a new sense of self.

The image James depicts a little earlier in the novel for the effect of the Verver millions on the Prince, who is concerned about a new sense of self, is a soothing balm that anoints or heals him as he anxiously awaits the new turn in his life. It seems to the Prince that he is floating on waters that have been "sweetened" by an "essence, poured from a gold-topped phial" (48). But this image, as the narrator indicates, is not exactly Amerigo's own creation. On the contrary, at this early point in the novel, the center of consciousness seems to be in great need of the narrator's ability to "represent": "we thus represent him as catching the echoes from his own thought while he loitered" (48). The metaphorical little vessel, despite all that is poured from it, is full - it cannot be emptied out - of a sweet and colorful essence that has enchanted and enticed him. Not only is the phial abundant in sumptuousness both internally ("essence") and externally ("gold-topped"), but at that point he, being harmoniously immersed "up to his neck" in an aromatic bath, is the beneficiary of all this abundant substance (48). The Verver monetary abundance sweetens and colors his unformed "unknown quantity," that is, it suffuses his sense of his unknown private self with a romantic essence. The image of water, then, even as the novel begins, is expressive of the Prince's impression of his own "personal quantity." And this dependence on the narrator for an image proves to be efficacious in that he is able to incorporate it into his own system of representation. Consequently, a little later in the novel, he builds his own story out of an image of a vessel on expansive waters, an image that has grown out of the narrator's image of an aromatic bath. Such is the inextricable connection between narrator and reflector that even when the narrative voice draws a distinction between the narrator and the reflector the relation is not severed. Thus, as Amerigo's conversation with Fanny whets his desire for a new sense of self, the water of the aromatic bath almost seems to extend into the expansive waters of "the unknown sea". According to Beth Sharon Ash, the Verver money is "an ideal nurturing substance for the Prince" and it is colored "with the promise of his own effortless and exquisite self-fulfillment."[7] But, as James indicates, the water in Amerigo's luxurious bath is circumscribed, and therefore cannot extend into the waters of the "unknown sea". Indeed, as James suggests through the narrator, the aromatic bath that immerses the Prince up to his neck is obviously associated with the monetary "bath" of his ancestors: "No one before him, never - not even the infamous Pope - had so sat up to his neck in such a bath. It showed for that matter how little one of his race could escape after all from history" (48). Thus, Amerigo's aromatic bath is just another version of the "chemical bath" that steeps him in his "race," and the sweetening essence turns out to be just another version of the "inexpugnable scent" that perfumes the "chemical bath" (52). Consequently the waters in his aromatic bath only keep his "old," princely, public self (that has grown out of his "antenatal history") afloat (52). And as the circumscribed water in the bath cannot unite with the water of the "unknown sea," Amerigo's sense of self-division persists. The activity to which Amerigo looks forward, that is, the creation of a personal identity that is to find expression in his perceptive flights, then, does not come with his marriage.

Thus at the Embassy party, with his picture of "Mr Verver's boat," the Prince paints another scene and continues to tell the same story of his inactivity to Fanny (228). His metaphorical ship at this point in the novel has been replaced by Adam Verver's boat. For, as Amerigo conceives his situation, his metaphorical ship has failed to embark on "the great voyage" in quest of a new sense of self and consequently has shrunk into a boat. The latter image conspicuously points out the diminution of the comparative stability and security of the "ship". As Amerigo conceives his relation with his father-in-law (who keeps him pecuniarily afloat), the latter is concerned with his princely public identity alone, and thus Adam's ship is nothing more than a "boat":

"The 'boat', you see" - the Prince explained it ... considerately and lucidly - "is a good deal tied up at the dock, or anchored, if you like, out in the stream. I have to jump out from time to time to stretch my legs, and you'll probably perceive ... that Charlotte really can't help occasionally doing the same.... Call our having remained here together to-night, ... call the whole thing one of the harmless little plunges, off the deck, inevitable for each of us." (230)

At this point Amerigo's sharp sense of the Ververs' unfathomable element has all but vanished. Hence he portrays himself as the bored young man who must stretch his legs and indulge in splashing about the boat. His "harmless" plunges signify his security against any apprehension of the veil of unknowability. Thus the white curtain or thick air of inexplicable mystery thins out and gives way to Amerigo's complacent sense of the Ververs' inanity, which looks forward to his notion that "knowledge wasn't one of their needs and ... they were in fact constitutionally inaccessible to it" (274). James, however, points out with one of his supreme twists of irony that at this point "knowledge" does not seem to be one of Amerigo's own needs as well. Thus he satisfies himself with the stagnant boat, for he finds relief in "harmless little plunges". Through his image of jumping into the water with Charlotte, Amerigo also tells the story of the bond that he has begun to develop with his father-in-law's wife, which after all is quite conceivable to Fanny, considering her awareness of "their little romance ...[which] was even their little tragedy" (89). Through his image of plunging "off the deck" with Charlotte, which comes in striking opposition to the implied picture of his superficial relationship (relationship on the surface) with his wife and father-in-law on the deck, Amerigo predicts the story of the depth of his intimacy with his father-in-law's wife. His metaphor of the "inevitable" little plunges with Charlotte is his allusion to his sense of her sympathetic awareness of his quest for his "unknown quantity," his unrealized personal self which Maggie, like her father, has failed to acknowledge and certainly to promote. To "jump out" into the water, for Amerigo, is to try to get in touch with his unformed, unrealized personal self. Thus, as this image of the "little plunges, off the deck" signifies, restricted alike by their social roles that Adam and Maggie have relegated to them, Amerigo and Charlotte find only in each other the desire to perceive and acknowledge their non-social, private, individual selves. The more that Amerigo learns to articulate his point of view in the stories of the relationships between the Verver father and daughter and their *sposi*, then, the more capable he seems to become of making analyses, as it strikes Fanny Assingham when she hears Amerigo's "eloquen[t]" short story (230). Thus he proceeds with "perfect possession of his thought ... to complete his successful simile by ... the supreme touch" (231).

And the more Fanny hears the stories that his "successful simile[s]" unravel, the more capable she herself becomes of making her own imaginative flights and "analyse[s]":

> She found his eloquence precious; there wasn't a drop of it that she didn't in a manner catch, as it came, for immediate bottling, for future preservation. The crystal flash of her innermost attention really received it on the spot, and she had even already the vision of how, in the snug laboratory of her afterthought, she should be able chemically to analyse it. (230).

The pictures he paints come together to form striking short narratives which express Amerigo's thoughts and ideas so lucidly for Fanny that they illuminate her faculty of perception with a "crystal flash". The "effect" of his story is so deep on Fanny, even when he begins to tell it, that she is already filled with a sense of "ominous intimation" (229). The narrative authority he exercises is so effective, and consequently, his point of view proves to be so overpowering for Fanny that she can do nothing to counteract it, and even hastens to acknowledge her "responsibility" to him (233). Hence she finds herself contemplating the "beaut[y]" of Amerigo's behavior: "I've thought it all along wonderful of him" (235). But James also points out that the "effect" of Amerigo's story is so deep on Fanny that it makes a storyteller out of her. Thus, supplanting the Prince as the center of consciousness in this scene, she contemplatively discusses with the Colonel her conversation with the Prince, and enters the "laboratory of her afterthought" with a considerable supply of analyzable material. And as she "chemically" analyzes this story in this laboratory of her meditation, she comes up with her perception of causal relationships. For she studies the cause of Amerigo's and Charlotte's present attraction for each other, which, she concludes, is not an uninterrupted continuation of their past attraction: "The great thing was that when ...[Charlotte's marriage] so suddenly came up for her he wasn't afraid... And ...Charlotte herself had [confidence] to any amount" (236). Fanny thus becomes aware of the role that Maggie, "the dear little person," plays in the renewal of this attraction (237). Likewise, she also becomes aware of the effect of Amerigo's and Charlotte's attraction for each other: "Maggie's the great comfort. I'm getting hold of it. It will be *she* who'll see us through. In fact she'll have to. And she'll be able" (237). The effect of Amerigo's story that is couched within his "successful simile" thus is so profound for Fanny that she herself manages to see ahead into the story of Amerigo's relationship with Maggie, and thus to go beyond his implied prediction of his relationship with Charlotte. Indeed, the amused storyteller in Amerigo brings out the sibylline storyteller in Fanny.

The story that he tells Fanny with such eloquence convinces Amerigo himself to such an extent that he "take[s] up" the "tale" of his relation of passion with Charlotte: "On that morning in the Park there had been ... doubt and danger, whereas the tale this afternoon was taken up with a highly emphasised confidence" (250). Interestingly, to take up the "tale" is to take up the relation. As James suggests in *The Golden Bowl*, then, tales or stories have a specific connection with personal relations. It is as though relation as the connection between events suggests relation as the connection between people. To relate or narrate a story is, in a manner, to relate or connect with another person through sympathy and understanding. On the eve of his marriage this "tale" comes up for him, but, filled as he has been at that point with his sense of "doubt and danger," he does not take it up. Now, however, as a result of the void in his relation with Maggie, who for Amerigo at this point belongs to the group of "little American daughters, little American wives," (246) and of the void in his relation with Adam himself, who gives his son-in-law a "rigged and appointed" ship, as it were, only to convert it into his own boat that "is a good deal tied up at the dock," the Prince feels deprived of his ability to act. Consequently, he feels free to take up the old story of his relation with Charlotte.

Hence to take up the "tale" is to take up the relation with a certain sense of self-justification. For to take up this "tale" is to read meaning in his life, the meaning that comes from his perception of his relation with his environment. And to find this relation, for Amerigo, is to be understood and to understand. Just as he does not comprehend Maggie, so he does not read a tale in his interaction with her. For there is hardly any interaction between them at this point. The Prince has saved, "for some mysterious but very fine eventual purpose, all the wisdom, all the answers to his questions, all the impressions and generalisations [which] he gathered; putting them away and packing them down because he wanted his great gun to be loaded to the brim on the day he should decide to fire it off" (155). He cannot, then, organize into the coherence of a story all the inadequate explanations that he has gathered about Maggie's need to emphasize her bond with her father at the expense of a bond with her husband. Meaningfulness is so absent from these explanations that they simply turn into chaotic, explosive material that may only lead to the absolute destruction of his mystifying relation with his strange little wife. The potential story disintegrates into the meaninglessness of a "senseless sound" (156). The void of his relation (an emotional bond) with Maggie is so great that there is only "the boundless happy margin" in the pages of their life together and not a story. That is, all the pages are blank for Amerigo. But in his interaction with Charlotte there is an intense relation, and thus there is a story that he wants to read. And in this old story of his relation with Charlotte that he takes up to read once again, he finds a coherence that is created by his communication and understanding with her.

As a result it seems to Amerigo that the old story continues in his present relation with Charlotte, and that consequently it invests him with his Roman life of the past: "The sense of the past revived for him ... as it hadn't yet done" (249). For, waiting alone at Portland Place with nothing more to entertain him than a cheerless meditation, he suddenly finds himself watching the "odd[ly] eloquen[t]" appearance of Charlotte, who has come to be alone with her lover of the old days, and therefore has carefully excluded the Verver finery from her attire to remind him of their old relation (249). His old life in Rome thus suddenly returns to him and fills him with a sense of his possession of the past. Charlotte's idea is to renew the old relation: "It's the charm ... of trying again the old feelings. They come back." (251). He comprehends the message that is written all over Charlotte's appearance. For he finds himself watching "the picture" that seems to be "exactly copied" from his old Roman days (249). And she realizes that he comprehends and is in accord with her idea of the return of the past: "'Everything,' she went on, 'comes back. Besides,' she wound up, 'you know for yourself'" (251).

Thus it seems to Amerigo that as he takes up the tale of his old relation with Charlotte, he is already in possession of the "climax" of this tale: "Charlotte Stant, at such an hour, ... turning up for him at the very climax of his special inner vision, was an apparition charged with a congruity at which he stared almost as if it had been a violence" (248). The "climax of his special inner vision" is the climax of his tale of passion because it is with his "vision" that he conceives and interprets, and thus reads and creates, meaning. The narrative thread that runs through the "fine embroidery of [his] thought" seems to have joined his old life in Rome with his present life to form the meaning of the story of his life, that is, an external harmony that leads to internal harmony (271). For in Charlotte's company Amerigo seems to find the possibility of the union between his private and public selves. Thus when he is with her he conceives himself as "a congruous whole" (270). The "intensity of his accord with Charlotte" is so forceful and focused for Amerigo that, at the Eaton Square dinner, everybody and everything become "a mystic golden bridge between them" (268). Ever since the renewal of his relation with Charlotte, he seems to have become such an acutely imaginative reader that he can even find a place for Fanny Assingham's exertions to be included in the Matcham party as the "last passage of the chapter" of the story that he now reads with interest and comprehension (271). Thus it seems to him he is "beset with perception" (267): "[At Matcham,] he found everything, for his interpretation, for his convenience, fall easily into place; and all the more that Mrs Verver was at hand to exchange ideas and impressions with" (272). It seems to Amerigo that there is such a coherent pattern in the "perfect parity of imagination" between them (283) that they share repeated "identities of impulse" (290). Such is the narrative authority of his point of view that even Maggie, later in the novel, is struck by the "depth of unanimity, and exact coincidence of inspiration," between Amerigo and Charlotte (354). The Prince reads such "meaning" in the tale of his relation with Charlotte that his "whole consciousness" almost "ache[s] with a truth of an exquisite order" as it flowers in Matcham: "There had been beauty day after day, and there had been for the spiritual lips something of the pervasive taste of it" (283).

But, even as the tale of Amerigo's passionate relation reaches its climax, it succumbs to inconsistencies. His tale of "the sun-chequered greenwood of romance" gives way to inconsistency and incoherence because, in spite of the "beauty" he is supposed to have tasted as a result of the "meaning" he is supposed to have read, his "lips" are still "thirsty":

> It [the truth of his harmonious relation with Charlotte] had already told them, with an hourly voice, that it had a meaning - a meaning that their associated sense was to drain even as thirsty lips, after the plough through the sands and the sight, afar, of the palm-cluster, might drink in at last the promised well in the desert... it was all ... as if their response had remained below their fortune. (283)

Having received "truth" and "beauty" already, it is rather odd that Amerigo's "thirsty lips" have not drained the "meaning". Not only can he not share the meaning with Charlotte ("their ... thirsty lips" have not tasted what they "might drink"), but also he himself fails to arrive at it. The consequence is a deep sense of emptiness, as the "desert" metaphor implies. The closer he gets to fulfillment the farther he finds himself from it. And clearly, the metaphor of the "desert" in the "greenwood of romance" is an element of incongruity and incoherence. Amerigo's incongruous juxtaposition of the desert and the greenwood shows the ways in which he tries to get rid of his sense of emptiness which persists despite his sense of fulfillment in the Matcham scene. His consciousness has whisked him away from his golden bridge and, in the middle of his greenwood, dropped him into a desert. The "palm-cluster" poses as a reduced version of a greenwood, but even this truncated form is only like a mirage in the desert, for it is alarmingly out of reach ("afar"). Thus, although Amerigo's consciousness ignores or resists the change, the story of the greenwood has begun to change into the story of the desert. Indeed, the unfulfilled ("thirsty") Prince is in the metaphorical desert because he thirsts for the meaning that he is already supposed to have found. Hence his tale of a fulfilling relationship of love and passion fails to produce a coherent picture of harmony.

Interestingly, James suggests that Amerigo's ideas and thoughts regarding his and Charlotte's "perfect parity of imagination" are represented through images that are manufactured by him alone and not in conjunction with the narrator. Thus the narrator uses such phrases in this passage: "to all his sense at these moments," and "[h]is whole consciousness..." or "the idea with which, behind and beneath everything, he was restlessly occupied, and in the exploration of which, as in that of the sun-chequered greenwood of romance, his spirit ..." and even "he found himself ..." (283). Once again, then, the narrative voice draws a distinction between the narrator and the reflective center in the production of images. But at this point the narrator does not seem to indicate that their relation remains connected. Clearly, at this point the center of consciousness does not depend on the narrator for his system of representation. And as a result the narrator suggests that the inconsistencies which the images of harmony demonstrate are the product of the reflector's imagination. Therefore James suggests here that the reflector's ground of narrative authority seems to be slipping away. This is why the metaphorical "golden bridge" of harmony between him and Charlotte itself "strongly sway[s]" and becomes "almost vertiginous" (268).

Indeed, because Amerigo's narrative authority has begun to slip away, his sense of harmony also breaks. As he himself is well aware, there are, in the tale of his relation with Charlotte, not simply "links" but "gaps" as well, which is why the links are "renewed and bridged" (249). In Amerigo's consciousness, his harmony with Charlotte is ironically associated with Lady Castledean's "spacious harmonies" with Mr. Blint (289). And Charlotte herself talks about their "harmonies" and not about their harmony (293). The use of the plural implies breakage, gaps, and divisions. Thus, even in the midst of Amerigo's simile of harmony - "I feel the day like a great gold cup that we must somehow drain together" - the narrator evokes the metaphor of a crack through Charlotte's symbol of "the gilded crystal bowl in the little Bloomsbury shop" which she uses, ironically, to associate with Amerigo's simile: "'But do you remember,' she asked, 'apropos of great gold cups, the beautiful one, the real one, that I offered you so long ago" (292). As Amerigo's "great gold cup" evokes the sense of true perfection or true harmony, so Charlotte's symbol of the "gilded" bowl that she calls "the real one" evokes the sense of false perfection or false harmony.

The image of the golden bowl, then, goes from representing the apparent symmetry in the passionate relation between the adulterous pair to representing the absence of symmetry in that relation. The old story of the golden crystal bowl, which the Bloomsbury antiquario has read, is the story of a "beautiful old process" of achieving harmony (119). In this story, then, the bowl is aligned with solid crystal, particularly because of the use of such words as "perfect," "single" (119), "hardness" and of the phrase, "lines and ... laws of its own" (121). To align the crystal bowl with solid crystal is to make it symbolically suggest a relationship of exquisite beauty and harmony. For solid crystal is a solidified substance whose components are ordered to form a specific pattern. This design is clearly repeated in three dimensions, and thus crystal develops an exquisite form, which shows that the external and internal structures are harmoniously bound. Solid crystal is composed of atoms that are arranged to have a geometrically ordered pattern and therefore crystal shows or figuratively suggests relationships that are definite and symmetrical. But to read a new story of the golden crystal bowl, which has grown as a result of Amerigo's outing with Charlotte on the eve of his marriage, is to align the bowl with flaws and vulnerability. Amerigo, unlike Charlotte, reads this story but his reading becomes ineffectual even for himself. For, as a result of Charlotte's insistence on seeing perfection in it in spite of its cracks, he fails to register that the old story of the "greenwood" (the romance) is turning into the new story of the "desert" (the tragedy). Likewise, the old story of flawless crystal, of harmonious design, and of symmetry in relations has changed to a new story of flaws and deception. For the golden bowl cracks and breaks up into three pieces, through which breakage at one level James suggests the eradication of the three dimensions that constitute the harmonious design of solid crystal and therefore the picture of perfect harmony. And although Amerigo is capable of connecting the new story of the bowl with himself, and therefore of seeing an "abyss of divergence" between Charlotte and himself, that is, an abysmal crack even in his passionate relation with Charlotte, he ignores it all to read the old tale of his relation of passion (258). But this old tale is not as meaningful as Amerigo would like to think. Thus the problem in his reading of his tale points out the problem of his narrative authority.

It is a problem that shows Amerigo's remissness of the new element of flaws that has changed the old story of a romantic relation. According to Leo Bersani, "[i]n a sense, it's irrelevant in *The Golden Bowl* that Amerigo and Charlotte were in love before the story began."[8]

But as James points out, this situation is imperative because it contributes to the demonstration of Amerigo's preoccupation with the old story. When Charlotte turns up at Portland Place the first time to be alone with Amerigo, even though he "remember[s] no occasion in Rome from which the picture could have been so exactly copied" for he "remember[s] ... none of her coming to see him in the rain while a muddy four-wheeler waited," it seems to him that the past, as I have mentioned earlier, revives for him with peculiar intensity (249). The new element of a "muddy" four-wheeler is significant, James suggests. There has been no "muddy," and therefore a defiling, smearing element (the context of adultery), in the past. And James points out that, although the designated reflector of the first volume sees the "muddy" four-wheeler, he does not read its implications. When he resumes his old relation with Charlotte, it seems to him that he is simply taking up the old tale. But merely to repeat for the center of consciousness is to fail to notice the difference between the past and the present, and thus the difference between the old and the new tale. As a result, just as earlier in the novel, through the repeated use of images of motionless boats, now through the image of muddy circularity (wheels), James shows how Amerigo fails to move his narrative forward.

Consequently Amerigo loses the narrative thread that connects the past with the present. His sense of the past "so handled and hustled the present that this poor quantity scarce retained substance enough, scarce remained sufficiently *there*" (249). Hence he loses his grasp over the present moment. It seems to him that the past has "interlock[ed]" with the future, but such an "interlocking," as James clearly indicates through the narrator, becomes suspect because of the virtual expulsion of the present (249). According to Margery Sabin, Charlotte evokes "a rich atmosphere of intimacy, continuous with their personal past."[9] But what appears to be the connection between the past and the present, on closer scrutiny, turns out to be the absence of connection, for the present has been "handled and hustled" out. As a result of Amerigo's loss of the narrative thread, he has begun to lose his sense of the past, and to be separated from his "present order":

> His old Roman life had had more poetry, no doubt, but as he looked back upon it now it seemed to hang in the air of mere iridescent horizons, to have been loose and vague and thin, with large languorous unaccountable blanks. The present order, as it spread about him, had somehow the ground under its feet, and a trumpet in its ears, and a bottomless bag of solid shining British sovereigns - which was much to the point - in its hand. (273)

The "poetry" of "iridescent horizons" has lost its charm for Amerigo because of the "large languorous unaccountable blanks" into which the narrative of his past seems to disintegrate insidiously. Thus it has lost its "ground" and seems merely "to hang in the air". In its stead Amerigo thinks he has found an "order[ed]" present that is replete with opulence, as his image of "a bottomless bag of solid shining British sovereigns" exemplifies. The bag seems to be perpetually replenished because we are told that it is "bottomless". But as James indicates, the "order" that spreads around him and that has "its" own feet on the ground, does not spread *under* him. Thus the "ground" that the Prince sees is not something he is sure of. The man who is unnerved by the "lapse of logic" (289), does not probe the precariousness of the "somehow" on which his "order" depends for a ground. Thus the propitious image he has in mind for the "order" that is associated with authority and ascendancy, "a bottomless bag" of gold coins, is also replete with ominous overtones. For a "bottomless" bag that supposedly contributes to the "order" of the present recalls how the Ververs have bought the "Personage[s,]" Amerigo and Charlotte, to represent them (255). And it also evokes the picture of a bag with such a big hole (on account of the "unaccountable blanks" of the past) that it has lost its bottom. The sense of the whole that the "order" of the present seems to evoke, then, disintegrates into the sense of the hole through which the "solid shining" gold coins implicitly tumble down into a bottomless abyss of disorder. Thus the narrator suggests something through the Prince's image, of which this reflector himself does not comprehend the full significance.

Amerigo also fails to comprehend the full significance of the role that Charlotte plays in ordering and organizing their "arrangements" (293). For all Amerigo's insistence on "the felt identity" between his own and Charlotte's plan to delay their departure from Matcham, the narrator points out that Amerigo "borrow[s]" from Charlotte, even if he does it "most effectively" and even if it is to do something that "he prefer[s]" (282). Despite all his earnestness, Amerigo acts in a rather laggard, leisurely, and dilettantish manner. Thus, early in the novel he professes to depend on Fanny Assingham to guide him in his perceptual quest, and now he finds himself depending on Charlotte to make the arrangements that he prefers. He wants Charlotte to order and organize so that he can have the pleasure of reading and following what she orders and organizes. Thus, after Charlotte's makes her excuse to Fanny for delaying her own and the Prince's departure from Matcham, Amerigo finds "himself making use five minutes later of exactly the same tone as Charlotte's for telling Mrs Assingham that he was likewise in the matter of the return to London sorry for what mightn't be" (283). But as the narrator points out, Amerigo does not simply follow Charlotte: he goes "a step further" (283). Thus he does not simply repeat Charlotte's "tone" but adds an ingenious touch. But just as he is indulgent of Charlotte's "arrangements" so he is quite oblivious of his own ingenious addition.

Therefore it seems that the Prince simply likes the idea of Charlotte's playing the role of a maker of arrangements in their otherwise inactive life that restricts them merely to their public selves and thus to the monotony of playing the social role of personages. For he simply enjoys reading the examples that demonstrate Charlotte's thinking: "Ever so quietly she had brought it out, as she had thought it, all out, and it had to be as covertly that he let his appreciation expand" (293). Hence he likes the idea of Charlotte's playing the role of a storyteller. For as he himself has played that role, it can only contribute to the meaningful relationship, that is, the harmony between them:

> He could only keep his eyes on her, "And have you made out the very train -?"
>
> "The very one. Paddington - the 6.50 'in'. That gives us oceans; we can dine, at the usual hour, at home; and as Maggie will of course be in Eaton Square I hereby invite you."
>
> For a while he still but looked at her; it was a minute before he spoke. "Thank you very much. With pleasure." (294)

Amerigo's silent look is full of his deep admiration for Charlotte's ability to order the events and to tell the story of their lives with the Verver father and daughter in advance. His "pleasure," then, is particularly for Charlotte's ability to act as a storyteller. For to be a storyteller is to be an actor, that is, to have the ability to act, and thus to fill up the "oceans" of time not simply with meaningful physical activity involving the expression of personal selves, but also with the intellectual activity of planning, ordering, and arranging the successful execution of those physical activities. To be a storyteller then is to be a perceiver, a thinker, an organizer, and a maker of connections. Consequently, to be a storyteller is to have a "vision" like Charlotte's that acts for "every relation" (114). This vision that enables her to perceive relations comes as such a contrast to Amerigo's prejudices that as he leaves the antiquario's shop to wait outside, the reader does not look with him inside the shop but with Charlotte as she looks outside. Amerigo does not hear the rest of the conversation between the antiquario and Charlotte as do James's readers. It is Charlotte's point of view then which informs us of this part of the action. It is she who has noticed the antiquario, and she who makes up the story about the price of the golden bowl, a fiction that exemplifies her narrative persuasiveness in that Amerigo accepts what she tells him.

Indeed, Charlotte plays the role of storyteller so impressively that it is not lost upon Maggie. Thus she goes to Eaton Square on the morning following her husband's and Charlotte's late return from Matcham with the express purpose of "hear[ing] all her story" (346). The story she hears from her husband only whets her "curio[sity]," and makes her emphatic about her need to hear as much "as possible of Charlotte's story" (348). And one of the effects upon Maggie of Charlotte's authoritative role as storyteller is for the former to feel the impact of the latter's ability to arrange. Charlotte has not only made arrangements for herself and Amerigo, but she manages to enlist Amerigo's support in making arrangements for Maggie as well: "She [Maggie] must be kept in position so as not to *dis*arrange them. It fitted immensely together, the whole thing, ... Amerigo and Charlotte were arranged together, but she ... was arranged apart" (356). And for Maggie to be "arranged apart" is to be "vault[ed]" and imprisoned "in a bath of benevolence" that threatens to drown her (355). So effective seems Charlotte's ability to control their lives that when Maggie wants her husband to take a trip with her father, Amerigo wishes Charlotte to take control of the proposal and thus arrange and organize their activities. Charlotte's authoritative arrangements force upon Maggie the "sense of a life tremendously ordered and fixed" (371).

But, like Amerigo, Charlotte clearly encounters problems as a storyteller because of her desire for the "fixed" life. It is her desire for the "fixed" life that draws her to the "old song" in Amerigo's "Glo'ster Glo'ster" (293). But the "old song" and thus the "old" harmony have given way to a new disharmony. Hence the events she predicts to Amerigo before leaving Matcham do not occur, and consequently the story she seems to be looking ahead into does not run its course. They do not find Maggie at her father's house, and consequently, Amerigo does not dine at Eaton Square or in Charlotte's company. The only notice that the intrigued Amerigo initially takes of this change is to resist it. Thus when Maggie wishes Amerigo to propose to her father to go off on a Continental trip with him, for she does not want the four of them to "simply go on as we are," he objects: "Well, we're going on beautifully" (370). Like Amerigo at this point in the novel, Charlotte is in possession of the old story of their lives, and resists any intrusion that threatens to change the "fixed" element. Thus the only notice she takes of the change that Maggie tries to initiate in the story of their lives is to work vigorously to maintain the old equilibrium. Consequently, like Amerigo (as we find him until his second encounter with the golden bowl), when Charlotte "rearrange[s]" it is only to circumvent Maggie's efforts at rearranging, and to hold on to their old arrangements (367).

But the effect of holding on to old arrangements is for Charlotte to limit her own point of view. As she tells Amerigo, "for things I mayn't want to know I promise you shall find me stupid" (294-95). To fail to perceive the new element that changes the old story is then to "stupid[ly]" resist the growth of her vision. Because Charlotte resists the growth of her vision, she fails to get an insight into Maggie's point of view: "I can't put myself into Maggie's skin... It's not my fit - I shouldn't be able, as I see it, to breathe in it" (259). Thus she fails to see the point of view that has begun to give a new shape to their old arrangements and to change the story of their lives. Charlotte's failure to comprehend this point of view shows how she limits the growth of her own point of view. Consequently, this failure is expressive of her ultimate failure as a storyteller and reader, as her pursuit and confrontation of Maggie in the drawing-room at Fawns reveals. For as storyteller she fails to convince Maggie of her own fiction (falsehood), and as a reader of stories she fails to make a hole in the wholeness of Maggie's fiction (falsehood). Clearly she cannot close the fiction that Maggie has opened.

And in the garden scene in which Maggie pursues Charlotte, the latter once again reveals her failure as reader and teller of stories. Not only is she unaware that she has the wrong volume of the old novel she borrows from Maggie, but although the latter offers her the first volume of the novel, she chooses to leave both volumes behind. Carren Kaston argues that in giving Charlotte the "right" volume, Maggie offers her "the new 'beginning' which she has imposed on her marriage and on the plot of the novel, to replace the 'wrong' beginning constituted by Charlotte's affair with Amerigo and the oedipal attachment to her father".[10] I would add that Charlotte's refusal to take the proffered volume, and consequently her retreat from the "ancient rotunda," signify the decisive moment of her ultimate failure as reader and teller of stories (538). As a reader and teller of stories, Charlotte takes a volume of the old novel and tries to seek refuge ("asylum") in the old "pillared and statued, niched and roofed" rotunda in a remote part of the garden at Fawns and which is therefore "admirably[y] shade[d]" by "the climbing rose and the honeysuckle" (538). As I see this old rotunda, with its "uncorrected antiquity, ... conscious hitherto of no violence from the present and no menace from the future," it represents the house of fiction where Charlotte seeks shelter in order to preserve the old story, and therefore the old harmony, of the father and daughter relationship, and of her own passionate relationship with Amerigo (538). But Maggie follows her right into this old house of fiction, as it were, and triumphs over Charlottle's old story, forcing her to change. It is Maggie then who finds a place within the rotunda, that is, takes possession of the old story. And thus it is Maggie who is left with the volumes of the old novel in their proper order, and consequently Maggie who executes the authority to order and to make a coherent design. In other words, Maggie triumphs over Charlotte as an acute reader and teller of stories. Thus it is Maggie who once again imposes her fiction ("I've failed!") on Charlotte (544). She then comes a long way from the time when she "couldn't read her pale novel" (333).

James's depiction of the bewildered and restless Maggie, early in the second volume, as literally struggling to read a story ("her pale novel") is significant because it is a symbolical comment on her struggle to comprehend the equilibrium that precedes or follows the problem in a story. When she first begins to ponder her own absence of interaction with her husband as opposed to Charlotte's intense interaction with him, she starts to ponder the "equilibrium" that governs her own and her father's as well as Amerigo's and Charlotte's lives (352). It is a strange equilibrium for Maggie because, although her husband and she, as well as her father and his wife, are supposed to be "a party of four," it balances her and her father on one side and her husband and her young and beautiful stepmother on the other (372). This equilibrium in the beginning seems to be a necessity because of what Fanny calls the "palpitating tale" of Fawns, which is about the tribulations assailing a millionaire as a result of his single status (177). This palpitating tale leads Maggie to tell her father the "story" about a remarkable young woman whose dignity continues to grow in the face of all her unsuccessful attempts at catching a husband, and which interests Adam enough to bring her into their palpitating tale (170). Charlotte's entry into the plot of the little "palpitating tale" establishes that very order and equilibrium that it has lacked. But this equilibrium, an arrangement which Maggie herself initiates, and with which the palpitating tale of Fawns ends and the little story of Maggie's life with her husband at Portland Place begins, turns out to be a strange equilibrium for her because it contains the problem of an absence of interaction with her husband. Indeed the disturbing disequilibrium that Maggie has begun to read in the story of the empty Portland Place is the result of the equilibrium of the palpitating tale of Fawns. Maggie wants to comprehend this strange equilibrium, and thus she exerts to grasp the narrative thread that runs through the episodes which connect her own life with the lives of the other three of the "party of four". This is why she conceives Charlotte's report of what the pair has "achieved" at Matcham and Gloucester as "Charlotte's story," and why she is so emphatic about listening to this story (348). She exerts to have a firm grasp over the causes and effects of their strange equilibrium.

Thus begins Maggie's constant and diligent study of causal relationships. Her desire to study the order of the events of their lives is her desire for a firm grasp over the narrative thread of causal relationships. Hence in her conversation with Amerigo regarding Adam's abandonment of the project for a Continental tour with herself she shows how she continues to trace a line of causes and effects: "'I was certain that was what father would say if I should leave him alone. I *have* been leaving him alone, and you see the effect. He hates now to move - he likes too much to be with us. But if you see the effect' - she felt herself magnificently keeping it up - 'perhaps you don't see the cause. The cause, my dear, is too lovely'" (363). Maggie's desire to grasp causal relationships is so consistent that she even begins to contemplate the "effect[s]" of Amerigo's presence and absence on herself (340). And she finds herself repeatedly analyzing the turning-point in all of their lives caused by her discussion with her father on an autumn day at Fawns regarding Charlotte: "It had been an hour from which the chain of causes and consequences was definitely traceable - so many things, and at the head of the list her father's marriage, having appeared to her to flow from Charlotte's visit to Fawns, and that event itself having flowed from the memorable talk" (341). Maggie's desire to grasp "the chain of causes and consequences" of the events of the past is her desire to move forward to an understanding of the events of the present.

To grasp the causal chain then is for Maggie to connect the episodes of her past life with those of her present, and thus to move forward with the narrative she has begun to read in her observations of her life as a daughter and a wife. Thus, unlike Amerigo, when Maggie remounts "the stream of time" she connects the past, that is, "the other time," when she has her first discussion with Adam in the park at Fawns as a result of the changes in their lives because of her marriage, with the present, that is, "now," when she has her second discussion with him in the same place late in the novel as a result of the complications that have generated because of those changes (503-504). To talk with her father about the past, for Maggie, is to talk about the causes that have led up to "the present situation" (500). Thus to talk about the past is to refer to their present situation indirectly. And thus this talk of the past is not quite what Sabin calls an "empty conversation,"[11] but rather, an indirect reference. If the talk of the past is an indirect reference to the present situation, then Maggie joins the past events with the present events to continue reading the narrative of her life. Hence she does not drown or stagnate in the past, that is, she does not constrict herself to reading an old story that is "fixed" in time, but journeys up the stream of time and watches the rapid movement of the "whirlgig of time" (500). The "whirlgig of time" that spins around for Maggie signifies the constant circular movement of time that enables her to fuse the events of the past with those of the present. For the "stream of time" keeps her on the move. Thus, as a contrast to Amerigo's image of the motionless boat or of his leisurely plunges off the deck of Mr. Verver's boat, Maggie's metaphorical "boat" pushes "off from the shore" and she moves forward with her life, and thus with the narrative she reads (501). Also, unlike him, Maggie does not accumulate all her unanswered questions with the purpose of watching them, or waiting for them to, explode into meaninglessness. Her "accumulations" are there, "like a roomful of confused objects" which she stores. On the one hand, as Sharon Cameron argues, this scene depicts "a picture of suppression" in which Maggie conceals meanings from her own mind.[12] But on the other hand, as Meili Steele argues, this is a means by which Maggie contains and controls the unknown.[13] I would also suggest that this is a means by which Maggie collects in order to preserve the unanswered questions. Thus she already starts to bring order by removing them from the corridor of her life where they may otherwise clutter and obstruct the forward movement of her consciousness (334). And Maggie's "later and more analytic consciousness" is the result of this forward movement (338).

For Maggie's imaginative "vision" continues to grow (521). As Leo Bersani argues, James's fiction is "full of visual shocks which constitute crucial turning points for his heroes and heroines."[14] In the beginning, perception for Maggie is associated with discomfort, fear, tension, and claustrophobia. Thus as she contemplates Amerigo's and Charlotte's reaction to her first effort at breaking away their equilibrium, she visualizes herself as suffering from a complete inability to move or stir, or as prevented from moving up: "it now arched over the Princess's head like a vault of bold span that important communication between them on the subject couldn't have failed of being immediate" (354). Perception at this point creates such violence in her imagination because all the observable material accumulating unconsciously in her memory has grown so considerably that it now arches out and forces its way into her shocked consciousness. She has to struggle to keep her "head," and thus her eyes, above "the dizzying smothering welter" of observable material that floods her consciousness so overwhelmingly that it tries to pull her down into the "submarine depths" of bafflement (354). Nicola Bradbury argues that the image of "the dizzying, smothering welter" depicts a picture of "stifling" but more importantly, of "rich immersion" of the self, and thus of being in the inside, as does

Maggie's image of the "bath of benevolence" (355), while her image of the goldfish bowl depicts a picture of looking from the outside.[15] Consequently for Bradbury, Maggie takes up "a double posture, ... doing what both author and readers attempt."[15] I would go further and say that James indicates Maggie's double posture of being inside and outside, of being and seeing, in the immersion image itself. For even when she is immersed in "the dizzying, smothering welter," or in a "bath of benevolence," she gets her head "above" and thus out of the water, and "manage[s] to see" what happens to and around her (354,355). Indeed, immersion and seeing have become such a habit for Maggie that she goes on to conceive herself and the other three members of her group as restless, tense, and wary watchers who continue to see and be seen while immersed in the watery element of instability, and who have become sufficiently conscious of seeing and being seen in this watery element to have become "like a party of panting goldfish" (524).

Maggie's determination to keep her head "always" above the submarine depths enables her to overcome each of her spells of perceptual "pauses and timidities" with "a further and lighter spring" (356). Consequently, every time her imaginative consciousness plummets into confusion, it soars higher up. Thus from the submarine depths of quasi-imperceptibility it ultimately rises up into the open upper air of intuitive perception: "Her comprehension soared so high that... [it seemed to her she was] hanging over a garden in the dark" (528). Hence her imagination moves from hearing what her father says "to himself" (510) to looking "with Charlotte's grave eyes" (521) and to visualizing Amerigo's "pale hard grimace" (529). For unlike Charlotte, Maggie gradually learns to get into others' "skin" with such frequency that she finds herself imagining their points of view. Mark Seltzer argues that Maggie's emphatic identification with Charlotte, her adversary or rival, is expressive of the "entanglement between love and power in *The Golden Bowl*": "Maggie controls precisely through a power of sympathy."[16] I would add that this intermingling of love and power enables Maggie to develop her perceptive imagination so thoroughly that she comes to be in possession of others' points of view.

Consequently, her imaginative consciousness moves from the darkness of "the first dawn" of soaring comprehension to "the immensity of light" and rises upward so considerably that, as she looks out her window at Fawns in the afternoon, it seems to her that she gazes out of a "castle-tower on a rock" (537). Unlike Amerigo, who finds himself "alienated" from "the Castello proper ... that had ... formerly stood up on the pedestal of its mountain-slope, showing beautifully blue from afar," and who therefore cannot quite reach this beautiful "head and front of the princedom" that seems to recede into a distance in space ("afar") and in time ("formerly"), Maggie finds herself perched within a "castle-tower" and thus in her house of fiction, as it were, high at the window of consciousness, like a Jamesian watcher who watches the human scene not directly but by way of the interpretive, creative imagination (156). And unlike Amerigo, who finds his own attempt at the acquisition of moral vision to be as frustrating as his attempt at climbing up a staircase of a quattrocento castle, Maggie finds that her own interpretive vision climbs higher and higher. As Carolyn Porter argues, Maggie has become "a transcendent seer," and the power she exercises as "author in charge of the play" "rests on her perceived status as a transcendent seer".[17] Further, because she has become a transcendent seer, Maggie looks out from her house of fiction and connects herself with her environment. Thus her "outlook" expands "all" around to include not simply one garden but many "gardens" and also "the woods," in a complete vision (537). As Susanne Kappeler argues, "what distinguishes the interesting character ...is his or her awareness of perceiving, and ...[h]e will, with this consciousness, fit his perceptions piece by piece into a larger scheme, a coherent vision, and make something of them, make sense out of them."[18] Consequently, a little later in the novel, it seems to Maggie that she reads "the *whole* history" of Charlotte's "relation" with Amerigo (552). The episodes between Charlotte and Amerigo then cohere into a wholeness for Maggie to form a complete story (with a beginning *and* an end, that is, about the growth *and* decline) of their "relation".

James emphasizes the center of consciousness's acute ability to read and thus take possession of a story by making the narrator's images blend with Maggie's own even in the beginning of the second volume. When Maggie first begins to ponder the remarkable situation in which she finds that "[s]he had surrendered herself to her husband without the shadow of a reserve or a condition and yet hadn't all the while given up her father by the least little inch" it seems to her that she has, "with the mere touch of her hand" created a change in their lives, a strange arrangement that has reared itself in "the very centre of the garden of her life, ... like some ... wonderful beautiful but outlandish pagoda" (328,327). Her image for her impression of the devotion she feels for her father and her husband is a pagoda, that is, a strange and mysterious house of devotion, because it embodies the strangeness of her own devotion that enables her "at once ... to separate and ... to keep together" with the two men in her life (328). Her metaphor also embodies her impression of the strange devotion between her husband and her stepmother which is an effect of her (Maggie's) strange devotion for her husband. My point, however, is not to go into the details of this metaphor but to focus on how James suggests the fusion of Maggie's consciousness with the narrator's. Clearly this image is Maggie's, for as the narrator tells us in connection with it, "that was what she felt, " or "to her considering mind," (327) or she "caught herself distinctly in the act of pausing," or "as she liked to put it" (328). But even in the midst of all these phrases the narrator states, "as I have called it" (328). The narrator, then, conceives Maggie's image as his own, and therefore blends her system of representation with his own: "we may add, with the ground soon covered by her agitated but resolute step..." (361). When James uses the first-person plural in the first volume it is to let his readers understand that Amerigo depends on the narrator for the construction of his image of the aromatic bath. But when he uses the first-person plural in the second volume he seems to suggest that the narrator is eager to establish an interdependent relation with Maggie. For James suggests that Maggie's image of the strange house of devotion influences the narrator into creating the image of "a Mahometan mosque" that is similar to Maggie's pagoda in that they (the pagoda and the mosque) are both eastern houses of spiritual devotion and therefore strange and mysterious to the western mind (328). And although the narrator creates only one more image - that of the spaniel - after that of the mosque, he preambles his third image in this connection (that of Maggie as "the frightened but clinging young mother of an unlawful child") with "might *I* so far multiply *my* metaphors" (330, my emphasis). The suggestion here is that the center of consciousness's metaphor of the pagoda too has become part of the narrator's metaphors. This connection or fusion between Maggie's and the narrator's images, and therefore an inseparable connection between the narrator and Maggie that the narrator is keen on making, depicts a clear picture of the way in which James emphasizes Maggie's (as opposed to Amerigo's and also the narrator's) exertion of narrative authority.

Thus James, even in the beginning of the second volume, shows Maggie as exercising the narrative authority that enables her to compose a short story through her image of the pagoda. For it paints a series of connected scenes. "She had walked round and round" this strangely adorned construction that has reared itself in "the garden of her life," that is, into her world of social and personal relations, and that has no doors through which she "might have entered" (327). At first she has not "wished" to enter, but now, as she continues "to stare and wonder" at this strange situation constituting of her life as a daughter and a wife and of its effects that is represented as a pagoda in her imaginative consciousness (327), she has "sounded with a tap or two one of the rare porcelain plates" that make up its exotic surface (328).

This scene, then, is followed by another scene, one that is suffused with climactic suspense: "Something *had* happened; it was as if a sound, at her touch, after a little, had come back to her from within; a sound sufficiently suggesting that her approach had been noted" (328). The significance of this passage to my discussion is that even in the first paragraph of the second volume, its center of consciousness demonstrates an ability to organize and connect, and thus even to condense the significant events of her life of the recent past into the coherence of a short story that concludes with a climax of imminent change. Like Amerigo's images, Maggie's pagoda image shows her desire to comprehend her situation by way of pictures that develop into little scenes. But, unlike his images, hers has not developed from the narrator's, and it also looks forward to change.

Also, Maggie shows herself as a more forceful storyteller than Amerigo in that, even near the beginning of the second volume, she passes a narrative thread through his image and her own to make them join into becoming parts of the same story. Thus she develops her image of dancing, through which she compares the desuetude into which her mental faculties have fallen with the desuetude into which her dancing steps have fallen:

> It had come to the Princess, obscurely at first, but little by little more conceivably, that her faculties hadn't for a good while been concomitantly used, the case resembled in a manner that of her once-loved dancing, a matter of remembered steps that had grown vague from her ceasing to go to balls. She would go to balls again - that seemed, freely, even crudely, stated, the remedy.... (330)

This image, which is constructed by Maggie without help from the narrator ("It had come to the Princess"), paints the scene of a nimble Maggie who has enjoyed a carefree existence literally on dance floors in the past. It articulates the theme of how she conceives her life of the past as following a coherent pattern, and of how in the present that pattern has broken. Through a scene it tells the little story of a sprightly young Maggie who has always taken an ordered, harmonious life for granted. Her image also tells the story of the social life that she has once enjoyed. Further, it continues this story in that it also paints the scene of Maggie's early notions of having found conjugal harmony. And it makes this miniature narrative longer by adding another scene to it through the picture of her being suddenly swept out of the social sphere and out of the matrimonial harmony (which thus stops even as it begins), and burdened by personal complications that have prevented her from enjoying that carefree existence. These complications have crept up so surreptitiously that she never realizes exactly when she ceases to dance in and out of the happy episodes of her life and out of society. Maggie's image then reveals her comparison of her life of the past with her life of the present. Also, it reveals her decision to analyze and plan. For this image particularly tells the story of a consciousness that has turned an eye on the self and found in it the reluctance and disinclination to cogitate. But her image does something that Amerigo's images do not. It shows the assiduous Maggie's determination to catch hold of a "remedy," that is, to make a new design of harmony, and thus to change, to grow, to act and not be acted upon. This image then also indicates the direction that the protagonist's life is going to take. It creates the picture of Maggie as a dancer and suggests the picture of Maggie as a choreographer, that is, a maker of harmonious patterns. For if she conceives herself as possessing "the constructive, the creative hand," the connection between Maggie as a dancer and Maggie as a dance composer is not hard to make (425). By extension her image looks forward to the performances she is going to put on as a playmaker and a player, that is, as storyteller and protagonist. This dancing image is also important because it picks up Amerigo's condescending image of his wife as "a little dancing-girl at rest, ever so light of movement but most often panting gently, even a shade compunctiously, on a bench" (266). Amerigo's image paints the scene of a "little character" that, on finding herself on the social stage, is overwhelmed by it (266). And Maggie's image reveals her vague and intuitive grasp of Amerigo's patronizing conception of his "little" wife. If Maggie has begun to make coherent "picture[s]" "touch by touch" which she forces upon Amerigo, and to organize the pictures into scenes and the scenes into short stories, then she has also begun to intuit the pictures within Amerigo's mind and connect them with those in her own mind (366). And if, as Teahan argues, "Maggie, in effect, becomes a Jamesian narrator who translates Amerigo's and Charlotte's consciousness" as she "construct[s]" their consciousness,[19] then she is in effect a Jamesian storyteller in that she picks up the scene that Amerigo's image paints of Maggie as a panting "little dancing-girl" who has retired from the dance floor, and extends his scene to make it a part of the story about her inactivity. She then runs her narrative thread through Amerigo's image and her own and thus continues the story that he begins to read about his "little" wife.[20]

And Maggie picks up this same narrative thread once again as she picks up the story of the former dancer of the social stage who decides to return to it, and continues this story through another image of herself as a dancer:

The Changing of Old Stories in The Golden Bowl 109

[A]nd when ...[Maggie] asked herself at Fawns to what single observation of her own, of those offered him in London, the Prince had had an affirmation to oppose, she but just failed to focus the small strained wife of the moments in question as some panting dancer of a difficult step who had capered, before the footlights of an empty theatre, to a spectator lounging in the box. (479)

This image of dancing, which again Maggie constructs without assistance from the narrator ("when she asked herself"), continues the story of the timid little wife who earlier forgets her dancing steps through desuetude but who now has taken her performances so seriously that she even rehearses on the stage "before the footlights of an empty theatre". And in this theater there is even a "spectator lounging in the box" who happens to be the very person for whom she has decided to take up her figurative dancing once again, and who has become sufficiently interested in his wife's performances to sit through her rehearsals, or sufficiently reassuring and encouraging to sit comfortably through them. Whatever Amerigo sees in his "small strained wife" now who has shocked his complaisance out of him with the "little story" (481) of the golden bowl that she tells him, as Maggie herself realizes, he no longer conceives her merely as "some panting dancer". For now not only has she taken up dancing again but has moved on from ball dances to "a difficult step". Thus whatever "observation of her own" that Amerigo resists as she tells him her little story of the golden bowl, he certainly does not resist her performances, which come after she tells him that story. At this point in the novel Maggie's perceptive imagination reads enough of Amerigo's indirect and non-verbal messages to begin to comprehend some of the workings of his mind. Through this image Maggie shows her understanding of Amerigo's transition from lounging inactivity to interested and supportive spectatorship.

Maggie's ability as the teller of the "story" of the golden bowl initiates this change in Amerigo as a spectator (461). She has been collecting and preserving material about the dubious element in Amerigo's relation with Charlotte which she learns to order and organize into the coherence of a story by studying the causal relationships that connect the events of the lives in the group of four ever since the Matcham party. And now she receives further material from the antiquario as a result of her act of buying the golden bowl with a high price without knowledge of the crack. The remarkably impressionable and impressive antiquario, in addition to unburdening what appears to be his guilty conscience to Maggie, also produces the scene that takes place in his shop long ago between Charlotte and

Amerigo as a result of his sight of their photographs which he observes as he waits for Maggie in a room at Portland Place. The antiquario does not possess enough information about the buyer or potential buyers of his golden bowl to be in complete possession of a story. He possesses disconnected scenes, for example, a scene about his potential buyers, which he offers to the actual buyer, and another about the actual buyer. He wants these scenes to be orchestrated and connected, which is why he passes his information to Maggie. Thus, although he cannot connect these scenes to form a little story about them, he passes his information because he is aware of the potential in it for a story of great significance to the actual buyer of the bowl. It is Maggie who takes hold of the scene and makes it a coherent part among the other scenes she has read in her observations of Amerigo and Charlotte, who draw her apprehensive attention because of their "vigilance of 'care'," which strikes her as their extreme precautions against "working harm" (268,369). Indeed she makes this scene that Charlotte and Amerigo enact in the little Bloomsbury shop the turning point of the story she now reads and tells about the golden bowl. The story she now tells Amerigo has such force for him that in all honesty he tells her she has become perhaps "more sacred" to him now than she has been even on the day of their marriage (462). For Maggie amazes Amerigo with the way she coherently and consistently develops her thoughts. She speaks with such coherence about the golden bowl that her speech becomes a "story". The "moral exchange" that occurs between them is the result of the story she begins to tell him and that reveals her "superior lucidity" (455). For it suggests unuttered words that Amerigo "might have inserted between the lines of her already spoken" (455). Consequently he follows "the clear train of her speech" so thoroughly that he gives the storyteller all his "attention" (457). Thus the storyteller in Maggie makes relations among events and talks about "relations" between Amerigo and Charlotte, and consequently, draws her husband into relation with herself (456).[21] If it seems that Amerigo "absolutely liked her to talk," then clearly he finds her narrative authority fascinatingly forceful (457). Hence he becomes the captivated listener, the spellbound audience member whom she has "straitened and tied" with her narrative thread (457). She has captivated him in this manner particularly because she is the accomplished storyteller who understands the value of "economy," and who understands when to throw in an element of "supreme clearness" and when to open up a chasm of uncertainty (463). Thus she is the storyteller who understands how to control "all the possibilities" in a story (488). Maggie does not know what her father knows or whether he suspects anything at all, but she understands what use to make of her own absence of knowledge in the story she tells. Thus she does not mention her father at all. It is the quality of suggestiveness in Maggie's story that entrances Amerigo most particularly. She is the serious storyteller who makes her "straight little story" spellbinding because of the interpretive activity she imposes upon her listener (481): "Find out for yourself!" she tells Amerigo at the end of her little story (465). For Amerigo to find out for himself, instead of relying on Maggie's or Charlotte's interpretive vision, is ultimately to change from an inactive, and dilettantish perceiver to an earnest seeker, and thus an active perceiver, reader.

Therefore Maggie winds her narrative thread around Amerigo to situate him in his "labyrinth," so as to bind him to the act of finding, but she also unwinds it to lead him out of his "labyrinth," and thus to lead him to the act of seeing:

> Hadn't she fairly got into his labyrinth with him? - wasn't she indeed in the very act of placing herself there for him at its centre and core, whence, on that definite orientation and by an instinct all her own, she might securely guide him out of it? She offered him thus assuredly a kind of support that wasn't to have been imagined in advance ... (454)

Maggie begins telling Amerigo her story by showing him the broken golden bowl and letting him know that she had placed the cracked but nevertheless intact bowl in "full view" exclusively for him to "see" it (454). Thus she passes her narrative thread to connect the broken bowl with the intact bowl, to indicate her own movement from ignorance to perception, and to move from a suggestion of her ability to mystify him to her desire to help him "see". She has placed Amerigo in a "labyrinth" with the thread of words with which she makes her little story and which leaves her interested but intrigued listener with much interpreting to do. She then evokes questions in her listener but gives him no answers. Thus with her story Maggie binds Amerigo to the act of finding out or creating the answers to his questions, that is, to making his own interpretations with his own imaginative consciousness. But as a result, he has also received a glimpse of a perceptive and contemplative Maggie who has already begun to work out a solution to the problem in their marriage. Thus, if to bind Amerigo is to thrust him into a perceptual quest, then Maggie paradoxically gives him the clue and enables him to be free to begin his journey, that is, to finally move forward instead of stagnating on Mr. Verver's boat. Thus she has also "fairly got into his labyrinth" in order to unwind the narrative thread and show him the way out of his labyrinth. She parallels herself with the mythological Ariadne, for she has been deceived by the man she loves, and as a consequence has even felt herself alone on a "strange shore to which she had been noiselessly ferried" (353). For John Carlos Rowe, however, Maggie "hardly [plays] the role of Ariadne": The Maggie who places herself at the center of the labyrinth is the only one whom Amerigo is forced to see "in his long and winding labyrinth" with the departure of Adam and Charlotte; and thus Maggie's "art transforms her into the minotaur - the destructive element itself."[22] But I would argue that it is not so much that Maggie is not an Ariadne as that she is a different and perhaps more complicated Ariadne than the old or mythological Ariadne. For she refuses to be a duped and victimized Ariadne who parts with her thread: She keeps a firm grasp over her narrative thread and therefore enters the labyrinth with the man she loves and helps, and even creates that labyrinth and places him in it. She then, in a manner, conflates the figure of Ariadne with the figures of Daedalus and Minos. Consequently, she is a new "Ariadne" who sees herself in the other and the other in herself, and as such, changes the old story of Ariadne (537).

Thus Maggie exercises her narrative authority through her ability to change an old story into a new one. Bersani argues that "[r]eality in *The Golden Bowl* consists in the novelistic arrangements of the first half; the second half gives us the correction, the unashamed, radical revision which Maggie then makes of her own work".[23] I would suggest that Maggie revises by changing old little stories into new little stories. This is why she reminds herself of "an actress who had been studying a part and rehearsing it, but who suddenly, on the stage, before the footlights, had begun to improvise, to speak lines not in the text" (348). For Laurence Holland, Maggie's ability to improvise is expressive of her realization that she has been "too passively" accepting the "'funny form'" of the lives of the group of four, and consequently, it is expressive of the beginning of her active sharing in their lives.[24] Maggie's ability to improvise also shows that after she has "rehears[ed]" her part and possessed herself of the old story, and after she has begun to perform as an actor in that story, she finds that the old story has changed and that she has to accommodate herself to the change. Thus she is an actor who is an author because she constantly studies her relation with her environment and takes part in the making of the change. She "'registers' the 're-perusal' of her work," as Bersani argues,[25] but she also moves on to register the changes that others have brought. Thus her observation of Amerigo's changed attitude towards Charlotte helps her to carry on her "show," that is, her fiction (475). Maggie studies the "repetition[s]" that occur in her actual world and comes to the conclusion that "a repetition" is not an exact duplication (539). For instance, when the roles are reversed between Maggie herself and Charlotte, and she sees herself as the pursuer and Charlotte as the pursued, she analyzes "the difference in intention" that brings the new element in the old story (539). Just as she takes note of the changes that occur around her which bring new elements into the old story of her life, so she herself changes the old story of her life by bringing new elements into it. Like Bersani, Kaston, too, argues that Maggie's revisions are like James's. Thus she writes, "in the second volume Maggie redesigns the plot of the first in an act of authorial revision similar to the ones James performed on his own works for the New York Edition": Through the act of looking again Maggie's vision enables her to change "old forms or fictions ... to become new," and to personalize and honor the "inherited forms" that she preserves.[26] I would go further and say that Maggie's revisions are not only with regard to the second volume. Her ability to revise is already in a vague and embryonic form even in the first volume. Thus she changes "an old story and a familiar idea that a beautiful baby could take its place as a new link between a wife and a husband, ... [for] Maggie and her father had, with every ingenuity, converted the precious creature into a link between a mamma and a grandpapa" (151). It is Amerigo who, as the central intelligence of the first volume, reflects on this change. But his reflection is geared to the irony of the increasing gap between himself and his wife, and he reserves this observation as a comment on the problem Maggie creates in their marriage. But James, at the same time, does something in addition: he reserves Amerigo's amused condescension as a comment on the latter's failure to realize the portent of this change of an "old story" into a new one. Maggie's ability to comprehend differences (for example, the difference between the past and the present) and changes enables her to grow, and consequently to transform an old story into a new one. Thus her revisions are not with regard to her "fictions" alone.

For Maggie's purpose is to change the old equilibrium of the story of her life into a new one. It is to work for this new equilibrium that Maggie tries to make new arrangements, that is, new pairings, among the group of four. For example, early in volume two she proposes the pairing of Adam and Amerigo, and of herself and Charlotte. Further, she accomplishes the pairing of Amerigo and herself and of Adam and Charlotte. And as a result of this new pairing, Amerigo is no longer the displaced father and her son "a hapless half-orphan" (151). Hence we see the picture of a father and son relationship as the Prince and principino come up together with the departure of Mr. and Mrs. Verver, a picture in which we see the child "clutching" his father's hand (578), followed by the picture of Maggie's and Amerigo's embrace in the concluding scene. Amerigo, then, finds a new relation with his son and his wife as the novel's concluding scenes suggest.

And as the novel's concluding paragraph points out, Amerigo finally is able to "see" for himself without having to follow the sight or vision offered by someone else (for example, either Fanny, or Charlotte, or even Maggie) who works as a guide:

> It kept him before her therefore, taking in - or trying to - what she so wonderfully gave. He tried, too clearly, to please her - to meet her in her own way, but with the result only that, close to her, her face kept before him, his hands holding her shoulders, his whole act enclosing her, he presently echoed: "'See'? I see nothing but *you*." And the truth of it had with this force after a moment so strangely lighted his eyes that as for pity and dread of them she buried her own in his breast. (580)

For Ralf Norrman these concluding lines of *The Golden Bowl* show how this novel has moved from the characters' use of pronominal referential ambiguity (that signifies insecurity) to Amerigo's use of the specific second person singular: "Amerigo cares for no other 'she'. He embraces his wife and uses the only pronoun he needs now".[27] I would add that Amerigo's confident and specific claim shows how his newly developing intimacy has engrossed him so thoroughly that he is no longer frustrated by what he does not understand about Maggie. He does not "see" what ...[Maggie] so wonderfully gave" but what he himself wishes to see. For Jean-Christophe Agnew, this scene depicts "a chastened Prince" who is once again "Maggie's dazzling and dazzled possession, and as such, fails to catch her meaning."[28] And for Porter, the Prince is still an "impotent observer" whose "personal single self" is absent and whose vision has "narrowed itself considerably" in the concluding scene.[29] But as James points out, Amerigo now sees in his own personal, individual way. He "trie[s] too clearly, to please her - to meet her in her own way," which indicates that he is aware of the difference between his own and her ways, and that he cannot meet her in "her own way" and has to meet her in *his* own different way. But because he "see[s]" in his own way, he finally does "see" her, and consequently, begins to comprehend something of one of those American minds that have so mystified him in the beginning of this novel. For Cameron, "if Amerigo sees nothing but her," he sees nothing but "what she has made him see," and consequently "she has nothing at all."[30] And for Jonathan Freedman, Amerigo's claim of seeing nothing but Maggie signifies that Maggie is the stern judge whose power is punitive and who releases her transgressing husband from imprisonment only "on promise of good behavior".[31] But as I see

Amerigo's claim, his vision indicates how his interpretive faculty has developed as a result of Maggie's refusal to let him see through her eyes. She has told Amerigo the story of the golden bowl, which includes the "story" he reads in it and the scene he enacts in the little antique shop, and which requires him to develop his own interpretive faculty. And as a result of what he sees, Amerigo has finally moved from inactive spectatorship to wholesome action: it is his "whole act" that "enclos[es]" Maggie.

What the conclusion suggests, then, is that a new state of equilibrium seems to have been established because the husband and wife meet each other on a new basis. For what the conclusion highlights is not a lop-sided relation, in which one borrows another's vision, but a balance between two different points of view which are implicit in Maggie's and Amerigo's own different visions or "way[s]". Each is aware of the other's different point of view, and through this mutual awareness James, in these concluding lines, shows how his protagonists finally do not supersede but parallel one another as centers of consciousness. Thus, if, as Teahan argues, Amerigo collapses as reflective center, and undergoes "an extinction of sorts" at the end of the first volume,[32] then at the end of the second volume he emerges once more with the capacity to establish his own point of view and not succumb to borrowing Maggie's. When Amerigo "echoe[s]" Maggie, James points out that, like Maggie, Amerigo sees. There is then harmony in the ability to see, for the force of his ability to see balances the force of her ability to see. Therefore the echo is not an echo in the subject of perception but in the equal ability to engage in perceptions. What Maggie and Amerigo have finally achieved is a relation that is balanced by what they comprehend about each other on one side with what they do not on the other side. For each of them vision is balanced by blindness: if the Prince sees nothing but Maggie, and therefore is in a manner blind, then so too is Maggie, who shuts and buries her eyes in Amerigo's breast as though she has been blinded by the strange light in his eyes. And as their passionate embrace suggests, such blindness acts as the stimulant required by them to continue to work at their newfound intimacy. If the strange light in Amerigo's eyes, or the "pity and dread" in Maggie's own, strikes us as a rather disquieting expression of a new equipoise based on emotional intensity, then we must remember that in all her humility, to quote Holland, Maggie "shields her eyes from the impact of ...[Amerigo's] faith and vision."[33] As Mark Reynolds observes, Amerigo's concluding words signify his "wonder at the as yet vague possibilities of what their romance might be."[34] The sense of vague possibilities finds expression not simply in his words but through his eyes and also through Maggie's. For Bersani, Maggie "saves an order which seems to be totally irrelevant to her passion."[35] And for Rowe, "[t]he marriages have been preserved by emptying them of all possible meaning."[36] But as James points out, Maggie does not simply save forms when she saves her marriage or empty them of "possible meaning". What the new equipoise between Amerigo and Maggie reveals, as the strange light in his eyes, and the mixture of "pity and dread" in hers imply, is a relation that is based not on sameness and therefore consolatory uniformity and certainty, but on difference and therefore the challenge of unpredictability and uncertainty. It is a difference that will lead them to wholeness together, and it is an unpredictability and uncertainty that will prevent their relation from becoming stagnant or superficial. James implies such a sharp sense of unpredictability in the new possibilities of the newly developing intimacy that even the narrator does not quite understand Maggie's act of burying her eyes. Thus he writes "*as for* pity and dread" and not "*for* pity and dread" (my emphasis). The new story that Maggie sets in motion is so full of uncertainty that the possibilities in it go beyond the narrator's perceptual control, which makes the conclusion a necessity at this point. According to David Craig, "having shaped her story to end in marital bliss, Maggie discovers that she cannot know the ending that she has imagined": "Maggie discovers the limits of the imagination, the loss of possibilities of an end."[37] But as I see the conclusion, it reveals not her "loss of possibilities of an end" but her nervous apprehension of her *continued* exertions in her efforts to create relations. Thus it reveals Maggie's apprehensive opening up to the uncertain new material for more new little stories, and to the uncertainties and instabilities of life that change old stories into new ones.

James, then, endows his center of consciousness with the narrative authority that he sees the author as exerting. According to Craig, "[t]he ending to *The Golden Bowl* presents James with special problems because he has displaced himself in the compositional process with his internal authors."[37] But clearly it is not so much that the author displaces himself as that he shows his art of storytelling *through* his "internal authors." Thus when James gets down into the "arena" and shares his narrative authority with his reflectors,[38] it is not to devalue or suspend his authority or to incarnate himself as a character, as Irena Auerbuch Smith reads him,[39] but to hold up the "clean glass" to the act of storytelling itself, and not to hold up "the muffled majesty of authorship" (*AN* 328). Indeed, James's opposition to the "mere *muffled* majesty of irresponsible authorship" is expressive of his aim to clearly depict his art of storytelling (*AN* 328, my emphasis). For it is to the art of composing narratives he alludes when he asserts that "as the whole conduct of life consists of things done which do other things in their turn, just so our behaviour and its fruits are essentially one and continuous" (*AN* 347). To make such connections of actions, or to connect one's actions to create coherence and continuity, is to exert narrative authority. And, as James suggests, this is what his centers of consciousness do as they act - being "actor[s] in the offered play" - and register or reflect the "whole thing," that is, the "thing" that is made whole by virtue of forged connections (*AN* 329). If, as James continues to write in the preface, it is imperative for "the artist" "[n]ot to *be* disconnected, ... but to feel ... the whole chain of relation and responsibility," then that artist is above all a storyteller (*AN* 348).

Notes

1. Henry James, The Art of the Novel (Boston: Northeastern University Press, 1984), 328. Cited parenthetically as AN.

2. Henry James, The Golden Bowl (1904; London: Penguin Books, 1985) 123.

3. Sheila Teahan, "The Golden Bowl and the Shattered Vessel of Consciousness," The Rhetorical Logic of Henry James (Baton Rouge and London: Louisiana State University Press, 1995) 133. Teahan's main argument in this essay is that the image of the bowl figures the vessel of consciousness and also signifies the doubly figuring and disfiguring capacity of metaphor itself because it (the bowl) "figures both the ground of narrative and its antithesis, both the decorative surface of James's standpoint and the abyss behind or beneath" (134).

4. Daniel Mark Fogel, Henry James and the Structure of Romantic Imagination (Baton Rouge and London: Louisiana State University Press, 1981) 97. Fogel's main argument is that The Golden Bowl is "an intricate but faithful enactment of the Romantic dialectic of spiral return" (95).

5. Paul Armstrong, The Phenomenology of Henry James (Chapel Hill and London: University of North Carolina Press, 1983) 145. Armstrong argues that through The Golden Bowl, James depicts the gap between the Self and the Other as unbridgeable. According to Armstrong, the Prince is aware of the discrepancy between the Ververs' Self for Others and their Self for Themselves, and that Maggie fails to see Amerigo's subjectivity and therefore does not see that "only a relation of mutual recognition and reciprocal exchange" would enable each to be "in freedom" with the other (146).

6. The quotation of Arthur Gordon Pym is from The Complete Poems and Stories of Edgar Allan Poe, Volume II (New York: Alfred A. Knopf, 1946) 852.

7. Beth Sharon Ash, "Narcissism and the Gilded Image: A Psychoanalytical Reading of The Golden Bowl," The Henry James Review 15.1 (1994): 73. In

this article, Ash argues that Maggie's bond with her father shapes her subjectivity and is expressive of "oedipal and preoedipal narcissistic wishes" (55).

8. Leo Bersani, "The Jamesian Lie," A Future for Astyanax: Characters and Desire in Literature (New York: Columbia University Press, 1984) 148. For Bersani, Amerigo's and Charlotte's "past is a concession on James's part to an order of psychological probability which the novel in fact dismisses, what is important is that they make love as a result of the arrangements contrived during the time of the novel itself" (148).

9. Margery Sabin, "Competition of Intelligence in The Golden Bowl," The Dialect of the Tribe: Speech and Community in Modern Fiction (New York and Oxford: Oxford University Press, 1987) 77. Sabin argues that in the first volume James offers, through Charlotte, "a compelling image of intelligence richly in accord with normative English values" and a "dramatic openness" (68), while in the second volume, he offers, through Maggie, a rejection of normative values and a "suppression of expressive speech" (82).

10. Carren Kaston Imagination and Desire in the Novels of Henry James (New Brunswick, New Jersey: Rutgers University Press, 1984) 153. Kaston argues that this scene "invites us to view the novel as an aggregate of competing authorial acts by the various characters" (153), and that Amerigo, Charlotte, and Fanny, fail as authors because they "have assumed authorial powers without consenting to be accountable," as opposed to Maggie, who succeeds because she has willingly paid "for the direction in which her design pushes the plot" (158). On a different note, Priscilla Walton, in "A Mistress of Shades: Maggie as Reviser in The Golden Bowl," in The Henry James Review 13.2 (1992), reads in this scene Maggie's figurative restoration of the order of patriarchy" (151). But clearly it is Charlotte who attempts and fails to restore the old order - an order which subscribes to a decadent patriarchal society in which even an intelligent, sensitive, and proud woman feels self-gratified in her role as another woman's husband's mistress. Maggie, on the other hand, works to break the old order of a female's role to please her father and her husband by effacing the self within her. Now she works to please the self within her by creating a connection with her husband. Thus she does not so much restore an order here as she creates one.

11. Sabin, 103.

12. Sharon Cameron, "Thinking Speaking: The Golden Bowl and the Production of Meaning," in Thinking in Henry James (Chicago and London: University of Chicago Press, 1989) 104. Cameron argues that The Golden Bowl is primarily concerned about meaning and not knowledge, and "meaning is subject to manipulation" (109). For Cameron, the first volume demonstrates that "speech is the medium through which one character exerts improper authority over another's understanding," while the second volume demonstrates that "thoughts become the medium in which meaning is made audible" (96).

13. Meili Steele, "The Drama of Reference in James's The Golden Bowl," Novel: A Forum on Fiction 21.1 (1987): 85. In this article, Steele examines the role of reference in "dialogue, ... and the presentation of the individual's experience" (73), and argues that "obscure dialogues" in The Golden Bowl "are an exploration of the ontological discontinuity generated by speakers with different referential languages" (79).

14. Bersani, 133. Bersani argues that the object of perception is the activity of the seer (138).

15. Nicola Bradbury, Henry James: The Later Novels (Oxford: Clarendon press, 1979) 172, 195.

16. Mark Seltzer, Henry James and the Art of Power (Ithaca: Cornell University Press, 1984) 62,71. And John Alberti, in "The Economics of Love: The Production of Value in The Golden Bowl," in The Henry James Review 12.1 (1991) discusses the entanglement between love and money by focussing on "economic metaphors" (10).

17. Carolyn Porter, "Henry James: Visionary Being," Seeing and Being: The Plight of the Participant Observer in Emerson, James, Adams, and Faulkner (Middletown: Wesleyan University Press, 1981) 161, 162.

18. Susanne Kappeler, Writing and Reading in Henry James (New York: Columbia University Press, 1980) 165.

19. Teahan, 137.

20. The image of the resting dancer is not the only picture that Maggie's consciousness picks up from Amerigo's. It seems to Maggie that she reads a tragically romantic story or follows such a story as she watches Charlotte's and Amerigo's movements in the second volume. For Maggie, watching them is like watching the performance of a "pair of operatic, of high Wagnerian lovers ... interlocked in their wood of enchantment, a green glade as romantic as one's dream of an old German forest" (519). Obviously, the scenes that Maggie contemplates are an extension of the scene that Amerigo depicts in his image of Charlotte and himself in the "sun-chequered greenwood of romance" (283). Also, Maggie's pictures of Amerigo's "privation that had left on his lips perhaps a little of the same thirst with which she fairly felt her own distorted," or of the "torment of the lost pilgrim who listens in desert sands for the possible, the impossible plash of water" (519), are reminiscent of Amerigo's pictures of his "thirsty lips" and of "the promised well in the desert" (283). It is as though, with her ability to comprehend others' points of view, Maggie picks up Amerigo's images, which he never articulates, and extends them to read the scenes that follow those that he portrays. She then repeatedly acts in the capacity of the narrator, and thus continues and completes the stories that Amerigo begins. And if his vision stops at a romance, her vision goes on to read the tragedy after the romance.

21. On a contrary note, Marcia Ian, in "Consecrated Diplomacy and the Concretion of Self," in The Henry James Review 7.1 (1985) argues that Maggie moves "from "sociability to solipsism, from relation to possession" (31).

22. John Carlos Rowe, 'The Deceptive Symmetry of Art in The Golden Bowl," Henry Adams and Henry James (Ithaca: Cornell University Press, 1976) 219. As I see the scene to which Rowe refers, after the departure of her father and Charlotte, Maggie, like the Ariadne deserted by her unfaithful lover, Theseus, is suddenly filled with the "terror" of uncertainty and disillusion: "Here it was then, the moment, the golden fruit that had shone from afar; only what were these things in the fact, for the hand and for the lips, when tested, when tasted - what were they as a reward?" (579). But into this moment of terror, anxiety, and disillusion, enters Amerigo, the effect of whose presence for Maggie is "the assurance of her safety ... making her terror drop," and making for the erasure of all sense of the unfaithful Amerigo (579). Amerigo's clasp of Maggie in a passionate embrace, in the final scene, is vaguely suggestive of Dionysus's clasp of Ariadne. Thus I see the conflation of a Theseus and a Dionysus in Amerigo who moves from being Maggie's adulterous husband to Charlotte's faithless lover, and finally to Maggie's faithful husband.

23. Bersani, 147.

24. Laurence Bedwell Holland, The Expense of Vision: Essays on the Craft of Henry James (Baltimore: Johns Hopkins University Press, 1964,1982) 381. Holland argues that the "grace of Maggie's histrionic performance and the actions she helps others perform become the foundation of the entire novel" (380): By forging "the lies, illusions, and devious pretences," Maggie helps to "redeem the promise of their lives" (387).

25. Bersani, 147.

26. Kaston, 137,166.

27. Ralf Norrman, "Referential Ambiguity in Pronouns," The Insecure World of Henry James's Fictions (London and Basingstoke: The Macmillan Press Limited, 1982) 65. Norrman argues that The Golden Bowl depicts pronominal referential ambiguity in a game of combinations of pairings, and that referential ambiguity dramatizes these combinations and thereby creates intensity (15).

28. Jean-Christophe Agnew, "The Consuming Vision of Henry James," The Culture of Consumption: Critical Essays in American History, 1880-1980, ed. Richard Wightman and T. J. Jackson Lears (New York: Pantheon Books, 1983) 100. Agnew argues that James depicts "a reified world," the product of modern consumer culture, that is "constructed by and for a consuming vision" (98).

29. Porter, 147. Porter argues that at the novel's end the Prince, as the "art object hoarded by the Ververs," is at last brought into "the stream of circulation," for he now sees his "use-value" for Maggie, who has exchanged her father for him. Thus, for Porter, Maggie becomes the "capitalist" who redeems the Prince's commodity value in the commodified world from which

her power generates (148). According to Porter, when Maggie pays for the Prince by giving up her father, the latter can "at least assess his own worth to her - although he is able to assess little else" (148). But as I see it, in assessing his own worth to her, the Prince also finds out his own individual difference, and thus his personal, single self. And thus when he embraces her, his "whole act" encloses her. Compressed within this phrase is the suggestion of Amerigo's having risen above self-division and found wholeness through action.

30. Cameron, 112.

31. Jonathan Freedman, Professions of Taste: Henry James, British Aestheticism, and Commodity Culture (Stanford, California: Stanford University Press, 1990) 233. Freedman's argument about The Golden Bowl is that when Maggie begins to act she "is transformed into a literal Belle Dame Sans Merci," whose power derives from a "combination of cruelty and boundless knowledge" (234). For Freedman, James does not simply inflate "the power of the decadent dark lady" but also domesticates it in Maggie: She is not the typical femme fatale, in that she works to establish "marital unity and familial harmony" (239). Thus for Freedman, The Golden Bowl shows how James moves beyond "the terms bequeathed him by the tradition of British aestheticism" as a result of his "aesthetic morality" (242).

32. Teahan, 136.

33. Holland, 407.

34. Mark Reynolds, "Counting the Costs: The Infirmity of Art and The Golden Bowl," The Henry James Review 6.1 (1984): 22. Reynolds particularly discusses the differences between Maggie's and Charlotte's art: While Maggie's fiction grants freedom to Charlotte by allowing her "a capacity for imagination and action," Charlotte's art attempts "to deny Maggie her freedom" (22).

35. Bersani, 153.

36. Rowe, 223. Rowe's main argument in this essay is that "[a]t the same time the golden bowl promises a perfect form" and "reveal[s] the impossibility of fulfilling" such a hope "in a world of time and change" (203).

37. David M. Craig, "The Indeterminacy of the End: Maggie Verver and the Limits of Imagination," The Henry James Review 3.2 (1982): 136,135. According to Craig, at the novel's conclusion, Maggie has "entered a world that is not her own" (133).

38. For a reading of "the contagious emanation of creativity" in this passage of James's preface see Daniel T. O'Hara's "Henry James's Version of Judgment," in Boundary 2 23.1 (1996): James maintains "a democratically aesthetic sovereignty" by which "the creative power of imaginative innovation contagiously disseminates itself among characters and readers so that they too become authorial" (68).

39. Irena Auerbuch Smith, "The Golden Goal: Toward a Dialogic Imagination in Henry James's Last Completed Novel," The Henry James Review 16.2 (1995): 173. Smith's argument is that James engages "in both a

monologue <u>about</u> and a dialogue <u>with</u> his characters" in <u>The Golden Bowl</u>, and thus engages himself "as author and antiquario" (178).

Chapter 4

The Changing Imaginative Consciousness of Lambert Strether

In the Preface to *The Ambassadors*, when James writes of his decision to employ "but one centre [of consciousness]" and therefore to keep "it all within my hero's compass," it is because "[t]he thing was to be so much this worthy's intimate adventure" that the author aims to "leave" as little as possible "a part of its value for [the protagonist], and *a fortiori* for ourselves, unexpressed" (*AN* 317).[1] Thus, although James does not make Lambert Strether a narrator, he endows him with a narrational role. By making one "centre" alone and by keeping it "all" within that center's "compass," James suggests that he situates the narrative itself in Strether's grasp. The verb "compass" connotes a successful reach, and the noun "compass" is suggestive of a circle with its center from which point the circumference is encompassed and grasped. Thus, in effect, James indicates that he invests his protagonist with authorial abilities. Indeed, to a certain extent, the author seems to associate the protagonist with the narrator, but he also allows the former's evolving imaginative consciousness to surpass the latter's. Thus in a sense, James allows the reflector to surpass the narrator in narrative abilities. The growth in Strether's imagination enables him to understand the principle of continual change within his environment, and thus to read and tell the stories of that environment, although he does not literally become a storyteller. Also, it enables him to understand the principle of continual change within his own consciousness. That is, he realizes that there is nothing final and stable within himself. Indeed, the growth in Strether's imaginative consciousness enables him to find the story of his life, which is the story of continual change. Consequently, it enables him to exert narrative authority, and thus to authorize his own point of view. For the growth in his imagination leads Strether to find his relation with his surroundings and to make narrative connections in his interpretation of events as well as to make connections between his own past, present, and future.

It is Strether's imagination that helps him to find his way when he becomes immersed in confusion. An example of this can be found in the image of his metaphorical immersion in water early in the novel:

> [T]here were days when Strether seemed to bump against [Waymarsh] as a sinking swimmer might brush a submarine object. The fathomless medium held them - Chad's manner was the fathomless medium; and our friend felt as if they passed each other, in their deep immersion, with the round impersonal eye of silent fish.[2]

Confronted by Chad's unexpected transformation, Strether's first reaction is to feel as helpless as though he is drowning out of exhaustion like a "sinking swimmer". He has tried to comprehend this transformation with his rational faculty, but the attempt to think "logically" has drowned him uncontrollably in a sea of "bewilder[ment]" (170,173). Despite Strether's logical thinking, Chad has become ungraspable by virtue of his transformation in a city that itself strikes Strether as continually changing, and therefore as continually trembling and melting out of his grasp. As Maud Ellmann asserts, "[t]he world twinkles with alterity".[3] At this point Strether is completely flabbergasted by the strange and unexpected phenomenon of Chad's change. But, once immersed in this unfathomably confusing element, although still flabbergasted, he finds *himself* transformed from a helpless "sinking swimmer" into a vigorous "fish". For, once immersed in it, Strether turns to his imagination to help him interpret.

James shows the process of development that Strether's imagination undergoes even through these two images of the swimmer and the fish. Perhaps the image of the sinking swimmer is *both* the narrator's and Strether's, or simply the narrator's own. Certainly the sentence does not suggest exactly whose image this is: "Strether seemed to bump against him [Waymarsh] as a sinking swimmer ..." This ambiguity, however, indicates how in the early phase of Strether's observation of Chad (and for that matter, of Waymarsh as well), James associates Strether with the narrator in regards to the protagonist's imaginative consciousness, and consequently, to his narrational abilities. But even in the same passage James points out that the reflector is also capable of creating his own image. For he clearly notes that Strether does not share the creation of the image of the "silent fish" with the narrator. This particular image is Strether's own: "and *our friend felt* as if they passed each other ... with the round impersonal eye of silent fish" (my emphasis). It seems as though Strether's imaginative consciousness continues to develop, resulting in the leap from a "sinking swimmer" to a "silent fish". Strether is "silent" because, at this early stage, words to explain the young man's transformation melt out of his grasp into silence like water. And he is vaguely and instinctively beginning to be aware that in this fathomless element which is like water itself, nothing is certain or stable or uniform.[4] Consequently, Strether does not conceive himself as in any way exerting narrative authority: "[E]ach of his remarks [in his discussions about Chad's situation with Miss Gostrey], as it came, seemed to drop into a deeper well" (189). For each of his utterances makes him increasingly aware of the fathomless ungraspability of things and takes him to a deeper level of contemplation. As a result he begins to be aware of his own meaning-making activities.[5] Chad's unfathomability, then, helps Strether to develop "the round impersonal eye" of acute observation, and thus to begin exerting narrative authority. His imagination makes an intuitive note of how everything glides out of his grasp and continues to change shape like water. For, as the imaginative faculty finds expression in fiction, it creates nothing final or absolute but everything that is dependent on interpretation. Therefore with his "deep immersion" Strether instinctively makes himself at home in the new, ungraspable and changeable, unpredictable and unstable environment that he finds in Paris. Unlike the unimaginative Waymarsh whose contact with Chad's fathomless element reduces him merely into an unconscious "submarine object," Strether, with eyes wide open, learns to wonder, to speculate and to discover by making imaginative guesses.

But, as Strether's image of deep immersion also reveals, at this point his imaginative thinking shows a certain analytical incoherence and inconsistency. As James points out, although there is coherence and consistency in his image of his transformation from a live but "sinking swimmer" into a live but "silent fish," there is questionable coherence and consistency in the image of the transformation of Waymarsh from a sunken and inanimate "submarine object" into a silent fish. (How, one wonders, especially after one has finished reading the novel and come back to this passage, has Waymarsh been subjected to the kind of transformation that Strether has?)

At this point, then, Strether's images do not consistently show signs of sophistication. Hence he conceives of Jeanne de Vionnet as "a faint pastel in an oval frame: he thought of her already as of some lurking image in a long gallery, the portrait of a small old-time princess of whom nothing was known but that she had died young" (247). If Strether's image for Jeanne as a portrait of an unknown dead princess shows his profound sensitivity to her mysterious young heart that has suppressed its own yearnings, and thus has died a figurative death, that is, if his image demonstrates his ability to catch an impression and make a picture out of a glimpse, (an ability that James lauds in "The Art of Fiction"), it also shows how this picture is "faint" and not vivid or striking, and how he objectifies the girl herself in the process. Without the use of his imaginative faculty, which seems to find fair ground for nourishment in the values of Paris, Strether's rational faculty, which conversely seems to have found a stimulating ground in the values of Woollett,[6] drowns his consciousness in the exhaustion of unrewarding activity. But now, with the use of his imagination, his rational faculty shows that, although it has not reached a high point, it has made a beginning in analytical contemplativeness.

Perhaps James suggests that because in the beginning Strether's imaginative faculty shows no sign of subtle refinement, early in the novel it becomes indistinguishable from the narrator's imaginative faculty. For instance, in the image for Strether's temporary respite at Notre Dame from his problem of confounding his ambassadorial mission of representing Mrs. Newsome, it is not at all clear how much of the construction depends on Strether and how much on the narrator: "he was able ... to drop his problem at the door [of the church] very much as if it had been the copper piece that he deposited, on the threshold, in the receptacle of the inveterate blind beggar" (272). Although, as Sheila Teahan observes, the rhetorical indistinguishability is inevitable in "indirect discourse,"[7] it also seems that because James sometimes even at this early stage in the novel gives Strether the power to create forceful images, he makes use of this rhetorical indistinguishability to suggest that the reflector potentially and nascently shows the narrator's imaginative abilities even at the beginning.

In tracing the gradual growth of sophistication in his protagonist's imagination, however, James points out that at the beginning of the novel Strether is obviously dependent on the narrator's imagination. Thus at this point it is the narrator who supplies an image for Strether's vaguely forming thoughts regarding his inclination and hesitancy in befriending the urbane and assertive Maria Gostrey who surprises him into an unlooked-for affinity. As the dazed protagonist does not see the parallel and contrast between her and himself, James points out that the reader has to depend on the narrator:

> She affected him as almost insolently young; but ...was however, like himself, marked and wan; only it naturally *couldn't have been known to him* how much a spectator looking from one to the other might have discerned that they had in common. It wouldn't for such a spectator have been altogether insupposable that, each so finely brown and so sharply spare, ... they might have been brother and sister. On this ground indeed there would have been a residuum of difference; such a sister having surely known in respect to such a brother the extremity of separation, and such a brother now feeling in respect to such a sister the extremity of surprise. (60, my emphasis)

As Millicent Bell observes, this image suggests that Maria "is a sort of twin" to Strether in that her "inability to live for herself" duplicates Strether's own inability to live for himself.[8] But as the image also reveals, he is unable to make relations on his own at this point. What strikes him about Maria's appearance is his own loss of youth and consequently, his own inability to live for himself. James also indicates that Strether does not contemplate the different forms of appearance. The "almost insolently young" appearance of a woman, who has used her eyes to a far greater advantage than he has used his own, is enough to confuse him. Although Strether soon learns to put "the extremity of surprise" under the service of his imagnative faculty, at this point, nursing his surprise as he does, and as the narrator humorously indicates, Strether is too busy to make efficacious use of his speculative eyes.

But as his imagination grows in refinement we notice how he learns to see more and more clearly. As James asserts in the Preface, it is Strether's "blest imagination" that "help[s] him to discriminate" (*AN* 316). For the more thoroughly he uses his imagination, the more sophisticated become his contemplative eyes. Thus, late in the novel while conversing with Maria on his clear understanding of Mrs. Newsome, Strether builds structures on Maria's foundation of the moral "block" that "[l]ittle by little looms up": "'I see it all,' he absently echoed, while his eyes might have been fixing some particularly large iceberg in a cool blue northern sea" (448). The inflexible Mrs. Newsome, as Strether sees her now, is as hard and cold as an iceberg. He now sees beyond her dignified surface into her essential interior "as I've never done" (447). The image of the "iceberg," as James points out through the use of the word "might," may very well be the product of a fusion between Strether's and the narrator's imagination. Or it may be Strether's own. For James shows a connection between this image and an earlier image that is unambiguously Strether's own. As he observes Gloriani for the first time in his garden and ponders the sculptor's great fame, Lambert Strether's lambent imagination comes in "contact" with "the light, with the romance, of glory" which envelops this great sculptor. As a result he "had the consciousness of opening to it, for the happy instant, all the windows of his mind, of letting this rather grey interior drink in for once the sun of a clime not marked in his old geography" (199). The narrator, then, indicates that this picture of a cool and even icy world has originated in Strether's imaginative consciousness. The protagonist knows this northern world well because it has been his home in Woollett. Under the influence of Paris, however, the imaginative world of "romance," and consequently the fervent and sunny light of a sympathetic imagination have begun, quite early in the novel,[9] to animate Strether's consciousness that of old has known only the cool atmosphere of his rational faculty. And now, late in the text, it has been sufficiently warmed to move out of that chilly picture in order to watch it from a distance. And as he watches it, his imaginative consciousness seems to develop it by adding the clear distinct details of a "large iceberg in a cool blue northern sea."

But if James points out the ascendancy of Strether's imagination over the narrator's only in a subtle manner in the image of the iceberg, he later illustrates it more directly. In the idyllic French country, losing himself in his reminiscences of the Lambinet he had failed to buy in his youth, and in his enamored admiration of Mme de Vionnet, it seems to Lambert Strether that he has himself stepped into a picture: "He really continued in the picture - that being *for himself* his situation - ... and had ... not once overstepped the oblong gilt frame" (457, my emphasis). And "the spell of the picture" is "essentially more than anything else a scene and a stage, that the very air of the play was in the rustle of the willows and the tone of the sky" (458). James suggests that Strether's dependence on the narrator's imaginative faculty for the creation of images, and thus of composing a vivid picture gradually diminishes, while the narrator's dependence on Strether's increases. Indeed, the center of consciousness's imaginative faculty grows with such force that the narrator at times has to make use of the former's images rather than coining his own. At this late stage in the novel, Strether's picture has even developed into a dramatic "scene" for him. And the scene continues to develop so smoothly that it flows into other scenes:

> Between nine and ten, [that is, just before Strether's last visit to Mme de Vionnet's] at last, in the high clear picture - he was moving in these days, as in a gallery, from clever canvas to clever canvas - he drew a long breath: it was so presented to him from the first that the spell of his luxury wouldn't be broken. (474)

The "spell of his luxury" has issued from "the spell of the picture" that Strether develops in the country. And if in the country he has conceived himself to be in one picture alone, now he conceives himself to be jumping in and out of several pictures, and with remarkable ease too. Clearly, Strether's imaginative faculty at last has developed the ability to create and sustain images without being aided by the narrator's imaginative faculty. And his imaginative independence shows how he has acquired his own narrative abilities, and thus reads not only the interior that Marie veils, but also his own contribution to the creation of that cover. Strether's shocked and climactic discovery of Marie de Vionnet's sexual intimacy with Chad at last forces upon him the realization "that he had really been trying all along to suppose nothing," that is, to imagine nothing about the Chad-Marie intimacy, simply to prevent any distortion of his own straight and narrow notion of a virtuous relationship, which seems to have grown out of the values of Woollett rationalism (468). To suppose nothing is to glide from one "vain appearance" to another, that is, as though from one picture to another in a gallery (204). And it strikes him now, just before his last visit to Mme de Vionnet, as he upbraids himself for his momentary desire to relieve himself from the ethical burden of "pay[ment]," that he is still indulging irresponsibly in fanciful illusions (473). In short, Strether rebukes himself for constructing naive theories about ideal conduct. Thus he directs his irony and mockery about his "spell of luxury" at himself, the incisiveness of which finds clear expression in the self-portrayal as a subject who cannot step out of the "clear" and unchanging, charming and illusory world of the "clever canvas" into the unclear, complicated and confusingly ever-changing world of his actual circumstances. At this late stage then, Strether's images show the coherence and consistency in meaning-making activities that earlier in the text they do not show. Late in the novel Strether's imaginative consciousness has indeed come a long way.

At the beginning, to be sure, Maria Gostrey helps Strether to develop his imaginative consciousness. For Maria shows him how to cultivate the wondering imagination by playing with ungraspable notions: "In ignorance she could humour her fancy, and that proved a useful freedom" (98). In ultimately refusing to let Strether attach a name to the nameless object of the Newsome industry, Maria arranges for herself the freedom to stray[10] into speculation. In treating this article as unnamable, she ensures the continual exercise of her imagination, and thus of her contemplative and analytical abilities. She teaches Strether that to "Guess" is to make a meaning through the imagination (179). As she "embroider[s]" with her imagination and lets it take its "own flight," she teaches him that in order to adapt himself to his new and unfathomable environment he must needs let loose his imagination (101,192).

Receiving his example from Maria, Strether realizes that the only way to come to terms with Chad's remarkable transformation is to let his imagination break out of "margin" (154). According to Strether, Mrs. Newsome has no imagination not because she cannot conceive a well-planned text about Chad's life in Paris, which she does, but because she does not use her imagination to speculate, to wonder and play with the unusual and the unknowable. Therefore she is like an iceberg that can thrive only in unchanging, frigid temperature and conditions, conditions that she can fathom, that is, those she is accustomed to, and therefore that must not change. She refuses to break away from the margins prescribed by social traditions. Strether on the other hand may begin as a sinking swimmer but, as he allows his imagination to break out of margins, he learns to be aware of, and thus to thrive in, unfathomable conditions.

As a result, Strether's imagination begins to stray and embroider, enabling him to form connections between the outer expressions and inner being of the people around him. As his sympathetic imagination strays or wanders and embroiders at Chad's first party, little Jeanne de Vionnet finds herself in the presence of a soothing and mollifying element because of the absence of the cold and direct medium of a piercing or inquisitive glance:

> [H]is fancy had ... begun so to stray and embroider that he finally found himself, absent and extravagant, sitting with the child in a friendly silence. Only by this time he felt her flutter to have fortunately dropped and that she was more at her ease. She trusted him, liked him, and it was to come back to him afterwards that she had told him things. (248)

To "stray" is to deviate, but to deviate is for his imagination to turn away from the prescribed way and thus to find a new way, its own way. Hence, emblematically, he "walk[s] round," engages in a "linger[ing] ... walk," or "a long vague walk," and a "slow reiterated ramble" (496,504, 287,79). Because he strays ("wander[s]"), he indulges in reveries ("wonder[s]"), as Strether himself realizes late in the novel: "I wondered and wandered" (493). Indeed, the first syllable of Strether's name ("stre") puns obviously on "stray". Even as Strether's straying imagination embroiders on the shy and reticent Jeanne, she becomes increasingly relaxed and receptive, which in turn enables his "deeply stirred" imagination to deeply engage in "contemplations" (273). And through these "contemplations," as he spends a few quiet moments with Jeanne, the imaginative Strether attempts to create connections between her inner being and outer expressions. Likewise, when Strether observes Mamie, who in like manner is deeply immersed in contemplations in the balcony of her hotel, he creates an imaginative connection between her inner being and outer expressions. Thus at last he is able to "read a meaning" into the element of "mystery" that envelops his encounters with her in Paris: "It had represented the possibility between them of some communication ... - the possibility even of some relation as yet unacknowledged" (378). There is no direct "communication" between them regarding Chad's transformation. Nevertheless, with his imagination Strether guesses about Mamie's perception of a remarkable change in Chad, and that therefore she is on his (Strether's) side rather than on Sarah Pocock's. And late in the novel, when he tries to make Sarah realize that "[e]verything has come as a sort of indistinguishable part of everything else," Strether reveals a firm grasp of causal relationships which becomes possible because of the growth in his orchestrative imagination (418).

Hence, by granting Strether the imaginative ability to make such narrative connections, James grants his center of consciousness a considerable degree of narrative authority. James is so emphatic about Strether's ability to forge connections that he makes the reflector pick the narrator's image of "brother and sister" that suggests a deep and strong but simple and innocent bond between Strether and Maria and connect it with his (Strether's) own "image of the Babes in the Wood" late in the novel: "They now took on to his fancy, Miss Gostrey and he, the image of the Babes in the Wood; they could trust the merciful elements to let them continue in peace" (488). Strether has developed his own understanding of what the narrator hints about his subsequent relationship with Maria and has found a concrete expression for it. Significantly, then, he has taken the narrator's image and made a story out of it. Also, he has taken the narrator's image farther with his suggestion of the melancholy irony and humor that he directs at himself for his ignorance and confusion. And Strether has also taken the narrator's image farther with his suggestion of the surprise that *both* Maria and he feel as a result of Chad's prolonged absence. Like the surprised and unknowing Babes in the Ballad who wait in vain for their relief from the Woods, the surprised and unknowing Strether and Maria, as he conceives, wait in vain for their relief from the confusion that Chad's mysterious disappearance generates. The element of "surpris[e,]" as Strether indicates to Maria a little earlier in the novel, has made him open-minded, observant, and receptive to change (447). Even as James connects the narrator's image with the reflector's, he allows the latter's to give an ironic twist to the former's, for he allows the latter's imagination to grow beyond the former's.[11]

Indeed, Strether's imagination gradually creates an epistemological pattern as it develops meanings. For the orchestrative imagination works in conjunction with the perceptive imagination. To comprehend a meaning is to rely on one's own ability to create coherence, and thus to gradually create a pattern with purpose and causality. Because meanings gradually emerge for Strether, even when the different parts of a perception make a meaning hang "beautifully together" to create an epistemological pattern, there is "still a loose end" that has to be put in place (397). Strether's vital, dynamic and interpretive imagination meanders forward through intricate passages - as James writes in his Preface, "through winding passages" - because of a desire to create or continue a pattern (*AN* 316). For instance, when Strether hears Jim Pocock's fable of the Newsome females' quiet feeding-time, he takes the metaphorical threads he finds in this fable and embroiders them into an intricate design:

> "They don't lash about and shake the cage," said Jim, who seemed pleased with his analogy; "and it's at feeding-time that they're quietest. But they always get there."
> 'They do indeed - they always get there!" Strether replied with a laugh that justified his confession of nervousness. He disliked to be talking sincerely of Mrs Newsome with Pocock ...But there was something he wanted to know, a need created in him by her recent intermission, by his having given from the first so much, as now more than ever appeared to him, and got so little. It was as if a queer truth in his companion's metaphor had rolled over him with a rush. She *had* been quiet at feeding-time; she had fed, and Sarah had fed with her, out of the big bowl of all his recent communication, his vividness and pleasantness, his ingenuity and even his eloquence, while the current of her response had steadily run thin. (333)

Strether develops Jim's metaphor of food by giving it a depth and a concrete and specific meaning: writing itself, that is, his own letters. The mother and daughter have been feeding "out of the big bowl of all his recent free communication". And to Jim's metaphor of keeping quiet in the cage Strether gives the specific meaning of Mrs. Newsome's decreasing current of response. Thus the pattern-maker gradually seems to diminish the loose ends and to continue to add to the pattern. Indeed "the growing rose of observation ... in which he could bury his nose even to wantonness" is Strether's romantic image for his gradually developing imaginative consciousness (397). Late in the novel Strether, then, comes a long way from the disillusioned protagonist whose "few germs" of consciousness that do sprout out of his second visit to Paris seem to be the butt of James's inexorable irony early in the novel (116). At that early stage Strether's erring "fancy" lavishes futile and "hungry gazes" at "lemon-coloured volumes" which create the illusion of "fresh ... fruit on the tree" and which tempt him to fall into the banality and barrenness of imperceptiveness (116). Now, however, the "few germs" of consciousness have produced the intricately patterned "rose of observation," which continues to blossom, that is, to grow. And such blossoming is exemplified in the growth of Strether's narrative authority.

The first stage of the blossoming of Strether's narrative authority can be seen in his decision to give Waymarsh a detailed account of his first visit to the Boulevard Malsherbes. James underlines the point that Strether, who earlier "can't talk of [Mrs Newsome]" to Maria (99), makes quite an ado about his role as a teller of the story of his meeting with Chad's friend: "'I've all sorts of things to tell you!' - and he put it in a way that was a virtual hint to Waymarsh to help him to enjoy the telling" (129). In his determination to "tell" Waymarsh about his first experience at the Boulevard Malsherbes, and in his desire to "enjoy the telling," Strether shows essential attributes of storytelling. He intends to develop his manner of telling, to entertain the morose and rigid Waymarsh, to find his own way out of confusions, and to be morally aware. Thus, inexperienced in the art of storytelling as he is at this point, Strether's burden becomes rather heavy and he winds up with "I guess I don't know anything!" (131). But to be "reduced" to the state of knowing "nothing" of Chad's story turns out to be an "enlarging" experience, for it makes possible the rejection of the story of Chad's affair authored by Mrs. Newsome, and the beginning of Strether's own readings of the story of the relation that he finds for himself when he comes to Paris (131). It also makes possible the rejection of his preconceived uneasiness with "any acceptance of Paris" (118). As a teller, Strether establishes his desire to begin at the beginning, that is, to be a reader, and thus to be a seeker with an open mind: "I'm not a bit sure [about my not liking little Bilham for his liking Paris] - its ... one of the things I want to find out" (132).

To be the teller of a story, then, is also to be a reader and thus to make the attempt to find out about the self and the other as seekers. The scene of the watcher (Strether) watching a watcher (little Bilham) at the end of Book Two is significant because it demonstrates Strether's first attempt to watch the watcher within and without. This scene illustrates Strether's first glimpse of his realization that watching is a continual activity because the subject of observation never yields stability and uniformity of interpretation: "[Strether's] interest [in watching] was affected by the young man's not being Chad. Strether wondered at first if he were perhaps Chad altered" (124). Just as he watches the other watcher, and realizes that the watcher is not Chad but an entirely different person, so, as he finds out, the Chad of the present is an entirely different person from the Chad of the past, and so too, as he will find out later, the present Strether is not the same as the past Strether. This scene foreshadows Strether's subsequent understanding that to be a continual seeker is to realize that nothing, which is subjected to growth, is ever final or unchangeable. The object of observation, whether the self or the other turns out to be entirely different from his initial impression of that object, and thus, entirely beyond his epistemological grasp:

> The balcony, the distinguished front, testified suddenly, for Strether's fancy, to something that was up and up; they placed the whole case materially, and as by an admirable image, on a level that he found himself at the end of another moment rejoicing to think he might reach. The young man looked at him still, he looked at the young man; and the issue, by a rapid process, was that this knowledge of a perched privacy appeared to him the last of luxuries. (125)

As "the distinguished front," the balcony is the alluring appearance that is well beyond Strether's imaginative grasp. The watcher's sense of being watched by another watcher, however, results in the sudden spark of an affinity between the two that places them together as though in "a perched privacy". For watching the watcher makes Strether faintly and vaguely aware of the self in the other and the other in himself.[12] Strether has become vaguely aware that the distance which separates him from the watcher on "the distinguished front" is also a distance that separates the Strether who "might reach" it from the Strether on the street. He is beginning to be vaguely and intuitively aware of the change in himself that is ahead. Thus the Strether on the street "rejoic[es] to think he might reach" such an emblematic "level" and height ("up and up")[13] and make some sense of what is beneath the "distinguished front". For at this point his self-identity is only a vain appearance: Who is this Lambert Strether, he wonders, whose name is on the "green covers" of a Review on "economics, politics, ethics" that after all is "no tribute to letters" (117). As in the Preface James mentions that Strether's "view" "change[s]" from "green" to "yellow" (*AN* 314), so in the novel he demonstrates how the reflector moves from the "green" of imaginative immaturity to the "yellow" of imaginative maturity, for he moves from the "green" covers to the "lemon" covers, that is, from a prosaic, and non-literary Review to imaginative literature, for example, the emotionally charged works of "the great romancer," Victor Hugo (276).

His movement towards literary narratives, then, represents his quest for self-identity. Although aware of his "reduced" condition, Strether struggles hard to preserve his "little scrap of an identity" by way of the Review (100-101). But the Review merely exemplifies to Mrs. Newsome's ambassador his dependence on Mrs. Newsome. As Susan Mizruchi claims, an effect of the "expanding consumer-capitalist world of mid nineteenth- to early twentieth century America" can be felt in the fragmentation within selves that "throw[s] into question the very possibility of an integrated personality".[14] The name on the green cover does not reveal an integrated personality, but the glaring absence of one: "it should have been, for anything like glory, that he was on the cover because he was Lambert Strether" (115). Consequently, it points out that Strether has become a disposable commodity owned by Mrs. Newsome, and as such he is as deficient in identity as the nameless product manufactured by the Newsomes. According to Michael Wutz, Strether's identity is "a borrowed one, existing as the extension of another person," and the green cover functions as "a paper carapace" that covers up his "real identity".[15] I, however, read James as underscoring at this point that finding himself immersed in the prosaic and non-imaginative world of economics, politics, and ethics, Strether is consumed by a sense of his own emotional barrenness. Hence, because of his emotionally unfulfilled state, at this point, Strether's sense of an identity is not so much hidden as absent: "But what am I to myself?" he laments to little Bilham (215). For Strether the Review only points to "a little scrap of an identity" because it is an ironical comment on a superficial life whose lack of substance reveals an economic, political and ethical plight. It seems as though his self-identity depends on his engagement in works that may fill up his emotional vacuum. Hence he turns the covers to plunge into depths of the imaginative world of narratives.

Likewise, Strether, an editor of a moderate Woollett Review, finds it necessary to develop into the reader of stories that are written in the appearances of other people. For, to make a meaning is to read a story. Thus, early in the text, he asks Maria, "You mean that just your hour with him told you so much of [Chad's] story?" (179). It then is the observant Maria's example that Strether follows as he tries to read "the whole of a story" in Chad's genial tone and protective attitude towards Jeanne (218). But he fails to read the "whole story" and reads only the story that Chad's appearance tells him. Likewise, it seems to Strether that he has read Mme de Vionnet's "whole story" when she talks to him about her trust in Chad: "Her face, with what he had by this time grasped, told him more than her words; whether something had come into it, or whether he only read clearer, her whole story - what at least he took for such - reached out for him" (365). Although Strether perceives Marie's "disguised suppressed passion" in her face, he takes this to be the "whole" story only to realize later that her disguise works in more ways than he has guessed, and that her "suppressed" passion is not quite the entire story (366).

Although these attempts to read the "whole" story contribute to Strether's development as a reader, ironically, when he abandons his presumption of reading the "whole" story he becomes a more acute reader. Thus when Mamie lets him know that her trip to Paris has "suited" her well, Strether reads the "story of her being ready to help him" (384). It is not the story of her entire life that he reads but a part of that entire story. And, in Waymarsh's straw hat and buttonhole adorned with a fresh rose, Strether reads the "story" of a particular phase in the former's life: his early morning "adventure" with Mrs. Pocock at the Marche aux Fleurs (406). Further, the "many pieces" of the story of ambassadorship, including the inflexible Sarah's representation of her mother, and the infatuated Waymarsh's representation of Sarah, "all" fall "into a close rapid order" for Strether as his conversation with Waymarsh reveals to him "what had happened" between Sarah and Waymarsh in Strether's absence (408). If there is a need to mention that "all" the "many pieces [that] ha[ve] to fit themselves" seem to have fallen in "a close rapid order," then James suggests that Strether has come to realize that the stories are never "whole" also because too often the "many pieces" do not fall into order, for too often the "ambiguous," puzzling, incoherent elements defy meaning-making attempts (408). It is with this acute awareness, then, that Strether becomes such a close reader of the discrepancies between the stories that people suggest or tell him and the stories he reads in their appearance that, as he goes over the scene on the river, he is quick to observe how Mme de Vionnet's appearance has not "matched her story" (467).

Because he develops into an acute reader of other people's stories, Strether develops into the teller of other people's stories. Thus he undertakes the telling of the "wonderful story" that he himself comes to read as a result of Mme de Vionnet and her work (362). In his letters to Mrs. Newsome, Strether tells the remarkable story of Chad's remarkable transformation at Mme de Vionnet's capable hands. This story, the product of Strether's sophisticated imagination, is reflective of his wonder and admiration for Marie de Vionnet's style. A "wonderful" story is a story about an admirably sophisticated and intelligent, sensitive and passionate woman who has separated from her husband a long time ago and who has amazingly accomplished a remarkable transformation in her lover. Therefore a "wonderful" story is about an amazing and unfathomable grace and clearly has nothing to do with petty and vulgar liaisons. Thus the point of view Strether establishes in this story is Mme de Vionnet's, and consequently the opposite of the Woollett point of view. As the teller of a "wonderful" story about the woman who fills him with wonder, Strether seems to be in possession of Keats's "Negative Capability, that is, when a man is capable of being in uncertainties, mysteries, doubts, without any irritable reaching after fact and reason."[16] Strether is repeatedly struck and fascinated by the "wonderful" Marie de Vionnet because she is "so odd a mixture of lucidity and mystery" (354).

But by using the words "lucidity" and "type" James subtly indicates that as teller of Mme de Vionnet's story, Strether often reaches out for an epistemological grasp with the arm of reason in defiance of negative capability. He depends upon her "lucidity" to guide him through the "mystery" just as he depends on the simplification of her mystifying character to a certain extent with the help of her "type". When he sees a "deep person" in Marie, it is important for him to smooth out some of his puzzlement with the help of "harmony and reason" (476). Indeed, Strether's imagination fails him whenever he separates his rational from his imaginative faculty and searches for "harmony" in "reason." And, as a result of the occasional encroachment of the Woollett values into Strether's consciousness, he often (and inharmoniously) does separate these two faculties. This may well have been one reason why James, in the Preface, emphatically points out that, although Strether possesses "imagination galore," he does not possess "imagination in *predominance*" (*AN* 310). As Strether himself is aware, he clings to "reason" so stubbornly that it might even appear perverse: It strikes him that he attempts "to show [Sarah Pocock] how, even perversely, he clung to his rag of reason" (420). He argues efficiently, as Maria Gostrey discovers early in the novel, and thus prefers to be consistently dependent on "reason" (190). But the "only logic" (the logic of conscience that prevents him from getting any tangible benefits) that he can cling to at the novel's conclusion and which does not tear into shreds as a consequence, is the result of the "wonderful impressions" he has received with the help of his imaginative faculty (512). Whenever he tries to make an epistemological grasp with the help of reason alone, Strether feels disturbed. For example, he comprehends, and is touched by, the sincerity in Mme de Vionnet's utterance about the happiness to give rather than to receive, but he is "puzzled" because there is another shade in "the quaver of her quietness" which he cannot reasonably explain, and thus he is "troubled" (481).

Strether's attempt to reasonably explain everything manifests itself in his troubled attempt to tell "All" about Marie de Vionnet (362). To try to tell "All" is to try to grasp something that is beyond his reach, for there will always be something about Marie or about her relationship with Chad that he will not be able to interpret or explain, as the metaphors of "the clouds of explanation" and "the wild weed of delusion" suggest (157). When Mme de Vionnet asks Strether to tell Mrs. Newsome "all," he takes the word in its literality, and therefore does not understand what she means (242). Thus in reply he asks in puzzlement "All?" (242). What she means is for Strether specifically to tell Mrs. Newsome "all" that is of any significance, that is, to tell Mrs. Newsome that he "like[s]" Marie herself and her daughter (243). For "truth" to Marie is not an all-inclusive concept but the interpreter's particular impression: "*any* truth" (242). As he attempts to tell "all" of Mme de Vionnet's story to Mrs. Newsome, Strether does not conceive of a particular impression but of several impressions. So voluminous are these impressions that Strether's letters to Mrs. Newsome are marked by an "unimpaired frequency," which only indicates that "their problem" has become "more complicated" (246). The problem, as James subtly implies, begins when Strether attempts to tell the entire story of Chad's relationship with a special woman and to explain why he (Strether) finds her so adorable. For soon after Strether thinks that he has told "all" about Marie to Mrs. Newsome he feels dissatisfied with himself as the teller of her story (282). Thus, in response to Mrs. Newsome's telegram, the frustrated Strether devotes himself to the "copious composition of a letter," which represents his role as storyteller, only to tear up "the numerous sheets of his unfinished composition ... into small pieces" (287). It seems to him that instead of conceiving and articulating all the facts that make up the whole story in his letters, he is left with the incoherence of its fragmentary "pieces."

The attempt to tell Marie's whole story, then, enables Strether ultimately to discover its ungraspability. Amidst all the relics of the past Strether finds the emblem of the grandeur of human accomplishments that have made a mark even on Chad. But as he looks around her apartments, he is overwhelmed by "all the indescribable," that is, "all" that he feels but that is beyond his ability to describe and narrate just as he feels it (362). The negatively capable Strether has not managed to read and therefore to tell Marie's whole story, for as he sees the wonderful story, it continues to change and therefore does not end. In regards to Chad, perhaps this incomplete story is full of the promise of future possibilities. As he tells the young man (who "might after all be capable of much [harm]"), "for you, from such a woman there will always be something to be got" (502). But this story is also incomplete because, mystified as he is by the woman in whom "there was always more behind what she showed, and more and more again behind that," Strether is hardly in the position to grasp and to narrate Marie's whole story (481). And as his interpretations continue to change, so his telling is never complete, and so the epistemological patterns he attempts to create are never complete and continually changing.

Nevertheless, when he abandons the ungraspable project of reading and telling a whole story about a person, Strether develops the ability to take control of, and not be controlled by, a point of view. He comes to realize, as he tells Miss Barrace, that certain "links" will be "missing" and certain "connexions" will remain "unnamed," but that does not prevent the tellers from entering "the heart of their subject" and interpreting a purpose (403). He now realizes that although the tellers may not receive and articulate the whole story, they may receive "the whole *point*" (403, my emphasis). Late in the novel, then, Strether comes a long way from the time when certain words appear "exorbitant" (244). He has acquired ease with words now as a result of the growth in his imaginative consciousness. If he laments that his relationship with Chad has become "horribly complex," then it is because he no longer expresses Chad's "point of view" (488). And although his point of view may be sympathetic to Mme de Vionnet's, in his decision to return home (discussed later in this essay) Strether shows how he also moves away from her point of view.

Mme de Vionnet herself urges upon Strether the need to develop his own specific view. Marie de Vionnet, the artist who creates a remarkable text in the transformed Chad, is interested in Strether's development and articulation of his own point of view and his own style. Thus to Strether's question, "Hasn't Chad talked to you [of his mother]?" she thoughtfully replies, "Yes, a great deal - immensely. But not from your point of view" (282). Strether's own manner of telling will reveal his own interpretive imagination. Marie de Vionnet is well aware that an interpreter, although aware of different points of view, cannot be emotionally and intellectually committed to various points of view, and therefore cannot be persuasive about the various points of view that circulate in the environment. The interpreter, then, needs to develop her own meaningful point of view alone, and thus her own convincing manner of conveying a perspective. She asks Strether to "[t]ell [Mrs Newsome] I've been good for [Chad]" because she is convinced that this is what Strether himself "think[s]" (244). She now sets her mind to helping Strether develop an eloquence and narrative authority that can persuade Mrs. Newsome into a new point of view.

Hence the discovery of his own point of view leads Strether to tell his own story. Thus after the Pococks' departure he gives Maria "the view, vivid with a hundred more touches than we can reproduce, of what happened for him that morning," that is, the morning of the Pococks' departure (442). As the narrator points out, Strether gives Maria a view of what has "happened for him" and not of what has happened for the Pococks. And to tell about what has "happened" on a particular occasion, James suggests, is to tell a short story, as it were. Strether, then, has begun to exert narrative authority over a short story about his own life. And if the narrator cannot "reproduce" the "hundred ... touches" that Strether produces, then in a manner, these hundred touches are beyond the narrator's narrative grasp. If Strether's imaginative consciousness continues to grow in refinement and thus his ability to create images moves beyond the narrator's, it is not surprising that the narrator at this late stage in the novel cannot "reproduce" the center of consciousness's copious and singular narrative "touches".

And now that Strether has found the narrative authority to tell a story about himself, he enters the picture he sees around him in his excursion into the country and becomes part of his surroundings: "Not a single one of his observations but somehow fell into a place in it; not a breath of the cooler evening that wasn't somehow a syllable of the text. The text was simply, when condensed, that in *these* places such things were, and that if it was in them one elected to move about one had to make one's account with what one lighted on" (458). James's emphasis on "these" brings out the significance of the environment for Strether's selfhood. Paul Beidler observes that in this scene Strether jumps out of the world of fiction, the painting within the frame, as it were, and steps on the frame of the painting, and thus "from his story to ours," for it is here that Strether "leaves his past as a fictional hero and steps back to read his own story as it unfolds from a detached vantage point".[17] And Armstrong observes that Strether's attempt "to understand others ...increases his understanding of himself."[18] I would go further and say that, as a result, he now realizes that his own story comes out of and blends with other people's stories: "he had never yet so struck himself as engaged with others and in midstream of his drama" (457-458). The center of consciousness has "elected to move about" these places because of his recognition of the interconnection between himself and the surroundings which include the space *and* the people. Indeed, Strether's understanding of his own connection with the human community has loomed so large for him at this point that he has "peopled all his space" (458). According to William Goetz, in the country Strether's imagination "sets him up for his greatest fall in the novel, a fall which will almost wreck him".[19] Certainly Strether indulges in some self-deception in this scene, but what makes it remarkable is that he is himself aware of his "happy illusion" (457). Thus, as he sits in the little building and watches the human scene on the river from his "post," a scene that "sharp[ly] arrest[s]" his attention, James suggests that he represents the artist in his house of fiction (460):

The "small and primitive pavilion that, at the garden's edge, almost overhung the water" and that includes a "platform, slightly raised" and "a protecting rail and a projected roof" (459), is a version of the Jamesian house of fiction because here Strether's imaginative consciousness indulges in reading and creating fictions as though he continues to look through "the oblong window of the picture-frame" even as he closely observes and interprets the human scene, as it unfolds for him on the symbolical water, from his balconied aperture (452). It may appear as though the connection he feels with his environment is only an ironic connection, and therefore simply a misreading on Strether's part. But because he becomes a part of this environment, he is able to comprehend that the couple in the boat have such an "expert, familiar, frequent" air about them "that this wouldn't at all events be ...[their] first time [on this river]" (461). And because Strether looks out of the house of fiction, he finds his emotional and social connections with this environment. These connections enable him to recognize and identify the young man and woman as Chad and Marie. Indeed, Strether's position (that of being planted in the house of fiction) illustrates his sense of connections, and hence his recognition of the complex "intimate" relationship between Chad and Mme de Vionnet, and his own "intervention" that has "absolutely aided and intensified their intimacy": "[H]e had absolutely become, himself, with his perceptions and his mistakes, ...almost an added link and certainly a common priceless ground for them to meet upon" (477-478). His own story in Paris, then, is part of "the typical tale of Paris," and to be "mixed up" with it is not simply to be mixed up with "the little" and the banal, "the fierce" and "the sinister," but also with "the acute" (472).

What makes his own story, which is part of the tale of Paris, especially "acute" is his understanding that, like Paris, there is nothing final and stable within himself: "[W]hat I want is a thing I've ceased to measure or even to understand" (443). He cannot measure and therefore does not understand what he "want[s]" because he understands the principle of constant change within himself. He now understands that there must be "room" for all the "alteration" of his interpretations (447). According to Kaston, Strether ultimately fails "to change enough to lay claim to the material of his life and the novel."[20] But as James implies, late in the novel Strether begins to understand that his life is to continue "transforming beyond recognition," and that he has come a long way from the time when he has conceived it as a "conveniently uniform thing" (497). As Bell asserts, Strether is "a man of artistic sensibility who finds his *life* to have been a story inadequately told - and must find a way of still telling it."[21] I would add that late in the novel Strether demonstrates his artistic sensibility in such a way that he makes his life the story that *continues* to change. His life becomes the story in which there will always be a "margin" for revisions. For "alteration" is the basic plot of the story of his life.

By contrast, as author of her own version of Chad's life in Paris, Mrs. Newsome is thoroughly opposed to any kind of "alteration". Julie Rivkin argues that Mrs. Newsome is "almost a parody of the absent author who 'works the whole thing out in advance' only to find the scheme revised in the act of execution".[22] Thus when a revision has been made by her first, deviating ambassador, she tries to annul the revision by sending a new delegation. As Mrs. Newsome resists change so she resists growth. In her opposition to any kind of alteration, it is also possible to see in Mrs. Newsome the stance of a historian who claims to have found an absolute truth, and who therefore does not acknowledge the role of the interpretive and orchestrative imagination, and thus of the inventive faculty, on the *narrative* of history.[23] As he notices Mrs. Newsome's unopened letter to her daughter while he waits in Sarah's hotel room, Strether becomes engrossed by "the sharp downstrokes of her pen" because "they ... stood for a probable absoluteness in any decree of the writer" (375). Mrs. Newsome's unopened letter to Sarah momentarily evokes the sense of "a sudden queer power to intensify the reach of its author" in Strether (375). In the past he has been persuaded so effectively by her narrative of Chad's life that the thought of seeing the woman in Chad's life does not even occur to him on his own. This is what Strether presumably remembers as he observes her unopened letter to her daughter, and what he finds "queer" about the "power" of this "author". It is a "queer" power that an author exercises when the impact of the text on the reader is to make the latter unquestioning. But James's attention to the sharp downstrokes points out that truth for Mrs. Newsome is rigid, stable and unchangeable: it is "absolute". Thus there is "no room [and] no margin" for revision in the text she authorizes relying on the fact of Chad's disinclination to return home (447). In turning away from the letter, then, Strether symbolically expresses his rejection of Mrs. Newsome's authoritative version of Chad's romantic relationship: "He looked at Sarah's name and address ...as if he had been looking hard into her mother's face, and then turned away from it as if the face had declined to relax" (375-376). It seems to Strether as he turns away from the sealed letter that he turns away from the impermeable Mrs. Newsome and the single-layered, flat and static story she has authored, and hence from whatever narrative authority she has exercised on him in the past.[24]

What James implies by making Strether see Mrs. Newsome in her letter is that, as a consequence of the collapse of her narrative authority, she has been stripped of the status of an author and reduced to the objectified status of the text that she has authored. Strether himself articulates this view when he tells Maria, "there's no room left; no margin ... for any alteration. She's filled as full, packed as tight, as she'll hold" (447). Strether's concept of "alteration" suggests his point of view that both reader and writer have nothing final or absolute to claim. But Mrs. Newsome, who adamantly refuses to budge from the text she authorizes, proves to be nothing more than hard "cold thought" (447). For she has become a self-limiting text that insists on a single interpretation. In Strether's eyes, then, she becomes equivalent to the text she has authored. Clearly, Mrs. Newsome's physical absence from James's novel corresponds with and is suggestive of her failure to establish herself as an individual. Hence we are given only a view of the cover and never of the content of her letter because her text lacks the depth that provokes continual interpretive efforts. For the cover of her text is expressive of the content that resists change. As she has become a superficial text, we are given only a superficial glimpse of her letter.

A way in which Strether's understanding of the principle of change manifests itself is through his awareness that his changing imaginative consciousness continually alternates between the stages of perceptual growth and decline. It is possible to see the cause of this perceptual decline in the periodic resurgence of the Woollett values in Strether that make him separate his rational faculty from his imaginative faculty mentioned earlier. Strether conceives the perceptual decline in his consciousness as an abyss of confusion and infirmity.[25] Thus his imaginative consciousness seems to plunge violently down into an abyss when he experiences a resurgence of Woollett rationalism: "He had wondered vaguely - turning over many things in the fidget of his thoughts - if Mamie *were* as pretty as Woollett published her; as to which issue seeing her now again was to be so swept away by Woollett's opinion that this consequence really let loose for the imagination an avalanche of others" (324). The Woollett air of sound sense brought in by the new ambassadors of Mrs. Newsome thrusts Strether's consciousness from its perch and overburdens it, and consequently, like an "avalanche," it plunges uncontrollably down to the stage of decline. And later, when the Woollett values encroach into him again and stir within him the thought of "wrongdoer[s]," and of "the silver stream of impunity," and thus when he "revert[s] in thought to his old tradition, the one he had been brought up on," it seems to him that he once again loses perceptual ground and tumbles down (473): "This was a deeper depth than any, and with no foresight, scarcely with any care, as to what he should bring up. He almost wondered if he didn't *look* demoralized and disreputable" (474). He feels "demoralized and disreputable" because at this moment his imaginative faculty has been overpowered by the world of Woollett rationalism. Clearly, whenever Strether's rational faculty is disconnected from his imaginative faculty, the result is his sense of abysmal confusion. But if his consciousness drops into a metaphorical abyss of imperceptiveness as a result of perceptual decline, then it also gains new ground as a result of perceptual growth. Hence the sexual element in Marie's relationship with Chad becomes, for Strether, a "technical" matter that does not displace the "virtu[ous]" element: "[Little Bilham's definition of the Marie-Chad relationship] was but a technical lie - he classed the attachment as virtuous. That was a view for which much was to be said - and the virtue came out for me hugely" (493). Consequently, on his last visit to Chad, his message "placed his present call immediately on solid ground" (499).

In his Preface, James illustrates his understanding of a rhythm of growth and decline in his protagonist's consciousness through the image of circular movement. Hence he writes, "[t]he revolution performed by Strether ...was to have nothing to do with any *betise* of the imputably 'tempted' state; ...his lifelong trick of intense reflexion ...was to bring him out ... through alternations of darkness and light" (*AN* 316). Strether makes a "revolution" not simply because his consciousness undergoes radical change as a result of his symbolical journey. Nor is it simply because, like a celestial body,[26] a planet, that makes its "revolution" around another celestial body, a star, Strether revolves around another character (for example, Mrs. Newsome or Mme de Vionnet) whom he has undertaken to represent. He makes a "revolution" also because, like a celestial body in a star system, he makes cyclical movements, and these motions (or this performance) suggest a circular rhythm, as does the image of "compass" discussed earlier. To make a "revolution," as Teahan argues, is to make a turn, a deviation.[27] To make a circular pattern is also to make a turn. For the circular pattern involves not simply a forward movement, but also a backward movement in the sense that the line of the circle returns, or turns back, to the point of origin. The line of the circle moves on forward until it reaches a climax and then arcs down to move backward, but from that downward arc it curves up to reach the climax again. When the author writes that Strether performs a "revolution," he implies that by continually moving out of and returning to the point at which he begins, the protagonist moves continually through "alternations of darkness and light," and thus his consciousness moves forward as it becomes refined, and turns backward as it falls into decline.

Interestingly, Strether too makes use of a circular image, the Berne clock, near the end of the novel in connection with his understanding of the rhythm of growth and decline, that is, of performance and waiting, within his consciousness. Thus, on the eve of his departure Maria and Strether look back in time at a succession of events they have lived through, and he talks about his having gone "in" after having come "out":

> He was out, in truth, as far as it was possible to be, and must now rather bethink himself of getting in again. He found on the spot the image of his recent history; he was like one of the figures of the old clock at Berne. *They came out, on one side, at their hour, jigged along their little course in the public eye, and went in on the other side. He too jigged his little course -* him too a modest retreat awaited. (509)

Strether has become so adept at creating coherent images late in the novel that he comes up with "the image of his recent history," that is, with a terse, subtle, and imaginative expression of the story of his visit to Paris. As a result of his interest in reading stories closely and in telling stories articulately, out of the incoherence of changeability and instability, he brings some kind of coherence into his life. As he now thoroughly realizes, this story is about the continual change in his consciousness as it alternates between the stages of growth or performing and of decline or waiting. After his own performance ("jigg[ing] ...in the public eye") comes his motionlessness ("modest retreat"). What he has not realized earlier is that the moment of motionlessness is as necessary as the moment of performance. Thus, early in the novel as he speaks with little Bilham in Gloriani's garden, he conceives himself as futilely waiting at the station from which the metaphorical "train" of life has pulled out without him (215). Now he realizes that the motionlessness signifies his moment of rest. If he has earlier failed to board the train of life, and if he feels himself waiting even as he speaks with little Bilham, then later, as his Berne clock metaphor of jigging figures signifies, he is engaged in action. A little earlier, although Strether begins to perceive the "charm" of "postponements," the charm is "melancholy": He wonders if he is heading towards "the wind up of his career" (488-489). But at the end of the novel Strether shows through his image of the jigging and waiting figures on the Berne clock, how he himself realizes the rhythmic relation between waiting and performing. Because of this understanding Strether now conceives himself as in "full possession of the key ... to what has lately happened," that is, as exerting narrative authority over the story of his life (498). "[A]nd the effect of it was to enable him quite to play with ... the key [to what had lately happened]" (499). To "play" with it, James suggests, is the effect of Strether's having made the narrative connection between the stage of growth, or performance, and the stage of decline, or waiting, in the story of his changing consciousness.

In the Preface James suggests that the protagonist's experience of waiting and performance bears a curious resemblance to the novel's experience of "breaks and resumptions":

> 'The Ambassadors' had been, all conveniently, 'arranged for'; its first appearance was from month to month, in 'The North American Review' during 1903, and I had been open from far back to any pleasant provocation for ingenuity that might reside in one's actively adopting--so as to make it, in its way, a small compositional law--recurrent breaks and resumptions. I had made up my mind here regularly to exploit and enjoy these often rather rude jolts-having found, as I believed, an admirable way to it (*AN* 317).

This same "compositional law" of "breaks and resumptions" that James makes up his mind to "exploit and enjoy" finds its way into the "scheme" he adopts for his protagonist. Clearly it is possible to see that "the admirable way" to handle the "rude jolts" is to create the consciousness of a similar pattern of "breaks and resumptions" for the protagonist. Strether then becomes a figure for the novel itself. Further, as the protagonist conceives his going "in" and waiting, so James conceives the "ins" which mark the composition's entry into its "problem" (*AN* 319). Likewise, as the protagonist conceives his coming "out" and performing, so James conceives the "outs" which mark the composition's exit from its "problem" (*AN* 319). And Strether realizes that although the stage of performance may be "little," and consequently it changes or breaks off and gives way to that of motionlessness, the rhythm of performance and motionlessness does not subside.

To "jig" is perhaps to engage in an act that is frivolous but that is also exhilarating. According to Pierre Walker, Strether's use of "jig" instead of "dance" indicates the protagonist's deprecatory attitude towards his own efforts to achieve anything. Walker argues that Strether's image of the Berne clock, which includes his image of himself as one of the mechanical bears, expresses Strether's "sense of futility".[28] But, as James points out through the indeterminacy of the image, it is also possible to see that the jig is a *lively* dance. And as such it is suggestive not simply of frivolities and belittling activities, but of a buoyant celebration of life, and thus of stimulating and rejuvenating activity. According to Allen F. Stein, the mechanical figures of the Berne clock are an image of circularity that expresses Strether's "despairing deterministic outlook": James depicts the circular quest romance of Romantic literature in "realistic" terms which show that, although he sees a victory of consciousness in his protagonist that separates him from the mechanical figures of the clock, Strether's impression of "having travelled in a circle" makes him sardonically "see himself as having run almost mechanically a preordained course of circularity."[29] But James gives his readers the freedom of choice to see the metaphor of the Berne clock not simply as Strether's image of circularity with a sardonic twist to his "victory of consciousness". For it also suggests Strether's ability to laugh healthily at himself. Thus it shows his coming to terms with, (that is, his own "ingen[ious]" "exploit[ation]" of) the breaks and resumptions in the perceptual growth of his consciousness, even without separating himself from the diminutive and mechanical figures.

By the end of the novel, then, Strether shows how with his imagination, and hence with his ability to make narrative connections, he comes to terms with transitoriness. If the figures of the Berne clock go into an enclosure, they also come out into the open and resume their course. Consequently, if Strether conceives himself as having no choice but to go "in," he also conceives himself as having the freedom to come "out" repeatedly. Thus he now shows awareness of how he receives and makes use of his little freedom of action over and over again. If early in the novel Strether laments not having even "the illusion of freedom," then late in the novel he realizes that he too has the freedom to act, however brief that action may be (215). The hour of freedom certainly is transient. This is why "the clock of ...freedom" that Strether has heard in Paris evokes his consciousness of his own "fleeting hour" (215). Indeed, as Adeline Tintner observes, the image of clocks in this novel is expressive of transience and the approach of death.[30] Early in the novel the clock of freedom ticks so loudly in Strether's consciousness that it reminds him more of transitoriness than of freedom. Thus, in the garden of the Tuileries, "[h]e watched little brisk figures, figures whose movement was as the tick of the great Paris clock, take their smooth diagonal from point to point" (111). At that point, the fleeting hour evokes such a sense of the diminution of the freedom of action in Strether that he reads the actions of humans as mechanically contrived and controlled movements of stiff little figures. For, at that point, he does not conceive their little movements as having the order and harmony of the pattern of a dance. But late in the novel, when Strether conceives himself as a figure among other figures, whose story is a part of the story of others, what he observes is his own "mistakes" and his "perceptions" just as he observes others'. Hence, by connecting the symbol of the clock-like movements of little human figures in the garden of the Tuileries with the metaphor of the Berne clock's jigging figures, Strether reveals that he has learned to connect himself with other little human figures. For, by connecting the symbol of the Paris clock with the metaphor of the Berne clock, he reveals that he has learned to connect "mistakes" with "perceptions". Consequently he observes not simply the little controlled movements of little figures but, as his use of the word "jig" reveals, also a pattern of steps that is created by these little figures who dance to the rhythm of gain and loss, and therefore who connect loss with gain. As his image of himself as a figure that jigs in and out on the Berne clock suggests, Strether demonstrates how he has learned to keep time with time. Indeed, it is because of the growth of his imaginative consciousness that Strether is no longer dejected or agonized by the transience of time and the sense of loss.

Consequently, to return home is the only logic that holds for Strether because with his return, although his consciousness once again faces the stage of decline and of loss, it no longer causes him unbearable disappointment and pain. According to Kaston, Strether's return home is the consequence of his filial relationship with Mrs. Newsome.[31] But as he no longer has any interaction with Mrs. Newsome, this relationship can hardly be in effect. More convincingly, as Nicola Bradbury, claims, Strether has to return home in order to preserve "the freedom of his imaginative experience".[32] Bradbury also claims that Strether's displaced position, his separation from his friends in Paris, and his consequent isolation are necessary for the preservation of this experience. Isolation, however, is not all that Strether is moving towards. For he now sees himself ready to live the life of an individual among other individuals. Thus, however secluded his life may become in Woollett, it will still be a life steeped in the awareness of other lives. Also, Strether has to go home because he refuses to be dependent upon anyone. To stay on with Maria would be to self-piteously depend on her "exquisite service, of lighted care, for the rest of his days" (511-512). Further, he has to go home because he cannot be Mme de Vionnet's, or *anybody* else's, ambassador anymore. He now has the ability to assert his own altering, fluctuating, diversifying points of view. Thus *The Ambassadors* ends when Strether's role as an ambassador ends. Having learned to authorize his own points of view, through his return to Woollett Strether figuratively announces his deviation from the ambassadorial role. In Paris we notice several ambassadors in Strether alone: he turns from representing Mrs. Newsome to Chad, and then he turns from representing Chad to Mme de Vionnet. Consequently, as Rivkin observes, in Paris Strether "denies himself experience in his own person" as a result of his ambassadorial functions.[33] I would add that late in the novel such a denial almost pushes him to a kind of metaphorical death: Strether's life is "essentially ...[brought] down ...to a function all subsidiary" to the lives of other people (427). In other words, as an ambassador if he moves up to finding himself as a part of a group, then as such he also moves down to losing his personal life. Thus, once he finds his own place in the pattern created by the figurative group of dancing figures, and thus once he understands the principle of constant change in the story of his own life, in returning to Woollett, although he may no longer actively be part of a group, as a result he will begin to live his own personal life. Also, the return to Woollett illustrates that he is now ready to establish connection with his remote past.

Early in the novel, Strether is far from grasping the narrative thread of his past, present, and future. It seems to him at the beginning of the novel that he lacks the connecting thread between his own past and present so thoroughly that the one seems irrevocably fragmented from the other. It is in Chester that he begins to be "quite disconnected from the sense of his past" (59). As a result he is agonized by his memories of his past failures as well as an unreachable past. And thus he is stuck with an "empty present" (114). For the sense of being disconnected from the past "had begun ...upstairs [in his hotel room in Chester] and before the dressing-glass that struck him as blocking further, so strangely, the dimness of the window" (59). The window represents Strether's bedimmed actual world of the present moment. And, as its view is blocked, he finds himself alienated from this actual world of the present moment. The dressing-glass on which he sees his reflected form, and which blocks the view, represents Strether's shadowy past. And the image on the glass represents the shadowy identity that is alienated from his present world.[34]

Late in the novel, however, Strether clearly finds his grasp of the narrative thread of his past, present, and future. According to Allen Menton, Strether finds his past through a direct experience of Paris and not an indirect experience of French literature.[35] And according to Armstrong, "by depicting a character's present perception of a scene through an anticipatory account of how he or she will remember it," James "couples future and past".[36] I would add that Strether connects his past, present, and future because he learns to draw the connection between the significant stages of his growth as a watcher. Walking to and from the Boulevard Malsherbes for the last time, James's reflector consciously draws a connection between his "first" and "last" days in Paris when he watches the figure on Chad's "balcony" (496-497), and again when he watches Chad's face "under the street-lamp" (504). As

James highlights Strether's ability to watch once again, so he highlights the "street-lamp," the light that enables him to watch once again. And if the word "street" subtly and vaguely evokes the first syllable of the reflector's last name, then the word "lamp" subtly and vaguely evokes the first syllable of his first name, drawing a connection between the past and future Lambert Strether. Indeed, when Strether first looks up at the continuous balcony of Chad's apartments and wonders about the possibility of being seen "in time" from that position, what he muses over is "the fine relation of part to part, and space to space," implicitly suggesting a connection between space and time (124). And when he takes his last look at that balcony he weaves the thread of connection between these two scenes (of the first and last days) through a few other scenes involving the watcher on the balcony. In one of these other scenes, as he waits alone for Chad on the latter's balcony late at night, he spends "a long time" seeing himself as part of a series of contemplative, solitarily waiting observers, little Bilham, Mamie, and Chad, as they have "hung over" the balcony (426). In each of these scenes, then, Strether sees himself through "time" - past, present, and future - as he takes up the posture of watching the watcher. Standing beyond the picture he watches, Strether shows a certain perceptive grasp over the stages of watching: He traces how he begins as a watcher who looks up at a watcher (little Bilham) on the balcony from a distance, moves up to observing the watcher (Mamie) from the room with which the balcony is attached, that is from a diminished distance, and then finally moves to the balcony itself as he watches the watcher within himself. As a result of the growth of his imaginative consciousness, Strether has found the narrative thread of the past, present, and future with which to connect the three stages he moves through as a watcher. Thus, standing in the *third story* of the Boulevard Malsherbes, in Chad's apartments, although at first he sees only a "vague vista of the successive rooms" (425), after his contemplation the vista is no longer vague, for "he passe[s] back into the rooms, the *three* that occup[y] the front and that communicate[] by wide doors," and which represent the past, present, and future (426, my emphasis).

To go a little deeper into James's depiction of Strether's grasp of the narrative thread of the past, present, and the future, let us focus on a few more details of this balcony scene. As he reflects, Strether finds himself "in possession as he never yet had been" as he "recall[s]" all that he has observed, which includes an emblematic "novel, half uncut" placed at his disposal in a "soft circle" (425). The "half uncut" novel, and therefore half read story is emblematically expressive of the story that continues into the unknown. The unread part of the novel is firmly connected with and grows from the part that has already been read as now Strether's yet-to-be-experienced future is connected with and grows from the past he has already experienced. Clearly, in his present consciousness, he is "in possession" of the narrative thread of his past and future instead of his earlier blanks. For the past, present, and future have all come together in a "circle". Hence, as the past is connected with the future, so it is connected with the present. For in the present moment he feels "the freedom that br[ings] him round again to the youth of his own that he had long ago missed. ... That was what it had become for him at this singular time, the youth he had long ago missed - a queer concrete presence, full of mystery, yet full of reality, which he could handle, taste, smell, the deep breathing of which he could positively hear" (426). If the past has become a "presence," then surely the past has become one with the present. That is, moving backwards into the past now is possible because, with the exertion of his narrative authority, such a movement circularly takes him forward into the present and future too. So forceful is his narrative authority that the events of his past come together in his negatively capable consciousness and condensed to form the image of a mysteriously tangible, living presence. It is not as if Strether has vanquished his sense of "loss," but that he has come to terms with it (426). In the past Strether's loss of a monetarily opulent future would have been an unbearable loss because in the past all he could conceive of the future was a blank. But now, because the "loss" of the past is no longer a blank but vividly substantiated as a "concrete presence," he has found the narrative thread of his life. Hence the future is no longer a blank. It may be unknown but is nevertheless material for potential stories waiting to be created and read. Thus in the concluding scene, to Maria's question "To what do you go home?" his reply is, "I don't know. There will always be something" (511). Although he does not possess the pieces of the ever-changing story of his life, he possesses the narrative thread to make connections within these pieces.

Consequently, through the exertion of his narrative authority, Strether ultimately finds his self-identity.[37] Early in the novel, it is his sense of the absence of connection between his past and his present, and thus his sense of fragmentation that prevents Strether from seeing any meaning in the name on the green cover. Kaston finds him "only Strether" despite his transformation (just as the latter finds Chad "only Chad" despite his transformation): "[implicitly] he is still prototypically ambassadorial."[38] As he has learned to connect his past with his present, Strether does not deny his identity as "Chad's mother's emissary" (497). But James suggests that at the end of the novel, the name that is no longer fixed on the green cover is suggestive of several meanings. And, as Teahan claims, his name also suggests the adjective "straighter": "'Strether' puns conspicuously on 'straight' and 'straighter.'"[39] As Strether learns to connect his present with his past and his future, he realizes that he can only try to be straight*er* now and in the future than he has been in the past. According to Ellmann, "[a]s the hero of the novel, Strether surrenders his identity to difference."[40] But it seems to me that he does not so much surrender his identity to difference as continue to create a different identity, and hence read or tell stories of his life on the basis of change. Thus now the name Strether also stretches to suggest the noun "stretcher": As he stretches because he learns to connect his past identity with his present, so he stretches because he changes. Thus if in the past he has been piqued by "his meagreness ... that sprawled ... *stretching* back like some unmapped Hinterland," then, as a result of all the changes he experiences, it is no longer his "meagreness" that stretches, but an ample imaginative consciousness that continually ventures into and reads stories about the "unmapped Hinterland[s]" within himself and about relationships between people (117, my emphasis). As Rivkin asserts, "what Strether will discover as he replaces one truth about experience with another is that there is no stopping point in this logic of revision, no superlative that will stand beyond all comparison".[41] It seems to me that this is why James uses the word "straighter" to indicate the comparative degree as for the growth of his composition, so for the growth of his protagonist (*AN* 307). Strether's understanding of the comparative case makes him come to terms as himself so with Chad as a "little" figure that is "only Chad" and as an example of remarkable transformation at the same time (494,482). It is this same understanding that James expects of his readers in coming to terms with his protagonist who is simultaneously a little figure and an example of remarkable transformation.

Notes

1. Henry James, <u>The Art of the Novel</u>, ed. R. W. B. Lewis (1934; rpr. Boston: Northeastern University Press, 1984) 317. Cited parenthetically as <u>AN</u>.
2. Henry James, (1903; London: Penguin Books, 1986) 181.
3. Maud Ellmann, "'The Intimate Difference': Power and Representation in <u>The Ambassadors</u>," <u>Henry James: Fiction as History</u>, ed. F. A. Bell (Totowa: Vision and Barnes and Noble, 1984) 100. According to Ellmann, "A site of transformation, Paris is most itself when least itself, passing towards a new translated form of being" (101). And in his reading of <u>The Ambassadors</u> in <u>Henry James and the Philisophical Novel: Being and Seeing</u> (Cambridge: Cambridge University Press, 1993), Merle A. Williams discusses "the

constantly changing phenomena that surround ...[Strether and] "the steady emergence of meaning in a variety of forms" (55,60).

4. The image of water, as I see it in The Ambassadors represents changeability and instability. On a different note, Reginald Abbott in his essay "The Incredible Floating Man," in Henry James Review 11 (1990), associates the image of water with dangerous "feminine forces of the deep" (178). And for Tony Tanner, in "The Watcher from the Balcony: Henry James's The Ambassadors," in The Critical Quarterly 8.1 (1966), the image of water in this novel is metaphorical of experience (41). Tanner observes that in this novel James depicts a "dual attitude to the great sea of life" without which "one starved" and in which "one drowned" (37). And for James Wise, in "The Floating World of Lambert Strether," in Arlington Quarterly 2 (1969) the water imagery signifies that Strether alternates between "a series of risings and plungings," and floats or drifts passively through the action, having been launched by it, rather than launching it (109).

5. For a detailed discussion of Strether's meaning-making activities, see Paul Armstrong's essay on The Ambassadors in The Challenge of Bewilderment: Understanding and Representation in James, Conrad, and Ford (Ithaca and London: Cornell University Press, 1987). As Armstrong observes, "Chad's transformation raises basic questions about meaning, interpretation, and reality" (67). And as Armstrong argues, bewilderment provides Strether with the "occasion for exploring the acts of reconfiguring his world to which it gives rise" (77).

6. I associate the world of Woollett with rationality, as opposed to imagination, because it is clearly and obviously governed by sense: It is sensible for Chad to return home and carry on his father's "big brave bouncing business" (96). It is also sensible for Chad to marry because then he will have children, and thus ensure the perpetuation of the Newsome line. There is no vagueness about the values of Woollett then. For everything seems to be clarified and well-planned to carry out the dictates of good sense.

7. Sheila Teahan, The Rhetorical Logic of Henry James (Baton Rouge and London: Louisiana State University Press, 1995) 2. In her essay on The Ambassadors, she argues that Strether's deviation from his ambassadorial mission both figures and is doubled by the novel's deviation from its narrative and causal line, a phenomenon that is inherent in narrative (98).

8. Millicent Bell, Meaning in Henry James (Cambridge, Massachusetts: Harvard University Press, 1991) 330.

9. The radiant and genial light of imagination has begun to act on Strether, and make him compose a picture, as it were, even as early as his solitary visit to the Luxembourg Gardens: "on a penny chair from which terraces, alleys, vistas, fountains, little trees in green tubs, little women in white caps and shrill little girls at play all sunnily 'composed' together, he passed an hour in which the cup of his impressions seemed truly to overflow" (112).

10. As Julie Rivkin, in "The Logic of Delegation in The Ambassadors" in PMLA 101.5 (1986) observes, Maria Gostrey's "name falls one consonant short of 'go straight' and leaves us with the open-ended sound and open path of 'go stray'" (824).

11. On a different or rather contrary note, William R. Goetz, who argues in Henry James and the Darkest Abyss of Romance (Baton Rouge: Louisiana University Press, 1986) that Strether's imagination fails and wrecks him, reads this image of the Babes as an expression of Strether's "return to second childhood" (205). But if this is Strether's image, as the narrator makes abundantly clear, the ironic tone is Strether's own and not the narrator's. As the image suggests, then, at this point Strether is being ironic about the past failure of his imaginative faculty. Goetz uses the image of the Babes as an illustration of Strether's being encaged and separated from "the position of the author" that earlier in the novel, according to Goetz, James encourages his readers to see (205).

12. The awareness that vaguely begins in this moment of watching a watcher reaches its culminating point in Strether's relationship with Mme de Vionnet. As Carren Kaston argues in Imagination and Desire in the Novels of Henry James (New Brunswick, New Jersey: Rutgers University Press, 1984), both Strether and Mme de Vionnet "recognize each other as other and affirm each other's sense of self" (105).

13. According to Tanner, Strether's "progress in Europe" can be regarded as the passive watcher's "ascent to a balcony" (40). Tanner observes that James is especially emphatic about Strether's ascent. But if James is particular about Strether's ascent, he is equally particular about his protagonist's descent.

14. Susan L. Mizruchi, The Power of Historical Knowledge: Narrating the Past in Hawthorne, James, and Dreiser (Princeton, New Jersey: Princeton University Press, 1988) 17.

15. Michael Wutz, "The Word and the Self in The Ambassadors," Style 25.1 (1991): 94-95.

16. Quoted from Keats's letter to his brothers George and Thomas, dated 21 December, 1817; taken from The Letters of John Keats, ed. Maurice Buxton Forman (London: Oxford University Press, 1947) 72.

17. Paul G. Beidler, in Frames in James: The Tragic Muse, The Turn of the Screw, What Maisie Knew, and The Ambassadors (B. C., Canada: University of Victoria, 1993) 85.

18. Armstrong, 97.

19. Goetz, 190.

20. Kaston, 90-91.

21. Bell, 326. She also points out that in remaining a man of imagination Strether remains a man of potentiality despite his coming across as "the man who has not lived" (330). Bell argues that James uses impressionism as "a personal program of perception implying an openness to chance and to a

multitude of personal impressions as they come, to a multitude of possible responses" (333).

22. Rivkin, 824.

23. But as J. Hillis Miller argues in "Narrative and History," in ELH 41.3 (1974), James shows his awareness that "Historians have always known that ["the narrating of an historical sequence in one way or another involves a constructive, interpretative, fictive act," and thus that] history and the narrative of history never wholly coincide" (461). As a contrast to Mrs. Newsome, Strether has come to realize that the search for pure history is an unrealizable goal, and hence that the narrative of history is dependent on the imaginative faculty. Early in the novel he looks at the site of the palace of the Tuileries and, as he tries to remember the palace, what strikes him is an "irremediable void" (111). The gap that history opens up for him is "irremediable" despite his memory. His "historic sense," confronted with an irrevocable gap, thus resorts to the "play" of his fancy (111). As Roslyn Jolly observes in Henry James: History, Narrative, Fiction (Oxford: Clarendon Press, 1993), to enter Europe, for Strether, is to enter "a new territory," which signifies that he begins to explore "the relations between fiction and history" (126). The "historic sense" is so thoroughly dependent upon the imaginative sense that the only way it can "freely play" is with the help of the latter: "He filled out spaces with dim symbols of scenes" (111). But at this point Strether is not aware of this dependence. This is why it seems to him that it is the historic sense that does the playing. Thus, when Maria gives him her interpretation of the story of Marie's past, although the narrator refers to "Miss Gostrey's sharp touch," her interpretation to Strether is "still history" (223). But late in the novel, after Strether himself has gained insight into the poor use to which Mrs. Newsome puts her imagination, he becomes aware that the historical voice of Paris is at best "vague" (475). Thus the narrator writes, "Strether had all along been subject to sudden gusts of fancy in connexion with such matters as ...[the voice of Paris] - odd starts of the historic sense, suppositions and divinations with no warrant but their intensity" (475). For Strether to be able to take his glimpse of the catastrophic truth of Mme de Vionnet's own turmoil of emotions, he has to make an imaginative comparison of her with the historical Mme Roland. Through this association of a historical character with a fictional character, James points out that his protagonist represents the reader who realizes the need to exercise the imaginative faculty. For such a reader realizes that in order to conceive the effect of a particular historical event, (s)he has to construct the narrative of the historical personage, for example, Madame Roland on the scaffold, with the imaginative faculty.

24. As Rivkin argues, The Ambassadors is a "tale of deviation from authority" (820).

25. According to Louise K. Barnett, in her essay "Speech in The Ambassadors: Woollett and Paris as Linguistic Communities," in Novel: A

Forum on Fiction 16.3 (1983), the image of the abyss is expressive of the irremediable gaps in knowledge that words cannot eliminate. These gaps that Barnett mentions remind me of Strether's metaphorical "well" that I have mentioned early in this essay, and into which he finds his remarks dropping as they increasingly move beyond his reach. In her analysis of the image of "sore abysses," Barnett asserts that "[a]bysses, always used in the plural for intensification, evokes weighty and complex matters whose properties to some extent exclude verbalization"; and thus, words in the Jamesian universe "can only point to the void, the sore spot, and then fall silent" (227).

26. At the risk of stretching interpretation to over-interpretation, I would like to point out that Strether's name, even if a little faintly and vaguely, is associated with the word ether, and thus is suggestive of the celestial. For if we break away the first three letters of his name from the rest we get "ether". It is interesting to note in this connection that, after he is joined by little Bilham in Gloriani's garden where he has been rather unceremoniously dropped by Mme de Vionnet, Strether gives the young man the impression that "if he had been overturned at all, he had been overturned into the *upper air*, the *sublimer element* with which he had an affinity and in which he might be trusted a while to float" (214; my emphasis).

27. As Teahan argues, Strether's "revolution" indicates his "inherent deviation from his appointed task" (97).

28. Pierre A. Walker, "Reading the Berne Bears in the End of James's The Ambassadors," Modern Language Studies 22.2 (1992): 13. For Walker, although Strether learns to comprehend "the duality of human nature and society," which enables him to "leave Paris with a far more complete understanding of the world and society" than the one with which he comes, what he receives from his understanding is a questionable gain (6,13).

29. Allen F. Stein, "Lambert Strether's Circuitous Journey: Motifs of Internalized Quest and Circularity in The Ambassadors," ESQ 22.4 (1976): 251.

30. Adeline Tintner, "A Source for James's The Ambassadors in Holbein's The Ambassadors (1533)," Leon Edel and Literary Art, ed. Lyall H. Powers (Ann Arbor: U.M.I. Research Press, 1988) 143. According to Tintner, as "death is hidden in ... [Holbein's] picture, so it is in James's novel... Death behind the idea of carpe diem stalks the book" (141). The suggestion of death certainly occurs in the suggestions of decay and loss, but these occur not so much in continuation as in alternation with the suggestions of growth and gain.

31. Kaston, 95-97.

32. Nicola Bradbury, Henry James: The Later Novels (Oxford: Clarendon Press, 1979) 67. On a different note, Leland S. Person, in "Strether's 'Penal Form': The Pleasure of Imaginative Surrender," in Papers on Language and Literature: A Journal for Scholars and Critics of Language and Literature 23.1 (1987), argues that James's protagonist builds "punishment into his very

experience of imaginative pleasure," and prefers relations that are imaginary rather than actual; and therefore, in returning home with the image of Maria Gostrey's offer, and thus "in not getting 'anything' for himself, ...[Strether] can have his pleasure and be punished for it too" (29,40).

33. Rivkin, 820.

34. Richard Hathaway, in "Ghosts at the Windows: Shadow and Corona in The Ambassadors," in The Henry James Review 18.1 (1997), argues that mirrors are "obscuring-revealing," for they veil and disclose "absence and presence, identity and non-identity" (87).

35. Allen W. Menton, "Typical Tales of Paris: The Function of Reading in The Ambassadors," Henry James Review 15 (1994): 287. According to Menton, Strether finds his past when he turns away "from the Paris of literary mediation and begins to experience Paris directly" (287). Menton explains that "the volumes of French literature that ...[Strether] has been reading since ... [his first] trip [to Paris] have colored his view of the city so thoroughly that the Paris in which he hopes to rediscover his lost youth is largely a product of that reading - a literary and mythological Paris" (286). But one wonders how far Strether pursues French literature when he returns home from his first visit. Certainly in his youth Strether bought books with great ardor, meaning to devote himself to a serious study of French literature. But these books have become "soiled" for reasons other than frequent handling: "They were still somewhere at home, the dozen ["lemon-coloured volumes"] - stale and soiled and never sent to the binder; but what had become of the sharp initiation they represented? They represented now the mere sallow paint on the door of the temple of taste that he had dreamed of raising up - a structure he had practically never carried further. Strether's present highest flights were perhaps those in which this lapse figured to him as a symbol ... of his long grind and his want of odd moments, his want moreover of money, of opportunity, of positive dignity" (116-117). With his return to Paris, however, the barrenness of the "lemon-coloured volumes" has transformed into or given way to the imaginative and emotional intensity of the "great" works of Victor Hugo. Therefore, however "indirect" his experience of French literature may be, it is possible to see that Strether has now learned to draw a connection between this "indirect" experience and his "direct experience of Paris".

36. Paul Armstrong, "Reading James's Prefaces and Reading James," Henry James's New York Edition: The Construction of Authorship, ed. David McWhirter (Stanford, California: Stanford University Press, 1995) 131. Armstrong argues that by doubling tenses in his fiction, James compels his readers simultaneously to perceive the scene and to engage in "an act of reflection that can only occur in a future where the perception it takes as its object is already past" (132). Armstrong also argues that a similar coupling of tenses occurs in the prefaces as well by which James "foreground[s] and thematize[s] the temporality of self-consciousness" (132).

37. According to Menton, Strether finds himself as well as Paris through his own past (299).

38. Kaston, 99.

39. Teahan, 99. She argues that "Strether aspires to follow a straight path in his capacity as center of consciousness ...[b]ut ...is condemned to deviation" (99).

40. Ellmann, 112.

41. Rivkin, 829.

Conclusion

Throughout this project on narrative authority in the Jamesian center of consciousness, my aim has been to focus on the reflectors' efforts to read and tell stories about themselves and their environments with the help of their wondering, interpretive, and creative imagination. I have tried to show that as a result of their activity as readers of stories the reflectors create meaning and therefore experience perceptual growth. As readers of stories they learn to make narrative connections between their interpretations of events, and thus to work for causal connections, coherence, and purposefulness, that is, for the creation of coherent epistemological patterns. Consequently, as readers of stories, because of their acute imagination, the Jamesian reflectors learn to develop their own systems of representation and figuration. And as tellers of stories, these reflectors achieve such representational sophistication that their imaginative abilities grow to become independent of the narrator's. Also, as these reflectors are storytellers who learn to develop meaning through the relation (narration) of events, so they learn to develop meaning through their personal relations, and their understanding of the need of such relations, with others. Thus the watcher in the "house of fiction" shows an acute awareness of "the human scene" (*AN* 46).

I have chosen my reading of *In the Cage* as my first chapter because the nameless telegraphist as center of consciousness, unlike Strether, Maggie, or Brydon, does not grow into a sophisticated teller of stories. That is, her attempt at storytelling is not as successful as the others'. This, perhaps, is why James makes the little post office more of a cage than a house of fiction. Although the house of fiction does not have "hinged doors that open straight upon life," and therefore the isolated watchers observe a "show" with their interpretive imagination much like the isolated and imaginative telegraphist who sits in "framed and wired confinement," James makes her isolation or her sense of isolation from the human scene more intense - a difference more in degree than in kind - than that felt by the watchers in the house of fiction. Indeed, the house of fiction is not a cage but a house, for James emphasizes the making and not the absence of connection between reflectors and their environment. Nevertheless, although not yet a successful storyteller, the telegraphist has the potential to grow into one. For as an "intense observer" she is an acute reader. Hence her reading of stories ultimately enables her to see that she herself, in a manner, has only tried to compose maudlin narratives. Consequently, her reading of stories about the romantic life of Captain Everard ultimately brings perceptual refinement in her life, and enables her to move beyond the cage of commonness. The break in the reflector's storytelling, then, is perhaps nascently suggestive of the storyteller's growth as process. Hence she continues to develop as an acute reader of stories. And as such she learns to exert the narrative authority that the third-person narrator of this novella exercises. For, as James demonstrates, she develops the narrator's ability of representation. Thus *In the Cage* is the only piece of fiction studied here that does not show the reflector's narrative authority at the expense of the narrator's. For this novella is the only one in which the reflector's narrative authority does not result in a reduction of the narrator's narrative authority.

The second chapter in this project, which is on "The Jolly Corner," and which shows that the arrangement of my readings of the four pieces of James's fiction is after all more topical than chronological, is obviously connected with the first chapter in that the center of consciousness in this short story, Spencer Brydon, like the telegraphist, seeks a life of refinement. While the telegraphist, who belongs to the lower classes and therefore is tormented by her socioeconomic plight, desires to create meaning through refinement in an environment that is stifled by the meaninglessness of poverty and coarseness, Brydon, who belongs to the upper classes and is affluent, desires to create refinement in his environment through a morally fulfilling aesthetic quest. Hence in Brydon we see a degree of sophistication that we do not notice in the telegraphist. As a storyteller, Brydon creates a metaphorical narrative of what he might have been if he had never left home and wandered in Europe, because in his actual life he does not read the coherence of a consistently developing story about a meaningful and purposeful life and thus about a self-fulfilling aesthetic quest. But although Brydon begins composing the fictional narrative, as it were, he creates a problem for his narrative authority because of a self-imposed isolation from his environment. Hence he is unable to complete his first attempt

Conclusion 161

at a figurative narrative about what he might have been. As James continues, however, Brydon's relationship with the actual human world, as it is represented for example by Alice Staverton, enables him to launch his metaphorical narrative, that is, make a beginning of it. And his realization and rejection of his self-imposed isolation enables him to grasp a fully developed narrative in a picture through which James demonstrates the power of representation and figuration. Hence when Brydon renounces self-isolation he is able to reassert his narrative authority. As a result, he ultimately finds self-fulfillment through his aesthetic quest.

As in the first two chapters I examine the reflectors' exertion of narrative authority in relation to their quest for refinement, so in the last two chapters I examine it in relation to their attitudes towards changes in their lives and in their environments. In the third chapter I discuss the center of consciousness in the first volume of *The Golden Bowl*, represented by the protagonist, Amerigo, as more resistant than receptive to changes. Thus, although he is capable of reading a new story that takes the place of an old one, he tends to ignore the changes that cause an old story to give way to a new one. As a result, late in the first volume the imagery he creates, and the story he creates through the imagery, break into irremediable incoherence and inconsistency. Consequently, he creates a serious problem in the exertion of his narrative authority. It seems to me that this is why James designates Amerigo as the center of consciousness of the first rather than of the second volume. For as a reader and teller of stories, Amerigo demonstrates the initial rather than the advanced stages of the exertion of narrative authority. Through the reflector of the second volume, however, James shows the continual development of the center of consciousness's assertion of narrative authority. Maggie Verver's intensely contemplative imagination enables her to create and sustain her imagery, to run a narrative thread not simply through Amerigo's imagery, but also to read the old story of his meaningful relationship with Charlotte Stant, and to register and examine changes in her own life and in her environment. Consequently, she exercises the narrative authority that enables Amerigo to make use of his own interpretive imagination instead of depending on another's. Further, it enables her, as a powerful storyteller, to replace the old equilibrium of the two couples with a new equilibrium, and thus to change an old story into a new one. Consequently, through Maggie, James implicitly suggests that the reflector's imagination is capable of evolving beyond the narrator's.

In *The Ambassadors*, however, as I see it, the author's suggestion that the reflector's imaginative abilities evolve beyond the narrator's is most clearly revealed. This is why James shows such a marked concern for

Lambert Strether's lambent imagination, and why I have chosen my reading of this novel as the fourth and final chapter in this project. As a result of the growth in his imagination, Strether learns to read and tell stories about his environment, and comes to realize that growth always suggests or is followed by change. Consequently, the exercise of narrative authority enables him to find the story of his own life, which is a story of change, and also to find his relation with others. Hence he comes to exert the narrative authority that enables him to make narrative connections between his past, present, and future. My choice of this particular arrangement of my chapters has also been determined by the point that, unlike the reflector examined in my second chapter, and unlike one of the reflectors in my third, as a storyteller Strether does not ever experience any loss of narrative authority. The growth in his imaginative consciousness enables him to gradually enhance his narrative authority. Perhaps it is because of this special focus on the subject of a changing growing imagination, and notable success with the technique of the center of consciousness through Strether that James considers *The Ambassadors* "as, frankly, quite the best 'all round,' of my productions" (*AN* 309).

Bibliography

Abbott, "The Incredible Floating Man." <u>The Henry James Review</u> 11 (1990): 176-188.

Agnew, Jean-Christophe. "The Consuming Vision of Henry James." <u>The Culture of Consumption: Critical Essays in American History 1880-1980</u>. Ed. Richard Wightman Fox and T. J. Lears. New York: Pantheon, 1983. 66-100.

Alberti, John. "The Economics of Love: The Production of Value in <u>The Golden Bowl</u>." <u>The Henry James Review</u> 12.1 (1991): 9-19.

Armstrong, Paul. <u>The Challenge of Bewilderment: Understanding and Representation in James, Conrad, and Ford</u>. Ithaca and London: Cornell University Press, 1987.

---. <u>The Phenomenology of Henry James</u>. Chapel Hill: University of North Carolina Press, 1983.

---. "Reading James's Prefaces and Reading James." <u>Henry James's New York Edition: The Construction of Authorship</u>. Ed. David McWhirter. Stanford: Stanford University Press, 1995. 125-137.

Ash, Beth Sharon. "Narcissism and the Gilded Image: A Psychoanalytic Reading of <u>The Golden Bowl</u>." <u>The Henry James Review</u> 15.1 (1994): 55-90.

Aswell, E. Duncan. "James's <u>In the Cage</u>: The Telegraphist as Artist." <u>Texas Studies in Literature and Language</u>. 8.3 (1966): 375-384.

Auerbach, Jonathan. "The Jamesian Critical Romance." The Romance of Failure: First Person Fictions of Poe, Hawthorne, and James. New York and Oxford: Oxford University Press, 1989. 118-171.

Aziz, Maqbool. "How Long Is Long; How Short Short! Henry James and the Small Circular Frame." A Companion to Henry James Studies. Ed. Daniel Mark Fogel. Westport, Connecticut and London, 1993. 207-234.

Barnett, Louise K. "Speech in The Ambassadors: Woollett and Paris as Linguistic Communities." Novel: A Forum on Fiction 16.3 (1983): 215-229.

Bauer, Dale and Andrew Lakritz. "Language, Class, and Sexuality in Henry James's 'In the Cage'." New Orleans Review 14.3 (1987): 61-69.

Beidler, Paul G. "The Ambassadors: The Oblong Gilt Frame." Frames in James: The Tragic Muse, The Turn of the Screw, What Maisie Knew, and The Ambassadors. B. C., Canada: University of Victoria, 1993. 74-92.

Bell, Millicent. Meaning in Henry James Cambridge, Massachusetts and London: Harvard University Press, 1991.

Benert, Annette Larson. "Dialogical Discourse in 'The Jolly Corner': The Entrepreneur as Language and Image." The Henry James Review. 8.2 (1987): 116-125.

Bersani, Leo. A Future for Astyanax: Character and Desire in Literature. New York: Columbia University Press, 1984.

Bier, Jesse. "Henry James's 'The Jolly Corner': The Writer's Fable and the Deeper Matter." The Arizona Quarterly. 35.4 (1979): 321-334.

Blackall, Jean Frantz. "James's In the Cage: An Approach through the Figurative Language." University of Toronto Quarterly. 31.2 (1962): 164-179.

---. "Henry James and Saintine." Notes and Queries 7.7 (1960): 266-268.

Boren, Lynda Sue. Eurydice Reclaimed: Language, Gender, and Voice in Henry James. Ann Arbor and London: U. M. I. Research Press, 1989.

Bradbury, Nicola. Henry James: The Later Novels. Oxford: Clarendon Press, 1979.

Burleson, Donald. "James's 'The Jolly Corner'." The Explicator. 49.2 (1991): 99-100.

Byers, John R. "Alice Staverton's Redemption of Spencer Brydon in James' 'The Jolly Corner." South Atlantic Bulletin 41.2 (1976): 90-99.

Cameron, Sharon. Thinking in Henry James. Chicago and London: University of Chicago Press, 1989.

Carroll, David. "The (Dis)Placement of the Eye ("I"): Point of View, Voice, and the Forms of Fiction." The Subject in Question: Languages of Theory and the Strategies of Fiction. Chicago and London: The University of Chicago Press, 1982.

Craig, David M. "The Indeterminacy of the End: Maggie Verver and the Limits of Imagination." The Henry James Review 3.2 (1982): 133-144.

Cramer, Kathryn. "Possession and 'The Jolly Corner'." The New York Review of Science Fiction 65 (1994): 19-22.

Culver, Stuart. "Representing the Author: Henry James, Intellectual Property and the Work of Writing." Henry James: Fiction as History. Ed. Ian F. A. Bell. Totowa: Vision and Barnes and Noble, 1984. 114-136.

Delfattore, Joan. "The 'Other' Spencer Brydon." The Arizona Quarterly 35.4 (1979): 335-341.

Dryden, Edgar. "The Image in the Mirror: James's Portrait and the Economy of Romance." The Form of American Romance. Baltimore and London: Johns Hopkins University Press, 1988. 109-136.

Edel, Leon. Henry James: The Treacherous Years. 1895-1901. Philadelphia and New York: J. B. Lippincott Company, 1969.

Ellmann, Maud. "'The Intimate Difference': Power and Representation in The Ambassadors." Henry James: Fiction as History. Ed. Ian F. A. Bell. Totowa: Vision and Barnes and Noble, 1984. 98-113.

Esch, Deborah. "A Jamesian About-Face: Notes on 'The Jolly Corner'." ELH 50.3 (1983): 587-605.

Fogel, Daniel Mark. Henry James and the Structure of the Romantic Imagination. Baton Rouge and London: Louisiana State University Press, 1981.

Freedman, Jonathan. Professions of Taste: Henry James, British Aestheticism, and Commodity Culture. Stanford: Stanford University Press, 1990.

Freedman, William. "Universality in 'The Jolly Corner'." Texas Studies in Literature and Language 4.1 (1962): 12-15.

Gabler-Hover, Janet. "The Ethics of Determinism in Henry James's 'In the Cage'." The Henry James Review 13.3 (1992): 253-273.

Goetz, William R. Henry James and the Darkest Abyss of Romance. Baton Rouge and London: Louisiana State University Press, 1986.

Gribble, Jennifer. "Cages." The Critical Review 24 (1982): 108-119.

Griffin, Susan M. "The Selfish Eye: Strether's Principles of Psychology." American Literature 56.3 (1984): 396-409.

Hathaway, Richard D. "Ghosts at the Windows: Shadpw and Corona in The Ambassadors. The Henry James Review 18.1 (1997): 81-96.

Hocks, Richard A. Henry James: A Study of the Short Fiction. Boston: Twayne Publishers, 1990.

Holland. Laurence Bedwell. The Expense of Vision: Essays on the Craft of Henry James. Princeton University Press, 1964.

Hutchinson, Stuart. "James's In the Cage: A New Interpretation." Studies in Short Fiction 19.1 (1982): 19-25.

Ian, Marcia. "Consecrated Diplomacy and the Concretion of Self." The Henry James Review 7.1 (1985): 27-33.

Jacobs, J. U. "The Alter Ego: The Artist as American in 'The Jolly Corner'." Theoria 58 (1982): 51-60.

James, Henry. The Ambassadors. Ed. Harry Levin. London: Penguin Books, 1986.

---. The Art of Fiction and Other Essays. New York: Oxford University Press, 1948.

---. The Art of the Novel. Boston: Northeastern University Press, 1984.

---. The Complete Notebooks of Henry James. Ed. Leon Edel and Lyall H. Powers. New York and Oxford: Oxford University Press, 1987.

---. The Golden Bowl. London: Penguin Books, 1985.

---. In the Cage and Other Stories. Middlesex: Penguin Books Ltd., 1972.

---. The Jolly Corner and Other Tales. Ed. Roger Gard. London: Penguin Books, 1990.

Jolly, Roslyn. Henry James: History, Narrative, Fiction. Oxford: Clarendon Press, 1993.

Kaston, Carren. Imagination and Desire in the Novels of Henry James. New Brunswick, New Jersey: Rutgers University Press, 1984.

Kappeler, Susanne. Writing and Reading in Henry James. New York: Columbia University Press, 1980.

Keats, John. The Letters of John Keats. Ed. Maurice Buxton Forman. London: Oxford University Press, 1947.

Krook, Dorothea. The Ordeal of Consciousness in Henry James. Cambridge: Cambridge University Press, 1962.

Lustig, T. J. Henry James and the Ghostly. Cambridge: Cambridge University Press, 1994.

MacCarthy, Desmond. Portraits. New York: Oxford University Press, 1955.

Maini, Darshan Singh. Henry James: The Indirect Vision. Ann Arbor and London: U. M. I. Research Press, 1988.

Menton, Allen W. "Typical Tales of Paris: The Function of Reading in The Ambassadors."The Henry James Review 15 (1994): 286-300.

Miller, J. Hillis. Ariadne's Thread. New Haven and London: Yale University Press, 1992.

---. "Narrative and History." ELH 41.3 (1974): 455-473.

Mizruchi, Susan L. The Power of Historical Knowledge: Narrating the Past in Hawthorne, James, and Dreiser. Princeton: Princeton University Press, 1988.

Moody, Andrew J. "'The Harmless Pleasure of Knowing': Privacy in the Telegraph Office and Henry James's 'In the Cage'." The Henry James Review 16.1 (1995)" 53-65.

Moon, Heath. "More Royalist Than the King: the Governess, the Telegraphist, and Mrs Gracedew." Criticism 24.1 (1982): 16-35.

Norrman, Ralf. The Insecure World of Henry James's Fiction: Intensity and Ambiguity. London and Basingstoke: The Macmillan Press Ltd., 1982.

---. "The Intercepted Telegram Plot in Henry James's 'In the Cage'." Notes and Queries 24.5 (1977): 425-427.

---. Techniques of Ambiguity in the Fiction of Henry James. Abo: Abo Akademi, 1977.

O' Hara, Daniel T. "Henry James's Version of Judgment." Boundary 2 23.1 (1996): 61-70.

Person, Leland S., Jr. "Strether's 'Penal Form': The Pleasure of Imaginative Surrender." Papers on Language and Literature: A Journal for Scholars and Critics of Language and Literature 23.1 (1987): 27-40.

Poe, Edgar Allan. The Narrative of Arthur Gordon Pym of Nantucket. The Complete Poems and Stories of Edgar Allan Poe. New York: Alfred A. Knopf, 1946. 723-854.

Porter, Carolyn. Seeing and Being: The Plight of the Participant Observer in Emerson, Adams, and Faulkner. Middletown: Wesleyan University Press, 1981.

Przybylowicz, Donna. Desire and Repression: The Dialectic of Self and Other in the Late Works of Henry James. Alabama: University of Alabama Press, 1986.

Reising, Russell J. "'Doing Good by Stealth': Alice Staverton and Women's Politics in 'The Jolly Corner'." The Henry James Review 13.1 (1992): 50-66.

---. "Figuring Himself Out: Spencer Brydon, 'The Jolly Corner,' and Cultural Change." The Journal of Narrative Technique 19.1 (1989): 116-129.

Reynolds, Mark. "Counting the Costs: The Infirmity of Art and The Golden Bowl." The Henry James Review 6.1 (1984): 15-26.

Rivkin, Julie. "The Logic of Delegation in The Ambassadors." PMLA 101 (1986): 819-831.

Rosenblatt, Jason P. "Bridegroom and Bride in 'The Jolly Corner'." Studies in Short Fiction. 14.3 (1977): 282-284.

Rovit, Earl. "The Ghosts in James's 'The Jolly Corner'," Tennessee Studies in Literature 10 (1965): 65-72.

Rowe, John Carlos. Henry Adams and Henry James. Ithaca: Cornell University Press, 1976.

---. The Theoretical Dimensions of Henry James. Madison: University of Wisconsin Press, 1984.

Rundle, Vivienne. "Defining Frames: The Prefaces of Henry James and Joseph Conrad." The Henry James Review 16.1 (1995): 66-92.

Sabin, Margery. The Dialect of the Tribe: Speech and Community in Modern Fiction. New York and Oxford: Oxford University Press, 1987.

Said, Edward. Culture and Imperialism New York: Alfred A. Knopf, 1993.

Salzburg, Joel. "Mr. Mudge as Redemptive Fate: Juxtaposition in James's In the Cage." Studies in the Novel 11.1 (1979): 63-76.

Samuels, Charles Thomas. The Ambiguity of Henry James. Urbana: University of Illinois Press, 1971.

Savoy, Eric. "'In the Cage' and the Queer Effects of Gay History." Novel: A Forum on Fiction 28.3 (1995): 284-307.

Schor, Naomi. "Fiction as Interpretation / Interpretation as Fiction." The Reader in the Text: Essays on Audience and Interpretation. Eds. Susan R. Suleiman and Inge Crosman. Princeton: Princeton University Press, 1980. 165-182.

Segal, Ora. The Lucid Reflector: The Observer in Henry James's Fiction. New Haven: Yale University Press, 1969.

Seltzer, Mark. Henry James and the Art of Power. Ithaca: Cornell University Press, 1984.

Shear, Walter. "Cultural Fate and Social Freedom in Three American Short Stories." Studies in Short Fiction 29.4 (1992): 543-549.

Shine, Muriel G. The Fictional Children of Henry James. Chapel Hill: The University of North Carolina Press, 1968.

Sicker, Philip. Love and the Quest for Identity in the Fiction of Henry James. Princeton: Princeton University Press, 1980.

Smith, Irena Auerbuch. "The Golden Goal: Toward a Dialogic Imagination in Henry James's Last Completed Novel." The Henry James Review. 16.2 (1995): 172-190.

Smythe, Karen. "Imaging and Imagining: 'The Jolly Corner' and Self-Construction." Dalhousie Review 70.3 (1990): 375-385.

Springer, Mary Doyle. A Rhetoric of Literary Characters: Some Women of Henry James. Chicago and London: University of Chicago Press, 1978.

Steele, Meili. "The Drama of Reference in James's The Golden Bowl." Novel: A Forum on Fiction. 21.1 (1987): 73-88.

Stein, Allen F. "Lambert Strether's Circuitous Journey: Motif of Internalized Quest and Circularity in The Ambassadors." ESQ: Journal of the American Renaissance 22 (1976): 245-253.

---. "The Beast in 'The Jolly Corner': Spencer Brydon's Ironic Rebirth." Studies in Short Fiction. 11.1 (1974): 61-66.

Tanner, Tony. The Reign of Wonder: Naivety and Reality in American Literature. Cambridge: Cambridge University Press, 1965.

---. "The Watcher from the Balcony: Henry James's The Ambassadors." Critical Quarterly 8 (1966): 35-52.

Teahan, Sheila. The Rhetorical Logic of Henry James. Baton Rouge and London: Louisiana State University Press, 1995.

Tintner, Adeline R. "A Source for James's The Ambassadors in Holbein's The Ambassadors (1533)." Leon Edel and literary Art. Ed. Lyall H. Powers. Ann Arbor and London: U. M. I. Research Press, 1988. 135-150.

Todorov, Tzvetan. The Poetics of Prose. Trans. Richard Howard. Ithaca: Cornell University Press, 1977.

Tuveson, Ernest. "'The Jolly Corner': A Fable of Redemption." Studies in Short Fiction 12.3 (1975): 271-280.

Van Slyck, Phyllis. "'An Innate Preference for the Represented Subject': Portraiture and Knowledge in The Golden Bowl." The Henry James Review 15.2 (1994): 179-189.

Veeder, William. "Toxic Mothers, Cultural Criticism: 'In the Cage' and Elsewhere." The Henry James Review 14.3 (1993): 264-272.

Walker, Pierre A. "Reading the Berne Bears in the End of James's The Ambassadors." Modern Language Studies 22.2 (1992): 4-14.

Walton, Priscilla. The Disruption of the Feminine in Henry James. Toronto: University of Toronto Press, 1992.

---. "'A Mistress of Shades': Maggie as Reviser in The Golden Bowl." The HenryJames Review 13.2 (1992): 143-153.

Wicke, Jennifer. "Henry James's Second Wave." The Henry James Review 10.2 (1989): 146-151.

Williams, Merle A. Henry James and the Philosophical Novel: Being and Seeing. Cambridge: Cambridge University Press, 1993.

Winnett, Susan. Terrible Sociability: The Text of Manners in Laclos, Goethe, and James. Stanford: Stanford University Press, 1993.

Wise, James. "The Floating World of Lambert Strether." Arlington Quarterly 2 (1969): 80-110.

Wright, Walter F. The Madness of Art: A Study of Henry James. Lincoln: University of Nebraska Press, 1962.

Wutz, Michael. "The Word and the Self in The Ambassadors." Style 25.1 (1991): 89-103.

INDEX

Abbott, Reginald 161n4
Abyss 13n13, 36, 37, 58, 103, 105, 125n3, 151, 152, 162n11, 164n25
Aesthetic 49-53, 55-56, 59-60, 62-63, 70-71, 75, 76n3, 129n31, n38, 168, 169
Agnew, Jean-Christophe 122, 128n28
Alberti, John 127n16
Art 1-2, 10, 24, 25, 34, 37, 42n2, 50-51, 56, 65-66, 74, 77n10, 78n22, 120, 124, 127n16, 128n22, n29, 129n34, 141
Artist 3, 6, 7-9, 12, 42n2, 44n19, 45n22, 66, 76n3, 125, 147, 148
Armstrong, Paul 3, 13n10, 93, 125n5, 148, 157, 161n5, 162n18, 165n36
Ash, Beth Sharon 96, 125-126n7
Aswell, Duncan 15, 36, 42n2, 46n31
Auerbach, Jonathan 13n5
Aziz, Maqbool 43n7, n9
Author 12n2, 126n10, 129n38, 130n39, 165n36, 169
 relationship with reader 112, 131, 150
 center of consciousness as 2- 4, 8, 49, 53, 56, 60, 67, 89-90, 120, 124, 126n10, 131-132, 156
 failings of center of consciousness as 12, 60, 162
 Lady Bradeen as 29-31, 33
 Mrs Newsome as 5, 141, 150-151

Barnett, Louise 163n25
Bauer, Dale 41, 47n36
Beidler, Paul 148, 162n17
Bell, Ian F. A. 12n2
Bell, Millicent 8, 10, 13n20, 14n26, 56, 70, 77n9, 78n22, 79n27, 135, 149, 161n8, 162n21
Benert, Annette 51, 62, 74, 76n4, 77n13, 78n16, 80n35
Bersani, Leo 103, 111, 120, 121, 123, 126n8, 127n14, 128n23, n25, 129n35,
Bewilderment 7, 27, 30-32, 74, 93, 109, 132, 161n5
Blackall, Jean 15, 42n3
Boren, Lynda S. 76n5
Bowl 5, 89-92, 99, 102-103, 107, 112, 117-120, 122-124, 125n2, n4, n5, n7, 126n9, n10, n12, 127n13, n16, 128n22, n27, 129n31, n34, 36, 130n39

Bradbury, Nicola 111, 112, 127n15, 156, 164n32
Burleson, Donald 73, 80n33
Byers, John 78n21

Cage 1, 4, 13n14, 15, 18, 22, 29, 30, 36, 38, 42n4, n7, 43 n11, 44n17, 46n26, 140, 162n11, 167, 168
 image of 17, 25, 36, 39, 42n3, n5, 43n7, n8, n9, 44n18, n19, 45n22, 46n29, 57n33, n36
 of commonality and commonness 17, 18, 24, 25, 30, 31, 39, 40
Cameron, Sharon 3, 13n11, 76n6111, 122, 126n12, 129n30
Carroll, David 79n25
Center of consciousness 1, 2, 3, 4, 6, 7, 9, 10, 13n8, 15, 16, 21, 22, 31, 49, 52, 55, 89, 95, 104, 124, 148, 166n39, 167, 168, 169
 narrative concerns of 8, 90, 115, 139, 167, 169
 as reader or teller of stories 5, 6, 8, 9, 11, 16, 25, 66, 89, 98, 113, 115, 124, 167, 168, 169
 imagination in 3, 4, 5, 9, 89, 132, 136, 139, 142, 167, 169, 170
 relationship with narrator 10-11, 16, 18, 32, 40, 42n5, 58, 96, 102, 113, 114, 131, 132, 134, 139, 148, 167-169
 as image-maker 9, 10, 16, 32, 49, 52, 53, 132, 148, 167, 169
Coherence 6, 25, 58, 63, 99, 101, 102, 133, 144, 146, 168, 169
 reflector's ability to create 29, 100, 113, 115-118, 125, 137, 153, 167
 coherent pattern or design 101, 109, 115, 140, 167
Confusion 7, 30, 31, 50, 51, 52, 60, 63, 70, 72, 75, 77n11, 93, 94, 111, 112, 132, 135, 137, 139, 141, 151
Connection 4, 5, 7, 8, 11, 12n4, 17, 18, 19, 20, 29, 68, 70, 71, 72, 73, 99, 106, 109, 117, 132, 157, 158, 165n35
 ability to forge 6, 11, 55, 68, 70-71, 74-75, 90-91, 95, 103, 115, 125, 132, 139, 156, 158-159
 causal 5, 22, 91, 109, 117, 167

narrative connections 5, 6, 15, 26, 28-29, 37-38, 54, 75, 90, 100, 104, 109-110, 115-116, 118, 132, 139, 154-155, 157-159, 167, 176, 170
  reflector's with surroundings 12, 64, 74-75, 113, 132, 148-149, 156, 168
  between people 29, 38, 99, 109, 116, 126n10
  between reflector and narrator 10-11, 41, 96, 114, 135, 139
  between scenes 11, 28, 29, 70, 114, 158
  between images 94, 116, 119, 135, 139, 156
  between narratives 71-74, 92, 94
  with past 70-71, 104, 110, 132, 157-160, 170
  loss or absence of 61, 63-64, 92, 102, 104, 118, 152, 157, 159
Craig, David 124, 129n37
Cramer, Kathryn 80n34
Culver, Stuart 12n2

Design 6, 7, 8, 9, 16, 25, 103, 109, 116, 121, 126n10 (See Pattern)
Drama 2,4,9, 26, 53, 54, 59, 70, 126n9, 127n13, 128n27, 136, 148
  reflector's attempt to create 32- 37, 42, 49, 55, 63-64
Delfattore, Joan 79n24
Dryden, Edgar 9, 13n22

Edel, Leon 42n6
Ellmann, Maud 132, 160, 160n3, 166n39, n40
Environment 8, 12, 34, 42n6, 51, 52, 59, 62, 64, 69, 70, 78n18, 79n25, 99, 113, 120, 131, 132, 133, 138, 147, 148, 149, 167, 169, 170
Equilibrium 90, 107, 109, 110, 111,121, 123, 169
Esch, Deborah 58, 77n11, n14

Fancy 18, 25, 36, 46n28, n32, 76n3, 137, 138, 139, 141, 142, 163n23
Fiction 12n2, 13n5, n8, 15, 16, 39, 40, 43n12, 45n21, 49, 50, 55, 56, 57, 76n6, 107, 108, 121, 133, 148, 149, 160n3, 163n23, 168
  watcher in house of 7, 8, 11, 12, 67, 68, 108, 113, 148, 149, 167, 168
  James's 1, 2, 3, 9, 46n29, 57, 67, 75, 89, 111, 134, 165n36, 168

Maggie's 8, 107-109,120-121, 129n34
Brydon's 9, 49-50, 54-56, 64, 66-68, 70, 74-75, 76n3, 168
Staverton's role in Brydon's 50, 70, 72-73
reflector as reader of 5, 27, 28, 92, 108, 109, 141, 142, 165n35
problems in 57-60, 63-64
Fogel, Daniel Mark 3, 13n12, 93, 125n4
Freedman, Jonathan 122, 129n31
Freedman, William 62, 78n17
Freedom 15, 18, 40, 41, 45n24, 77n7, 125n5, 129n34, 137, 155, 156, 159

Gabler-Hover, Janet 45n23
Goetz, William R 4, 13n13, 148, 162n11, n19
Gribble, Jennifer 17, 34, 42n7, 43n7
Griffin, Susan M 9, 14n23
Growth 7, 15, 27, 44n19, 68, 95, 108, 113, 131, 141, 142, 150, 152, 160, 167
  of reflector's imaginative consciousness 8, 131, 132, 135-136, 139, 147, 152, 156, 158, 167, 170
  of reflector's images 9, 69, 94, 96, 140-141, 148
  as process 6, 15, 42, 134, 142, 151-154, 158-159, 164n30, 168, 170
  perceptual 2, 5, 151-152, 155, 157, 167

Harmony 55, 71, 100, 102, 103, 106, 107, 108, 115, 116, 123, 129n31, 145, 155
Hathaway, Richard D 165n34
Hocks, Richard A 45n20
Holland, Laurence Bedwell 2, 3, 13n6, 120, 124, 128n24, 129n33
Human 2, 7, 8, 17, 21, 22, 49, 50, 55, 61, 62, 63, 64, 66, 67, 68, 74, 75, 113, 146, 148, 149, 155, 156, 164n28, 167, 168
Hutchinson, Stuart 36, 46n30

Ian, Marcia 128n21
Identity 19, 20, 21, 22, 23, 43n8, 44n15, 45n22, 57, 61, 73, 74, 78n20, 79n24, 80n32, 92, 95, 96, 105, 142, 143, 159, 160, 165n34
Image 8, 9, 10, 11, 13n22, 42n3, n5, 43n9, 44n15, 51, 52, 53, 55, 56, 58, 59, 61, 65, 68, 69, 70, 76n4, n5, 77n7, n10, 90, 93, 94, 95, 103, 104, 113, 114, 115, 116, 125n3, n7, 126n9, 132, 134, 135, 137, 142, 152, 155, 157, 162n11,

Index 175

164n25, 165n32
narrator's 10, 16, 31-32, 95-96, 114,
  132, 134-135, 139, 168
role in reading or telling stories 9, 11,
  16, 32, 49, 53, 54, 56, 59, 65, 66, 69,
  70, 72, 74, 89, 90, 91, 93, 94, 95, 97,
  98, 102, 113, 114, 115, 116, 117, 139,
  144, 148, 153, 167, 169
reflector's 30-32, 35, 52-53, 90, 95, 102,
  113-115, 117, 132-137, 162n11
reflector as constructing 2, 17, 21, 23,
  29, 49, 52-55, 94-97, 105, 111-112,
  115-117, 127n20, 139-140, 153-156,
  159, 169
reflector as connecting 94, 115-116,
  127n20, 139, 169
unconnected or inconsistent 61, 102,
  105, 133, 169
narrator's dependence on reflector's 114,
  134, 136, 139, 148
reflector's independence from narrator's
  31-32, 40, 102, 167
of water 11, 16, 31, 32, 40, 68, 94, 95,
  96, 97, 112, 127n20, 132, 133, 149,
  161n4,
Imagination 4, 6, 7, 8, 9, 13n12, n21, 16,
  25, 26, 33, 36, 39, 42n5, 43n8, 44n19,
  45n22, n23, n24, 46n33, 47n33, n36,
  52, 64, 76n3, 102, 125n4, 126n10,
  129n34, n37, n38, n39, 138, 139, 142,
  145, 148, 151, 161n6, n9, 162n12,
  n21, 164n32, 165n32, 169
as meaning making faculty 6, 137,
  140, 167
narrator's 134-137, 169
narrative abilities of reflector's 4, 69,
  89, 131, 137, 139, 143-144, 147, 150,
  153, 155, 163n23, 167, 169
connecting 70, 101, 138-139, 169
connection with rational faculty 132,
  134, 136, 145, 151-152
reading with 4, 5, 8, 23, 100, 131-132,
  142, 160, 167
wondering 4, 33, 45n22, 67, 69, 133,
  137, 138, 167
interpretive 3, 4, 8, 56, 66, 90, 113, 119,
  132, 133, 140, 147, 149, 150, 167, 169
sympathetic 73, 112, 136, 138
the growing 8, 39, 69, 111, 131, 132,
  134, 139, 140, 147, 156, 158, 167, 170
and perception 3, 4, 42n7, 93, 111-112,
  117, 135, 140, 167, 169

analytical abilities of 4, 37, 40, 98, 132,
  134, 137
reflector's imaginative consciousness
  89, 112, 114, 119, 131, 132, 133, 136,
  137, 140, 148, 149, 151, 160
limitations of 4, 47n36, 102, 124, 133,
  134, 145, 152, 162n11
Impressions 1, 6, 9, 16, 18, 21, 23, 31, 32,
  33, 35, 38, 43n7, 53, 54, 68, 69, 95, 99,
  101, 113, 134, 155, 161n9, 163n21,
  164n26
Interpretation 2, 3, 4, 5, 9, 20, 27, 33, 36,
  38, 43n12, 45n21, 47n36, 53, 65, 90,
  132, 147, 151, 167, 169
as devoid of absoluteness or finality
  141, 146, 147, 149
Isolation 11, 12, 17, 24, 45n22, 50, 62, 63,
  64, 66, 71, 74, 93, 156, 167, 168, 169

Jacobs, J. U. 76n3
Jolly, Roslyn 163n23
Journey 9, 24, 92, 93, 94, 95, 111, 119,
  152, 164n29

Kappeler, Susanne 113, 127n18
Kaston, Carren 8, 12, 13n21, 14n28, 39,
  47n33, 74, 80n36, 108, 121, 126n10,
  128n26, 149, 156, 159, 162n12, n20,
  164n31, 166n38
Keats, John 145, 162n16

Lakritz, Andrew 41, 47n36
Lustig, T. J. 77n12

MacCarthy, Desmond 66, 78n23
Maini, Darshan Singh 46n29
Margin 9, 25, 26, 35, 44n20, 65, 99, 138,
  150, 151
Meaning 3,4, 6, 8, 13n20, 29, 30, 36,
  45n23, 50, 52, 53, 55, 63, 69, 70,
  71, 72, 73, 74, 75, 91, 95, 99, 100,
  101, 102, 111, 122, 124, 126n12, 133,
  137, 139, 140, 143, 144, 147, 159,
  161n3, n5, n8, 167, 168, 169
absence of 95, 99, 101, 102, 144, 159
Menton, Allen W 157, 165n35, 166n37
Miller, J. Hillis 7, 13n18, 163n23
Mizruchi, Susan L 143, 162n14
Moody, Andrew J 43n11
Moon, Heath 46n25

Narrative 1, 8, 9, 12n4, 15, 18, 26, 33, 35,

39, 41, 44n13, 54, 55, 56, 59, 60, 64, 65, 66, 68, 69, 70, 71, 72, 73, 74, 76, 76n3, 80n32, 90, 91, 92, 94, 96, 105, 107, 119, 120, 124, 125n3, 143, 161n7, 163n23, 168, 169
- composing figurative narratives 8,-11, 15, 49-51, 56-57, 65-67, 71, 75, 169
- reading figurative 25-29, 65, 74, 89, 110-111, 131, 150
- confusion in 60-61, 63-64, 157
- loss of control over 58, 60-61, 63, 104
- break of consistency in 7, 58, 102
- image and 11, 29, 53, 66, 70, 72, 94, 98, 102, 104, 114, 115
- attempts at composing coherent or complete 33-35, 37, 42, 95
- rejection of sentimental 4, 16, 39-41

Narrative authority 1-3, 5, 12, 31, 40, 50, 52, 53, 66, 67, 68, 73, 75, 89, 90, 91, 92, 101, 103, 107, 109, 114, 120, 124, 124, 131-133, 148, 153, 159, 167, 168, 169, 170
- through reading stories 4, 15, 27-29, 31-32, 32, 37-41, 89-91, 109, 131-132, 137, 141, 147, 167-168
- through storytelling 49, 67, 89-90, 107, 109, 114, 120, 125, 141, 147-148, 153, 167-170
- through narrative connections 125, 132, 139, 169-170
- growth of 141, 147, 169-170
- Maggie's over Amerigo's 90, 114, 118
- reflector's over narrator's 114, 131, 148, 169
- problem in exertion of 11, 30, 50, 57-58, 91, 102-105, 150, 168-169

Narrator 1, 8, 52, 53, 80n34, n38, 116, 117, 127n20, 163n23
- relationship with reflector 10-11, 16, 18, 31-32, 40-41, 42n5, 95-96, 105, 113-114, 131-132, 134-136, 139, 168
- conscious separation from reflector 18, 58, 102, 104-106, 133, 135-136, 147, 162n11, 163n23
- reduction of authority 10-11, 114-115, 124, 131, 136-137, 139, 148, 167-169

Norrman, Ralf 18, 31, 43n10, 45n24, 46n24, 61, 78n15, 122, 128n27

Observer 1, 3, 7, 12, 13n8, 13n9, 32, 44n19, 122, 127n17, 135, 139, 144, 149, 150, 155, 156, 158, 168

O' Hara, Daniel T 129n38

Order 7, 52, 53, 56, 63, 71, 74, 78n19, n20, 90, 101, 103, 104, 105, 106, 107, 108, 109, 110, 111, 115, 117, 124, 126n8, n10, 144, 155

Past 22, 23, 24, 29, 31, 38, 43n7, 51, 52, 54, 56, 57, 62, 63, 68, 70, 71, 76n5, 78n19, 92, 98, 100, 104, 105, 110, 111, 115, 116, 121, 126n8, 132, 142, 146, 148, 150, 157, 158, 159, 160, 162n11, n14, 163n23, 165n35, n36, 166n37, 170

Pattern 6, 7, 22, 25, 26, 52, 61, 75, 101, 103, 115, 154, 167
- reflector as maker of 6-8, 115-116, 140-141, 147, 157
- 152, 155-156, 167
- as never complete 6, 115, 140-141, 146-147, 152, 157
- 152, 157

Perception 2, 3, 5, 7, 9, 10, 11, 18, 27, 32, 43n7, n8, 67, 70, 90, 92, 93, 94, 96, 97, 98, 99, 101, 105, 106, 108, 111, 112, 113, 117, 119, 123, 127n14, 139, 140, 141, 144, 149, 151, 152, 153, 155, 156, 157, 158, 162n21, 165n36, 167, 168

Person, Leland S 164n32

Picture 9, 10, 11, 18, 28, 29, 30, 32, 33, 35, 53, 56, 58, 63, 66, 68, 69, 70, 73, 78n20, 79n26, 93, 96, 97, 98, 100, 102, 103, 104, 105, 111, 112, 114, 115, 116, 121, 127n20, 134, 136, 137, 148, 149, 158, 161n9, 164n30, 169

Poe, Edgar Allan

Porter, Carolyn 3, 13n9, 113, 122, 127n17, 128n29

Power 1, 2, 3, 4, 10, 11, 12n4, 24, 36, 41, 44n20, 46n32, 70, 109, 112, 113, 122, 126n10, 127n16, 129n29, n31, n38, 134, 150, 160n3, 162n14, 169

Present 24, 34, 43, 60, 63, 68, 69, 70, 71, 78n19, 94, 98, 100, 104, 105, 108, 110, 111, 115, 116, 121, 132, 142, 152, 157, 158, 159, 160, 165n35, 170

Przybylowicz, Donna 62, 78n19

Quest 3, 11, 17, 42n7, 43n8, 44n13, n15, 49, 50, 51, 56, 60, 75, 76n 3, 77n13, 80n32, 94, 95, 96, 105, 119, 143, 155, 164n29, 168, 169

Reising, Russell J. 70, 78n14, 79n26
Refinement 8, 15, 17, 18, 19, 24, 25, 36, 39, 50, 53, 56, 69, 134, 135, 148, 168, 169
Reflection 2, 7, 8, 9, 18, 20, 32, 44n15, 89, 90, 102, 121, 123, 125, 144, 157, 158, 165n36
Reflector (See Center of Consciousness)
Relation 67, 96, 99, 102, 104, 114, 122, 124, 125n5, 128n21, 165n32
  as connection 5,6, 11-12, 18, 20, 26, 61, 70, 72, 96, 98, 99, 106, 110, 117, 132, 135, 139, 158, 163n23, 170
  establishing by relating story 12, 74-75, 98-100, 106, 118, 120, 125, 141, 167
  pictures about 29, 103, 135, 139, 153
  understanding need to form 66, 99, 123-124, 139
Relationship 10, 17, 20, 21, 28, 36, 37, 42n3, 45n24, 79n26, 97, 108, 121, 137, 146, 152, 156, 162n12
  between self and other 134, 141-142, 148-149, 157-158, 162n12
  narratives about 15, 19-20, 22-23, 25, 33, 35, 57, 98-103, 113, 117, 141, 146-147, 149-150, 160, 167-169
  failures in 21, 24-25, 34, 64, 99, 103, 114
Represent(ation) 2, 4, 9, 10, 11, 12n2, 14n27, 16, 19, 20, 23, 25, 32, 43n11, n12, 45n22, 49, 53, 54, 55, 56, 57, 76n3, 80n38, 89, 95, 102, 103, 105, 108, 114, 134, 139, 160n3, 161n5, 169
(Also see Image)
Revision 30, 120, 121, 126n10, 150, 160
Reynolds, Mark 123, 129n34
Rivkin, Julie 150, 156, 160, 162n10, 163n22, n24, 165n33, 166n41
Rosenblatt, Jason P 79n28, 80n38
Rovit, Earl 79n29
Rowe, John Carlos 120, 124, 128n22, 129n36
Rundle, Vivienne 1, 12n3

Sabin, Margery 104, 110, 126n9, n11
Said, Edward 12n4, 14n27
Salzburg, Joel 20, 24, 39, 44n14, n16, 47n34
Samuels, Charles Thomas 42n2
Savoy, Eric 46n28
Scenes 7, 26, 34, 35, 39, 44n18, 49, 53, 70, 71, 115, 116, 117, 118, 123, 136, 144, 157
  in reflector's image 11, 53, 54-55, 90, 92-94, 96, 114-116, 136, 163
  reflector's ability to connect 28-29, 94, 114-116, 118, 127n20, 136, 158
Schor, Naomi 26, 45n21
Self-fulfillment 49, 51, 96, 168, 169
Self-identity 21, 74, 80n32, 142, 143, 159
Self-isolation 50, 64, 66, 67, 157, 168, 169
Segal, Ora 3, 13n8
Seltzer, Mark 2, 12n4, 112, 127n16
Shear, Walter 56, 62, 77n7, 78n18
Shine, Muriel G 44n19
Sicker, Philip 17, 43n8, 44n15
Smith, Irena Auerbuch
Smythe, Karen 56, 61, 70, 77n6, n8, 77n14, 79n27
Spectator 3, 5, 7, 90, 117, 123, 135
Springer, Mary Doyle 63, 78n20
Steele, Meili 111, 127n13
Stein, Allen F 74, 80n30, n31, n37, 154, 164n29
Story 1, 4, 5, 6, 7, 8, 11, 13n14, 21, 22, 26, 27, 32, 40, 43n7, n9, 56, 76n5, 77n13, 80n34, 91, 109, 119, 123, 127n20, 159, 163n23
  reading or telling as an act of creating meaning 4, 5, 8, 12, 16, 17, 18, 19, 20, 22, 25, 50, 63, 70, 71, 91, 100, 106, 143, 144, 153, 167
  reading or telling as an act of drawing connections 5, 6, 11, 12, 22, 23, 24, 28, 29, 37, 56, 70, 90, 92, 94, 99, 100, 103, 106, 109, 116, 117, 118, 125, 144, 148, 149, 155, 157, 158, 167
  relationship between reading and telling 8, 9, 11, 15, 38, 98, 141, 144, 168
  new 103, 120, 121, 124, 169
  old 35, 37, 89, 90, 99, 100, 103, 104, 107, 108, 111, 120, 169
  developing 56-57, 93, 95, 115-116, 168
  elements of 55, 57, 64, 74, 75, 100, 101, 109, 113, 115, 118, 121, 141
  perceptual growth through reading or telling 5, 28, 32, 39, 92, 97, 98, 106, 141, 147, 148, 149, 167, 168
  interpreting as reading or telling 15, 89, 91, 100, 147
  problems in reading or telling 15, 16, 24, 32, 34, 35, 37, 58, 61, 99, 107, 108,

143, 144, 145, 146
James as teller of 1, 6, 8, 9, 49, 53, 55, 56, 64, 66, 89, 91-92, 124
  changing of 90, 103, 107, 108, 120, 121, 124, 146, 147, 150, 159, 160, 169, 170
  about change 132, 150, 153, 154, 157, 160, 170
  reading in surroundings 8, 17, 131, 148, 167
Surroundings (See Environment)

Tanner, Tony 3, 13n7, 30, 45n22, 161n4, 162n13
Teahan Sheila 8, 10, 13n19, 14n25, 91, 116, 123, 125n3, 127n19, 129n32, 134, 152, 159, 161n7, 164n27
Telegram 4, 15-18, 20, 25, 27-33, 35, 38, 45, 146
Tintner, Adeline R 155, 164n30
Todorov, Tzvetan 20, 44n13, 73, 80n32
Tuveson, Ernest 75, 78n24, 80n39

Upper Class 4, 15, 17, 18, 19, 20, 22, 24, 25, 27, 34, 37, 43, 45, 46, 168

Van Slyck, Phyllis 11, 14n27
Veeder, William 44n17
Vision 2, 3, 4, 13n6, 18, 25, 29, 31, 35, 37, 41, 43n9, 46n29, 52, 56, 60, 63, 65, 68, 71, 72, 73, 98, 100, 106, 108, 111, 113, 119, 121, 122, 123, 127n17, n20, 128n24, n28
Voyage 9, 11, 24, 92, 93, 94, 95, 96, 111, 119, 152, 164n29
Vulgar 25, 33, 34, 36, 50, 51, 67, 72, 73, 74

Walker, Pierre A 154, 164n28
Walton, Priscilla 43n12, 44n20, 46n28, 126n10
Watcher 2, 3, 6, 7, 67, 112, 113, 141, 142, 157, 158, 161n4, 162n12, n13, 167, 168
Wicke, Jennifer 25, 44n18
Williams, Merle A 160n3
Window 7, 8, 43n8, 56, 64, 65, 66, 67, 68, 112, 113, 136, 149, 157, 165n34
Winnett, Susan 34, 46n26
Wise, James 161n4
Wonder 4, 13n7, 22, 31, 32, 37, 45n22, 53, 54, 67, 69, 71, 75, 91, 114, 123, 133, 138, 141, 142, 144, 145, 146, 151, 153, 158, 167

Wonderful 91, 98, 113, 122, 144, 145, 146
Wright, Walter F 77n10
Wutz, Michael 143, 162n15